AF785021

PIPE FITTINGS

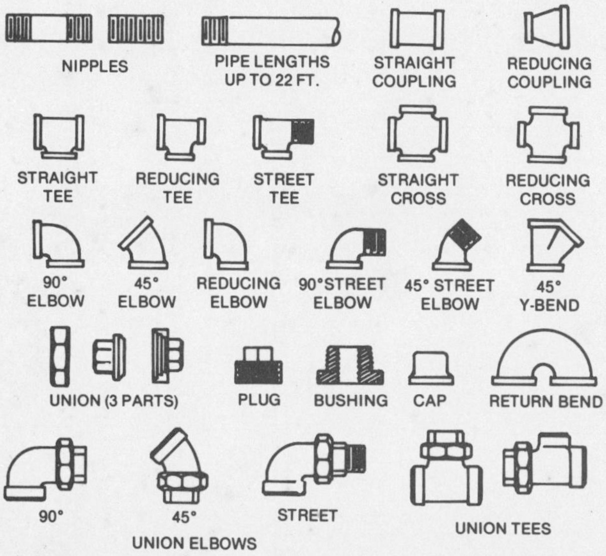

Here are the common steel pipe fittings. Nipples are simply short lengths of pipe threaded on both ends. Reducing fittings join two different sizes of pipe.

Compression fittings of the flared-tube type are the easiest for the novice to handle when working with copper tubing.

STANDARD STEEL PIPE (All Dimensions in Inches)					
Nominal Size	Outside Diameter	Inside Diameter	Nominal Size	Outside Diameter	Inside Diameter
1/8	0.405	0.269	1	1.315	1.049
1/4	0.540	0.364	1 1/4	1.660	1.380
3/8	0.675	0.493	1 1/2	1.900	1.610
1/2	0.840	0.622	2	2.375	2.067
3/4	1.050	0.824	2 1/2	2.875	2.469

SQUARE MEASURE
144 sq in = 1 sq ft
9 sq ft = 1 sq yd
272.25 sq ft = 1 sq rod
160 sq rods = 1 acre

VOLUME MEASURE
1728 cu in = 1 cu ft
27 cu ft = 1 cu yd

MEASURES OF CAPACITY
1 cup = 8 fl oz
2 cups = 1 pint
2 pints = 1 quart
4 quarts = 1 gallon
2 gallons = 1 peck
4 pecks = 1 bushel

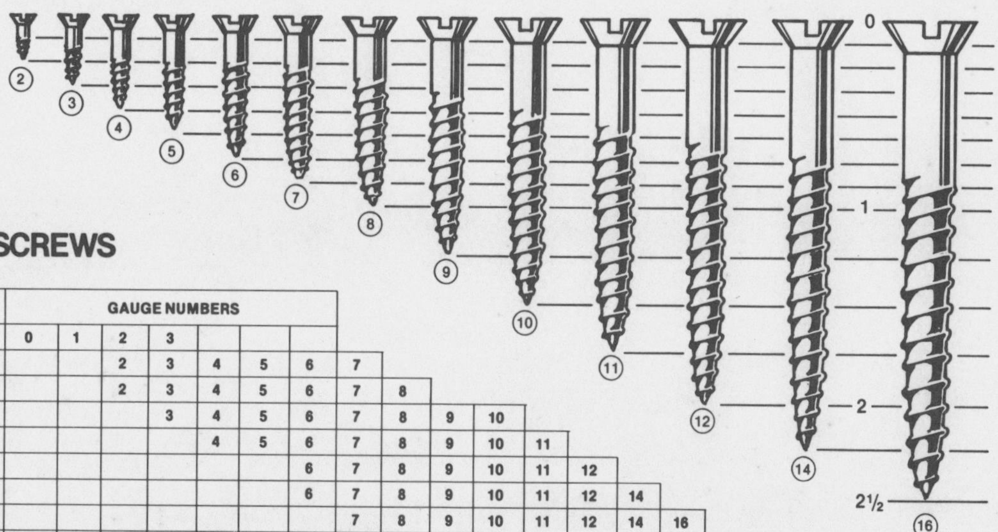

WOOD SCREWS

LENGTH	GAUGE NUMBERS																
1/4 INCH	0	1	2	3													
3/8 INCH			2	3	4	5	6	7									
1/2 INCH			2	3	4	5	6	7	8								
5/8 INCH				3	4	5	6	7	8	9	10						
3/4 INCH					4	5	6	7	8	9	10	11					
7/8 INCH							6	7	8	9	10	11	12				
1 INCH							6	7	8	9	10	11	12	14			
1 1/4 INCH								7	8	9	10	11	12	14	16		
1 1/2 INCH							6	7	8	9	10	11	12	14	16	18	
1 3/4 INCH									8	9	10	11	12	14	16	18	20
2 INCH									8	9	10	11	12	14	16	18	20
2 1/4 INCH										9	10	11	12	14	16	18	20
2 1/2 INCH													12	14	16	18	20
2 3/4 INCH														14	16	18	20
3 INCH															16	18	20
3 1/2 INCH																18	20	24
4 INCH																18	20	24

WHEN YOU BUY SCREWS, SPECIFY (1) LENGTH, (2) GAUGE NUMBER, (3) TYPE OF HEAD—FLAT, ROUND, OR OVAL, (4) MATERIAL—STEEL, BRASS, BRONZE, ETC., (5) FINISH—BRIGHT, STEEL BLUED, CADMIUM, NICKEL, OR CHROMIUM PLATED.

In this volume . . .

THIS BAR OFFERS everything. Open or closed it's a beauty. There's a bar-type sink, a refrigerator, a roomy storage compartment and a drawer for accessories. Find plans on page 194.

A BIKE is a personal thing. How do you go about selecting one that's exactly right for *you*? An authority gives detailed tips on what to look for—and what to avoid—in searching for a bike that's just right. See the article on page 304.

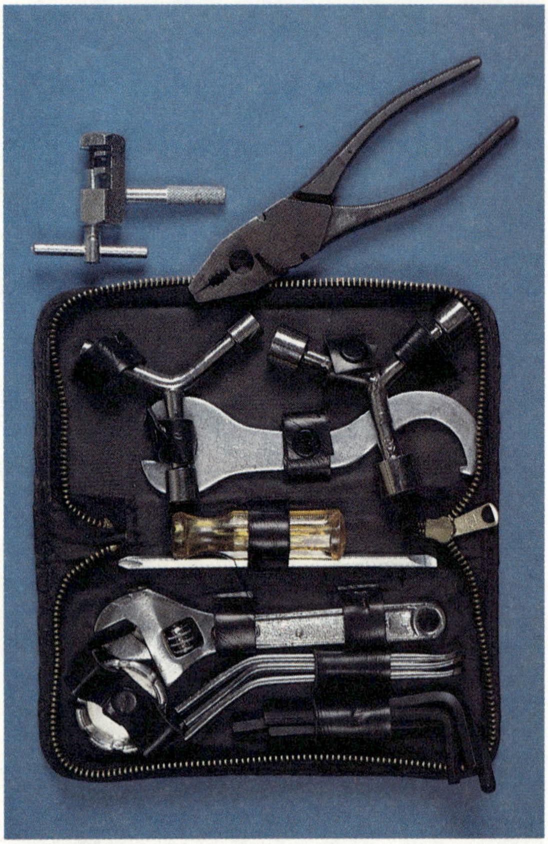

HERE ARE ALL the tools you need to make most of the basic bicycle repairs yourself. The article on page 313 explains how to make those repairs—and when to take your bike to a professional.

NEED BENCHES for your deck? We show some fine design ideas at the right. And you'll find detailed plans for building two others in "Benches to build for your deck" on page 264.

THIS MULTIPURPOSE TABLE, made of wood-grain laminate, earns its keep in several ways. With leaves extended it's an attractive buffet serving counter. Straddling a twin bed, it's a handy bed table with raised bookrack. You'll find complete plans on page 246.

LOOKING FOR MORE IDEAS for basement rooms? These two photos show attractive yet simple-to-execute designs. You'll find still more basement remodeling ideas in another article on page 198. And no matter what your design, you'll want to know ''How to frame a basement partition'' (page 200) and how to ''Finish your basement like a pro'' (page 202).

Look what you'll find in other volumes!

INTERESTED in wildlife photography? You can do it from an armchair in your living room! That's where this beautiful picture was taken. You'll find the secret on page 339 of Vol. 3.

TO A PHOTOGRAPHER, nothing is more frustrating than to discover something is wrong with the camera just when he wants to take a picture. Check page 516 of Vol. 4 to keep your camera shooting.

EVERY CRAFTSMAN CRAVES a large workshop with plenty of space for his bench and tools but even a small area can be utilized efficiently. See "How to lay out your workshop," Vol. 20, page 3142.

A BEAUTIFUL LAWN sometimes needs sprinkling, but it also needs fertilizer, and weed and pest control. Read the latest tips in "How to have the best lawn in your neighborhood" on page 1688 of Vol 11.

TRY CAMPING at the water's edge, either in a tent or in your boat. Then try "Camping away from campers." For details, see Vol. 4, page 545.

WHAT A STRIKING PHOTOGRAPH of a boat! And you can take equally dramatic pictures. An article on page 356 of Vol. 3 tells you "How to get your boat to pose for better pictures."

UNDERWATER PHOTOGRAPHY offers a double challenge: the challenge of existing in the depths, and the challenge of photographing this beautiful but strange environment where light and color are not what they seem. Read "The fascinating world of underwater photography," Vol. 19, page 2980.

YOU'LL FIND PLANS for gifts galore throughout all 20 volumes. Here are just a few, including a pipe rack with humidor, a cheese tray, toy cars, a treasure chest, and a dresser-top valet. Anyone would be proud to be on the receiving end—or the giving end—of such gifts. You'll find plans for them in the article "Gifts to make for Christmas" on page 1352 of Vol. 9.

Popular Mechanics

do-it-yourself encyclopedia

in 20 volumes

a complete how-to guide for the homeowner, the hobbyist—
and anyone who enjoys working with mind and hands!

All about:

home maintenance
home-improvement projects
wall paneling
burglary and fire protection
furniture projects
finishing and refinishing furniture
outdoor living
home remodeling
solutions to home problems
challenging woodworking projects
hobbies and handicrafts
model making
weekend projects
workshop shortcuts and techniques
hand-tool skills
power-tool know-how
shop-made tools
car repairs
car maintenance
appliance repair
boating
hunting
fishing
camping
photography projects
radio, TV and electronics know-how
clever hints and tips
projects just for fun

volume 2

ISBN 0-87851-067-2
Library of Congress Catalog Number 77 84920

© 1982 THE HEARST CORPORATION

All rights reserved. No part of this book may be reproduced or used in any form or by any means—graphic, electronic, or mechanical, including photocopying, recording, taping or information storage and retrieval systems—without written permission of the publishers.

The Hearst Corporation cannot assume responsibility for proper application of techniques, implementations or proper and safe functioning of any of the manufactured or reader-built items, products or projects resulting in whole or in part from all or any part of any plans, prints, projects or instructional materials published in this volume.

The Hearst Corporation cannot assume responsibility for the continuing availability of any special parts listed in articles in this volume.

MANUFACTURED IN THE UNITED STATES OF AMERICA

contents

VOLUME 2

Bandsaw basics

A bandsaw can be the most useful power tool in a shop. Not only does it rip and crosscut, but it also resaws and cuts curves

By HARRY WICKS

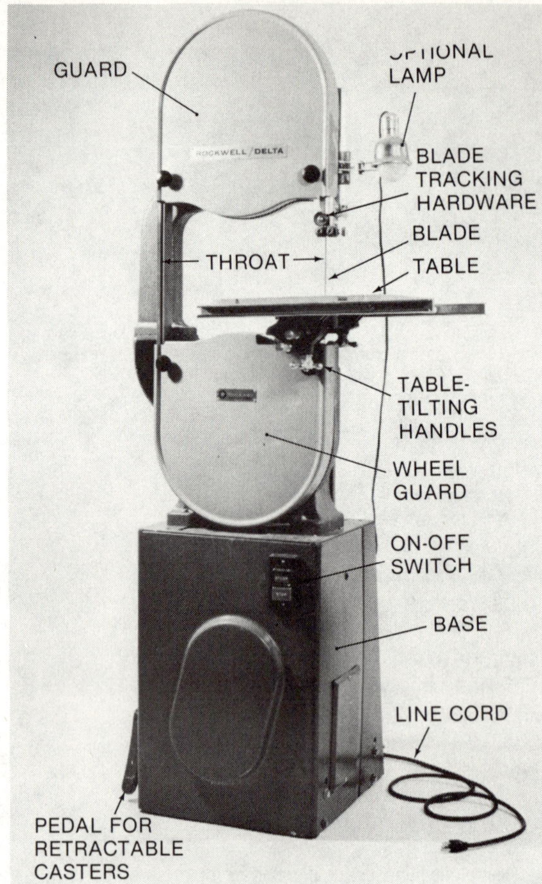

BANDSAW PARTS are identified on this 14-in. Delta. Capacity is blade-arm distance, or throat.

■ IF FOR SOME reason stationary tools had to be stripped from my shop, but I could choose just one to keep, it would probably be the bandsaw. A bandsaw is a relatively simple machine consisting of a pair of wheels around which a blade travels, a table for supporting the workpiece, and guides for keeping the blade running and cutting in accurate fashion. A well-maintained bandsaw, in my opinion, is one of the most valuable tools you can add to your workshop. With it, you can make simple rips and crosscuts while the better-quality tools also are equipped with adjustable tables for making compound cuts.

If you own a model with a fair-sized throat—that's the distance from the blade to the vertical blade enclosure—you can handle most of the ripping and crosscutting chores that you're likely to encounter. And the bandsaw gives you super-capacity for cutting scrolls, curves and the like, which are impossible on the table, or radial-arm saw.

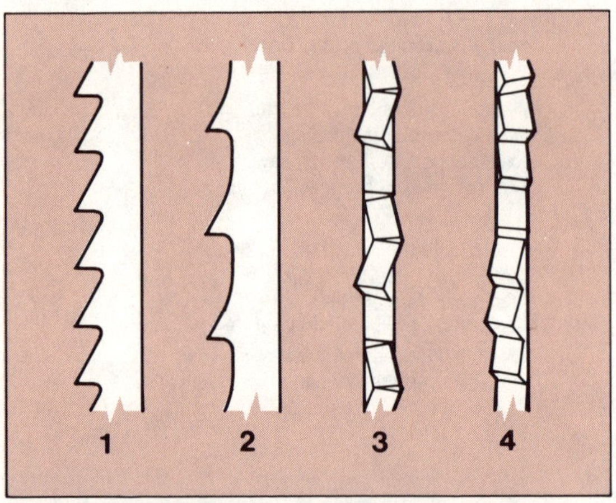

BANDSAW BLADES you should know: **1** Regular teeth for ferrous metals and wood. **2** Skip tooth has wide-spaced teeth for high-speed cutting, fast chip clearance. **3** Wavy-set hacksaw-like blade for tubing and pipe. **4** Raker set, a general purpose blade usually used on thick stock for a fast cut.

SEE ALSO

Bandsaws, sharpening . . . Bandsaws, tables . . . Circular saw blades . . . Motors, shop . . . Power-tool maintenance . . . Power-tool stands . . . Safety, workshop . . . Table saws . . . Workbenches . . . Workshops

Like the table saw, the bandsaw is a bench tool. It should be well fastened to a rigid base—either legs designed for it, or a bench that puts the saw's table at a comfortable height. Position the saw in your shop so that there is room in all directions for swinging a workpiece. I have my bandsaw legs fitted with lockable casters. When the tool is not in use, I park it along a wall. When I need plenty of working room, I simply push the table to shop center and lock the casters.

If you are buying a bandsaw, do read the manufacturer's instructions for using and maintaining the tool.

Be aware that there is a wide variety of blades available. Since they vary in tooth size and configuration, you should know which types are best for your purposes; there really isn't one general-purpose blade. Make no mistake, you need a number of different blades in order to get the maximum performance from your bandsaw.

The blades come in widths ranging from ⅛ to

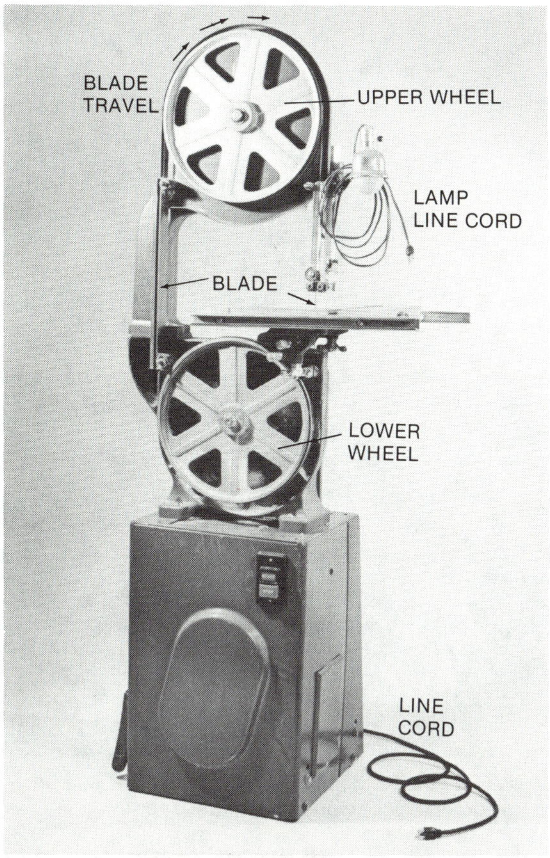

WITH WHEEL GUARDS (covers) removed, it is easy to understand principle of bandsaw cutting. Under tension, blade travels around both wheels.

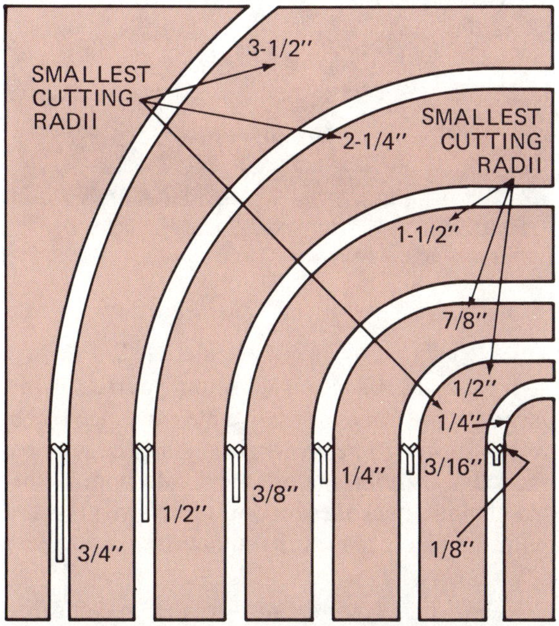

BLADES ARE available in widths from ⅛ too ¾ in. Narrower ones can make the tightest turns; wide ones are useful for heavy stock.

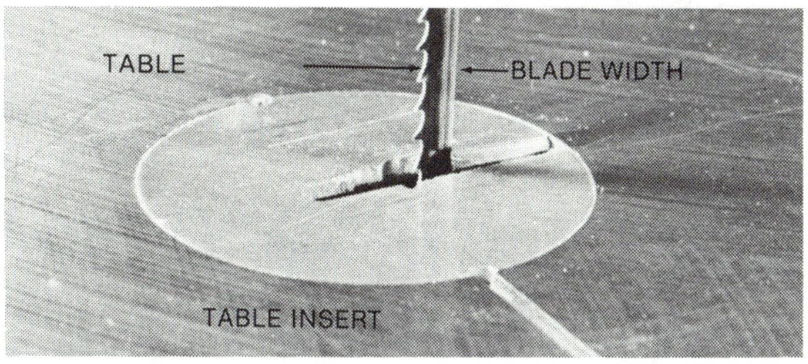

TABLE INSERT should always be in place when the saw is in use to support the workpiece. It is removed to get the blade in and out (using the table slot visible in the foreground).

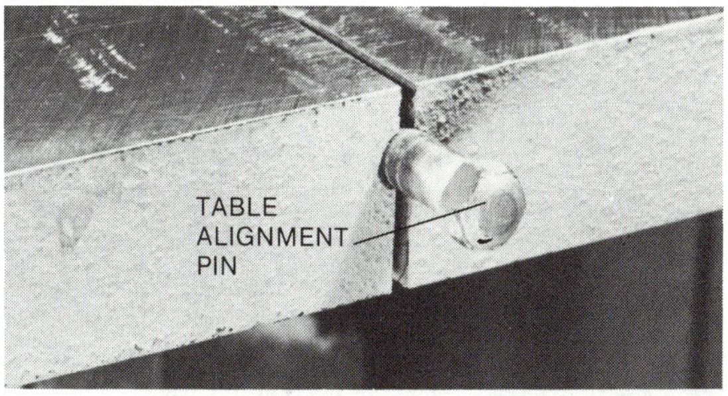

TABLE-ALIGNMENT pin keeps the saw table level on both sides of the blade-changing slot.

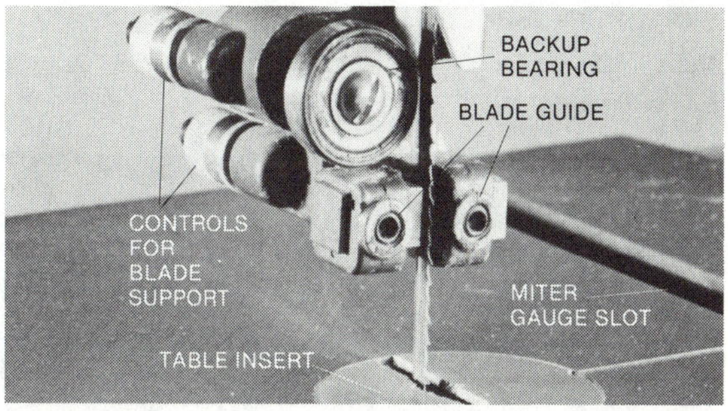

CLOSE-UP VIEW of blade support and guides reveals the basic simplicity of design. Blade guides should ride just behind the gullets while the backup bearing supports the blade as the work is fed into the teeth. Entire assembly can be adjusted up or down to suit depth of cut required.

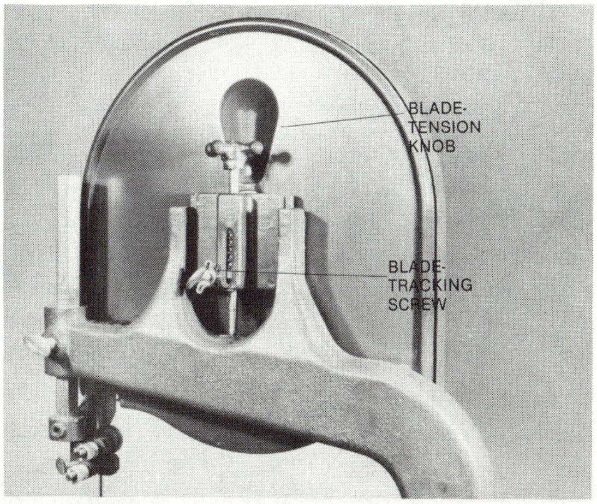

AFTER A BLADE is installed it must be tensioned and tracked using this hardware.

MAKE CERTAIN thumbs are not in the cutting line as you push workpiece into the blade.

WHEN ACCURACY is a must on a long rip, use rip fence and position hands as shown.

TO COMPLETE a rip on narrow stock, push work through with a wide board (arrow).

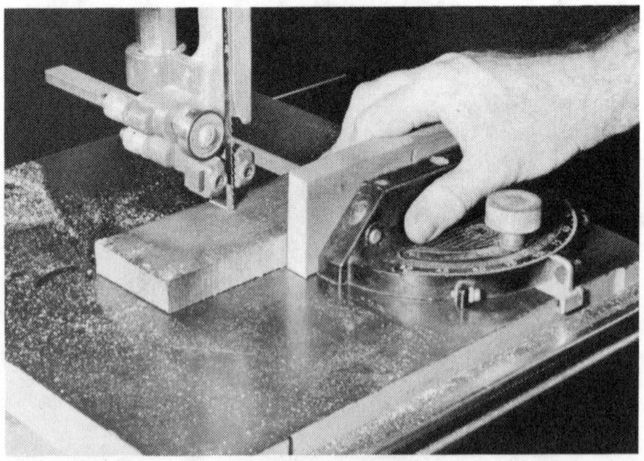

A MITER GAUGE comes with a quality saw; add an extension block of wood for greater support.

GRIP WORK and gauge firmly with your fingers when making crosscuts with the miter gauge.

TO CUT round stock (i.e. dowels), clamp guides on both sides so the work can't drift.

¾-in. The narrow ones can cut to a tighter radius than the wide ones. If you try to turn too sharp a radius with a wide blade, you're sure to break it.

It is best to use the small-tooth blades when you want a fairly smooth cut that won't require a great deal of sanding. These cut slower than the large-tooth blades, which leave saw marks that have to be removed with sandpaper. When making cuts where roughness doesn't matter at all, use a skip-tooth blade, which permits extra-fast cutting.

To use the bandsaw, position yourself comfortably in front of the table and feed the work slowly. The workpiece should not be shoved forcefully against the blade and, if the blade binds, back the work off to remove pressure until the blade again runs smoothly.

Keep your saw adjusted to the maker's instructions. Correct tension is necessary for proper tracking. When possible, use one of the cutting guides as shown in the photos above.

A rip fence for your bandsaw

By PAUL FIEBACH

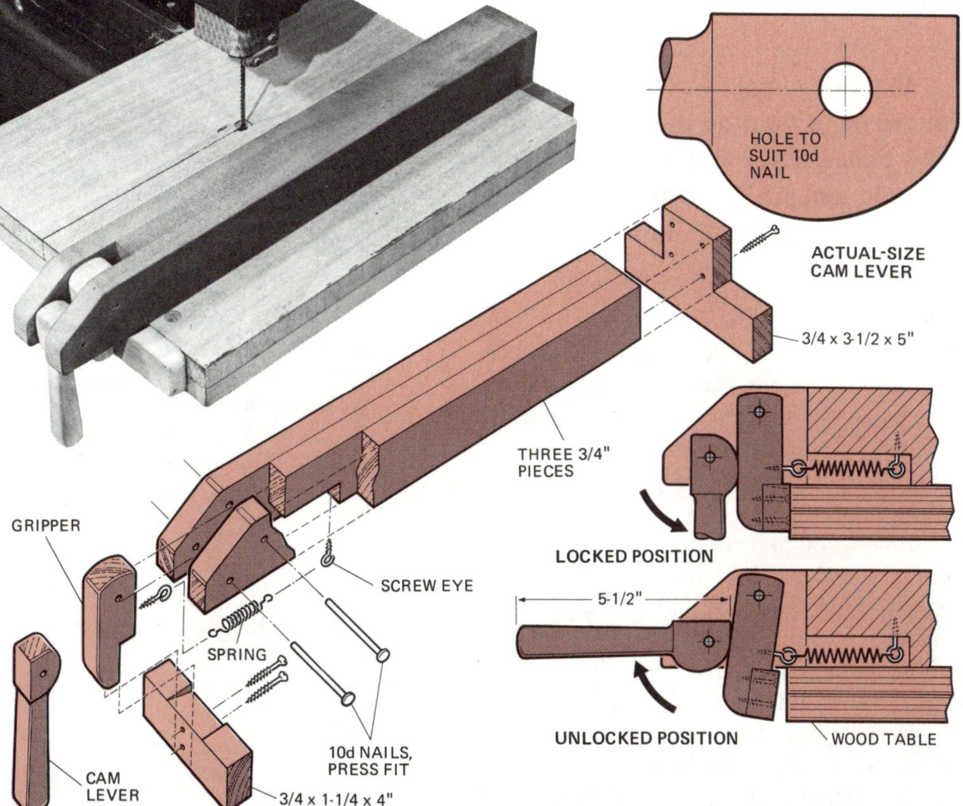

■ A RIP FENCE on a bandsaw can be as handy as the one on a table saw, yet how many bandsaws come with a fence as standard equipment? I made this wooden one for my bandsaw, and it works as well as any fence you can buy—and costs a lot less. Its cam-locking action is positive and holds the fence securely to front and back edges of the table. When the clamping lever is released, the fence stays put yet can be moved back and forth or lifted from the table.

The drawing shows how the fence is made, its length being determined by the depth of the bandsaw table. The cam is given full size for tracing. The coil spring, housed in a 2¼-in.-long notch which is made in the center member of the three-piece fence, keeps the fence snug against the saw table when you make lateral adjustment. Overall length of the center piece should be ⅛-in. less than table depth.

While the cutaway drawing, which illustrates the fence in an unlocked position, shows the spring-fitted pressure pad backed off from the table, this is shown exaggerated for the sake of clarity. Actually, the spring causes the pressure pad to hug the table even when unlocked.

SEE ALSO

Bench saws . . . Circular saw blades . . . Motors, shop . . . Power hacksaws . . . Power-tool stands . . . Table saws . . . Workbenches . . . Workshops

Make a jig to sharpen bandsaw blades

By WILLIAM G. WAGGONER

With this simple wooden frame you can do your sharpening right on the machine. It can be built quickly and easily, and will do the job with amazing precision, insuring reliable tooth-to-tooth spacing

■ THE UNIQUE ADVANTAGE of this sharpening jig is that you can sharpen your bandsaw blades right on the machine. It insures tooth-to-tooth spacing with such reliability that you can sharpen a 96-in.-long blade in less than 10 minutes.

The simple wooden jig for the saw table can be built quickly and easily—there are no critical dimensions, even though it will do the job with amazing precision. I used a regular bandsaw sharpening guide and simply made the brackets to hold it. This can be made of ¾-in. aluminum or steel angle. Just saw along one side of the angle and fold back the remaining flaps as indicated in the drawing. Then place the bracket on a drill press and carefully drill a pair of aligned ¼-in. holes.

Assemble the wooden portion of the jig as detailed and cut a cross member to fit into the groove on the saw table. If no miter-gauge groove is provided on your particular bandsaw, simply attach the cross member so it rides along the edge of the table. In either event, locate the cross member so that the smooth section at the end of the file will contact a tooth at the end of the first filing stroke. Then lift the handle of the file-carrying frame to bring the next tooth into position.

When initially setting up the jig, loosen the locking controls on the file-carrying frame and place the file into the space between two teeth.

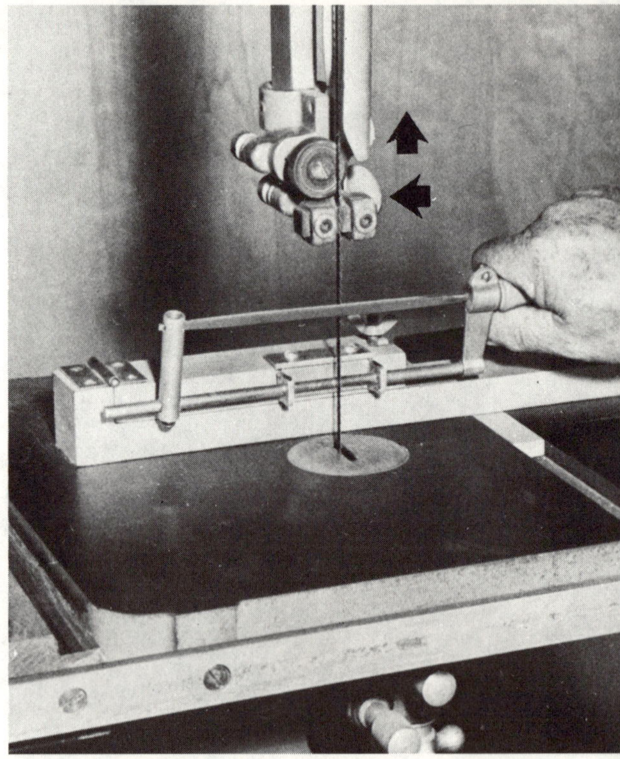

TWO-STROKE ACTION is shown by the arrows. Push forward to sharpen; pull up to position the next tooth.

FORWARD MOVEMENT should stop when the tooth rests on the file's smooth shank (indicated by pencil point).

SEE ALSO

Bench saws . . . Circular saw blades . . . Cutoff machines . . . Motors, shop . . . Power hacksaws . . . Power-tool stands . . . Radial-arm saws . . . Sharpening, tool . . . Table saws . . . Workbenches . . . Workshops

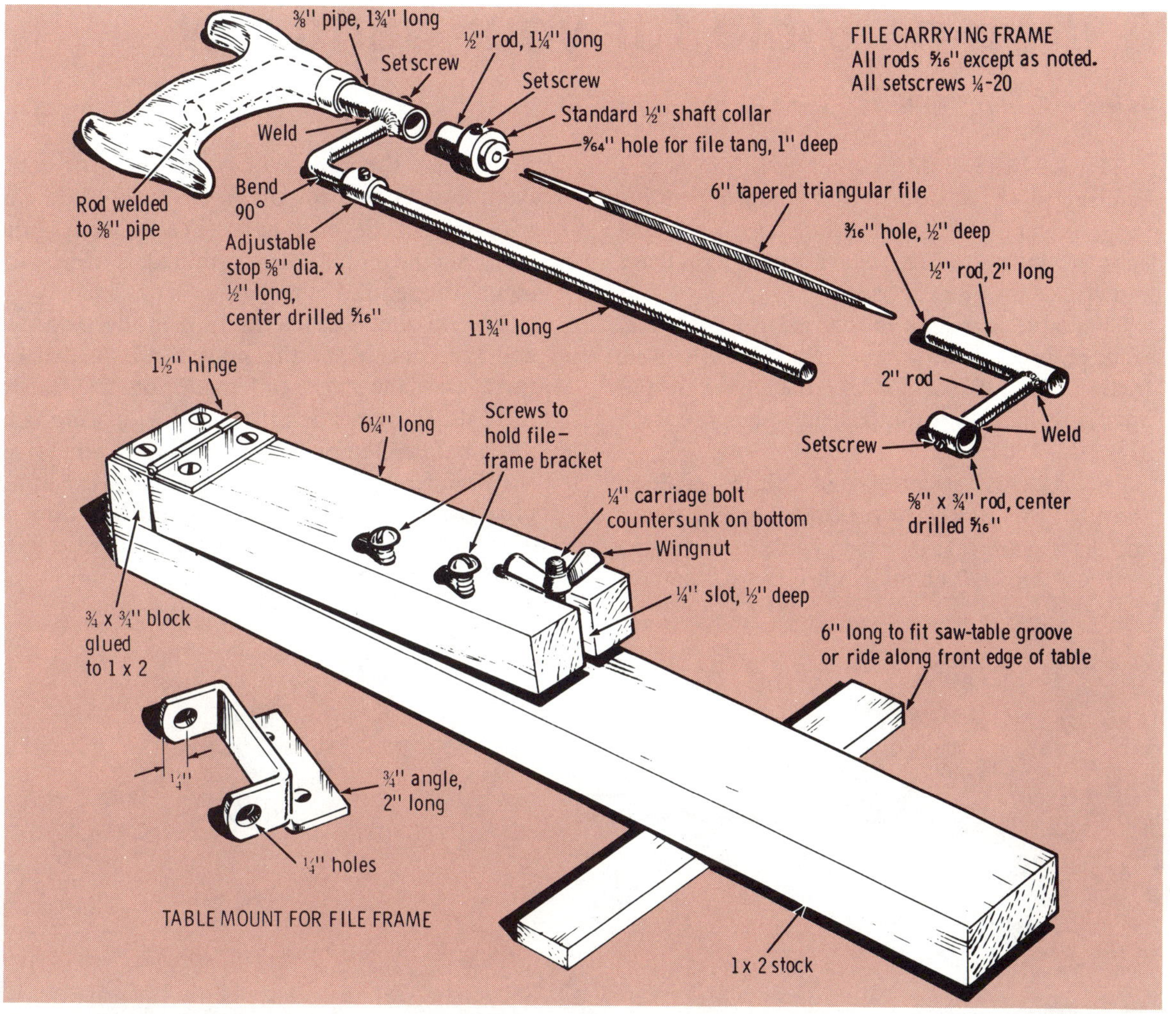

ADJUST WINGNUT to stop upward movement and position the teeth. Then hold the blade lightly and sharpen.

Then lock the controls and secure the entire jig to the table with a C-clamp. Make certain the smooth shank of the file is contacting a tooth and lift the handle until the next tooth is in the correct position. Turn down the wingnut to limit the travel of the hinged arm at this point and you're ready to begin the sharpening operation.

Give each tooth the same number of file strokes. Unless the saw has been badly neglected, one stroke per tooth should be sufficient.

In the event you don't use a commercial bandsaw-sharpening guide, you can make the file-carrying frame shown in the drawing. However, because the dimensions for the bracket were derived so the commercial (¼-in. shank) tool could be used, the substitute frame will require 5/16-in. holes drilled in the bracket. Otherwise, operation and adjustments are the same.

But whether you make or buy the file-carrying frame, you're sure to appreciate the convenience of being able to quickly sharpen your bandsaw blades.

A drop-on table for your bandsaw

By GEORGE S. WATSON

■ THERE ARE TIMES when even the largest bandsaw table is too small for the job. By adding this auxiliary wood table, I increased a small table to a king-size 20 x 37-incher with a rip fence and circle-cutting attachment.

This table is unique in that the rip fence and pivot point stay put in any set position by mere friction. To shift position of either fence or disc pivot, just pick it up and place it where you want it.

Three cleats, attached underneath, position and hold the plywood over the table. Rip fence and pivot point ride in a ¾-in.-wide dado having a strip of No. 120 emery cloth glued to the bottom. Make the dado with your router or saw's dado cutter, and cut the ¾-in.-wide blade slot with parallel cuts on your table saw. Depth of the dado should equal the combined thickness of metal, rubber and emery cloth.

The two metal hooks rest in ⅛-in.-deep dadoes and are bent. Make the short bends first, hook them over the edge and mark for the second bend. Bend by heating the metal with a propane torch before clamping and bending in your vise.

I found bike inner tube better than car inner tube to cover the metal pieces. Clean and cement with Skotch Super glue. Pivot pin in a No. 6 x ½-in. FH stovebolt filed to a point.

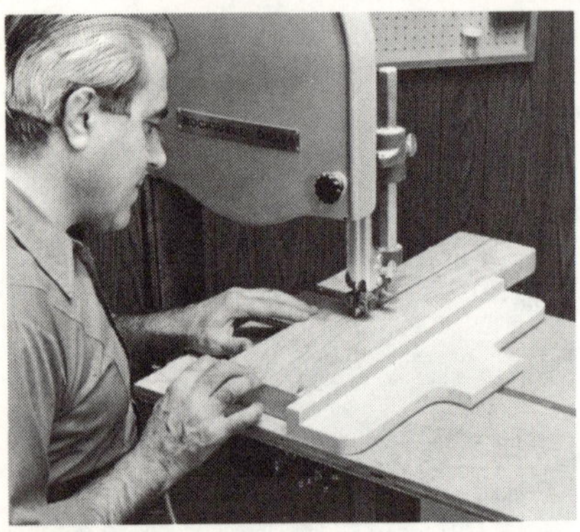

TABLE CAN BE made to fit any size saw. Here it's on a 14-in. Rockwell with its rip fence in use. Photo below shows how pivot point is used to saw a perfect disc. Cleat spacing at right is for 12-in. Craftsman. Cleats are placed to suit saw's table.

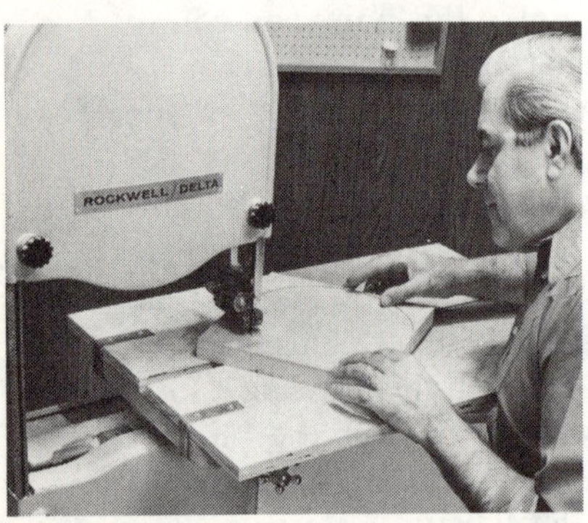

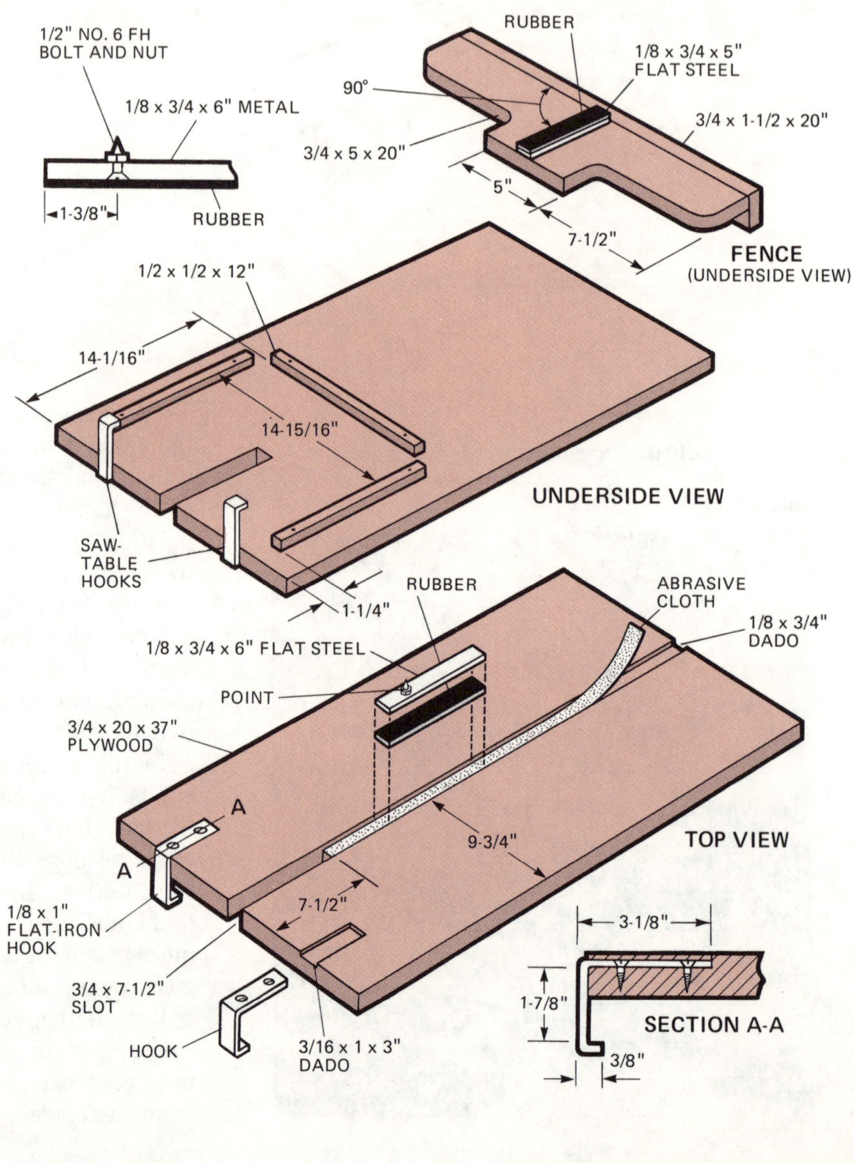

SEE ALSO
Bandsaws . . . Bench saws . . .
Discs, wood . . . Motors, shop . . .
Safety, workshop . . . Saws, bench . . .
Shop tools . . . Table saws . . .
Workbenches . . . Workshops

BARBECUE BAR with Jenn-Air cooktop, refrigerator (inset) and Nutone food center is easy to build.

Build a barbecue bar for your family room

By RICK EICKHOFF

■ ALTHOUGH THIS BARBECUE bar is designed with special convenience features, it is easily constructed and finished with a durable plastic laminate. A twin-grill convertible cooktop, refrigerator and food center are incorporated into the bar. It is finished with Nevamar's Butcher Block and Classic Cane laminates and trimmed with rattan.

Materials left over from the bar will make a companion coffee table. A hinged top covers the table's storage area.

Cut bottom **I** and kickplate pieces **F, J.** Using glue and ringed nails join pieces, keeping assembly square.

Lay out and cut the two end panels **G** and attach to assembly with 8d finishing nails and white glue. Nail **Z** and **Y** to the refrigerator end panel, and nail a temporary 1 x 2 brace across the refrigerator opening.

Lay out and cut partitions **G** and **H.** Mark their locations on the plywood bottom. Turn the cabinet on its face (drawer) side, glue and nail partitions through the bottom with 8d nails.

Cut out the back **E.** With cabinet face down and everything square, nail and glue **E** in place. Nail rail **K** in partition notches.

Measure and cut facing pieces: horizontal rails **O, P, Q, R** and vertical stiles **S**. Use doweled joints on the facing frame. Dry assemble, then glue joints and clamp with 6-ft. bar clamps. Make sure assembly is square.

When facing frame is dry, nail and glue it to cabinet base, ends and partitions, checking alignment. Cut, nail and glue **AA** and **X.** Add corner blocks **BB** for securing top.

Plane or sand all facing joints flush. Cut vertical laminations to run full length of stiles; apply contact cement to mating surfaces. Butt-cut and apply end laminate. Cut and apply back laminate in one sheet. End and back edges will be covered with trim.

SEE ALSO
Barbecue tables . . . Barbecues . . . Bars . . .
Cookout bars . . . Family rooms . . .
Serving carts . . . Snack tables

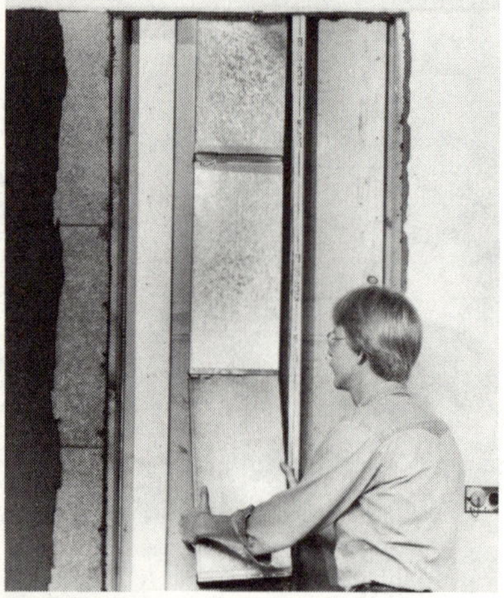

TO RETAIN effective exhaust system, use large ducts. For good air flow, use a minimum of elbows. A 5-in. elbow, 3 x 10-in. duct and Broan No. 435 roof jack worked here.

ASSEMBLE the unit in your shop, then install it. As shown below, all duct joints should be wrapped with tape to prevent exhaust leaks.

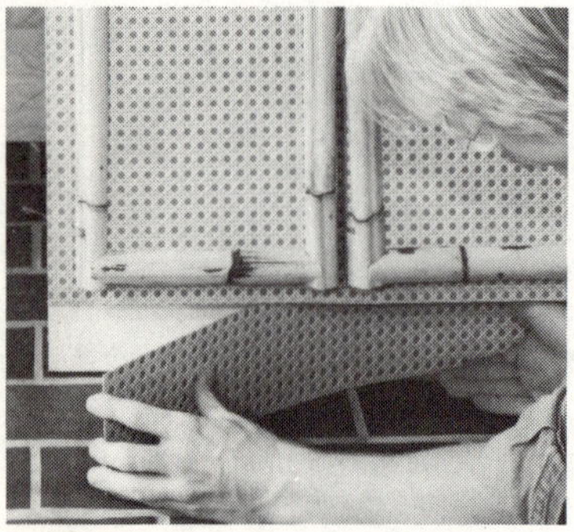

CUT AND FIT cane plastic on the kickplate with bar in position.

BARBECUE BAR/COFFEE TABLE—MATERIALS LIST

Key	Pcs.	Size and description	Key	Pcs.	Size and description
A	1	¾ x 29 x 80½″ particleboard	R	2	¾ x 2 x 8¼″ pine
B	1	¾ x 2½ x 29″ plywood	S	4	¾ x 2 x 30½″ pine
C	2	¾ x 2½ x 73″ plywood	T	2	¾ x 6⅜ x 9⅝″ plywood
D	1	¾ x 5 x 29″ plywood	U	1	¾ x 6⅜ x 30¼″ plywood
E	1	¾ x 29¼ x 78¼″ plywood	V	2	¾ x 9⅝ x 21⅜″ plywood
F	1	¾ x 5¼ x 78¼″ plywood	W	2	¾ x 15 x 21⅜″ plywood
G	3	¾ x 24½ x 34½″ plywood	X	1	¾ x 1½ x 29¼″ pine
H	2	¾ x 24½ x 28½″ plywood	Y	1	¾ x 1 x 2½″ pine
I	1	¾ x 24½ x 51¼″ plywood	Z	1	¾ x 1½ x 5¼″ pine
J	1	¾ x 5¼ x 52¾″ plywood	AA	1	¾ x 1 x 22½″ pine
K	1	¾ x 2 x 76¾″ plywood	BB	4	¾ x 5 x 5″ pine
L	2	½ x 4½ x 22¼″ fir plywood	CC	1	¾ x 5 x 22″ plywood
M	2	½ x 4½ x 6¼″ fir plywood	DD	2	¾ x 12¼ x 22½″ fir plywood
N	1	¼ x 6¾ x 22½″ plywood	EE	2	¾ x 12¼ x 14¾″ fir plywood
O	2	¾ x 1¾ x 28¾″ pine	FF	1	¾ x 13¼ x 22½″ fir plywood
P	1	¾ x 2 x 28¾″ pine	GG	1	¾ x 16¾ x 26″ particleboard
Q	4	¾ x 1¾ x 8¼″ pine	HH	8	1¼″-dia. rattan poles

Misc.: 3 4x8 sheets Nevamar Classic Cane plastic laminate (No. RC-2-2 701); 1 4x8 sheet Nevamar Butcher Block plastic laminate (No. WV 830); 2 Grant 22-in. drawer slides (No. 336); 4 magnetic catches; 4 prs. Amerock burnished brass hinges (No. 1238); 8d finishing nails; 4d nails; 1¼-in. No. 8 fh wood screws; 1½-in. No. 8 fh wood screws; 1¼-in. ringed nails; 1 pr. 1½-in. brass butt hinges; ⅜-in.-dia. dowel; white glue, shelving hardware; contact cement, varnish or shellac.

Lay out and cut plywood doors **T, U, V, W.** Cut laminate for door edgings (¼ in. oversize), facings and backs. (Laminate backs to guard against warpage.) Glue laminate to backs, edges and then fronts, routing edges flush after each gluing. File corners smooth.

Cut drawer sides **L** and **M.** Dado the lower edge for bottom **N.** Cut, then slide the bottom in place and attach lamination to the front. Fit piece **CC** to the cabinet and hardware to the drawer and cabinet. Screw on laminated false drawer front.

Hang the doors next. After adjusting the blade for depth, use a circular saw to cut a slot in the door for the pin hinge. Screw-fasten the hinge to the door, assemble doors to cabinet stiles and install magnetic catches.

Halve rattan **HH** or bamboo poles on the circular saw and keep matching halves together. Cut trim to length and apply it with dark areas opposite each other. Put cabinet on its back and apply vertical trim to the front with white glue and 4d finishing nails. Cope horizontal rails into the stiles. Trim outside corner with matching

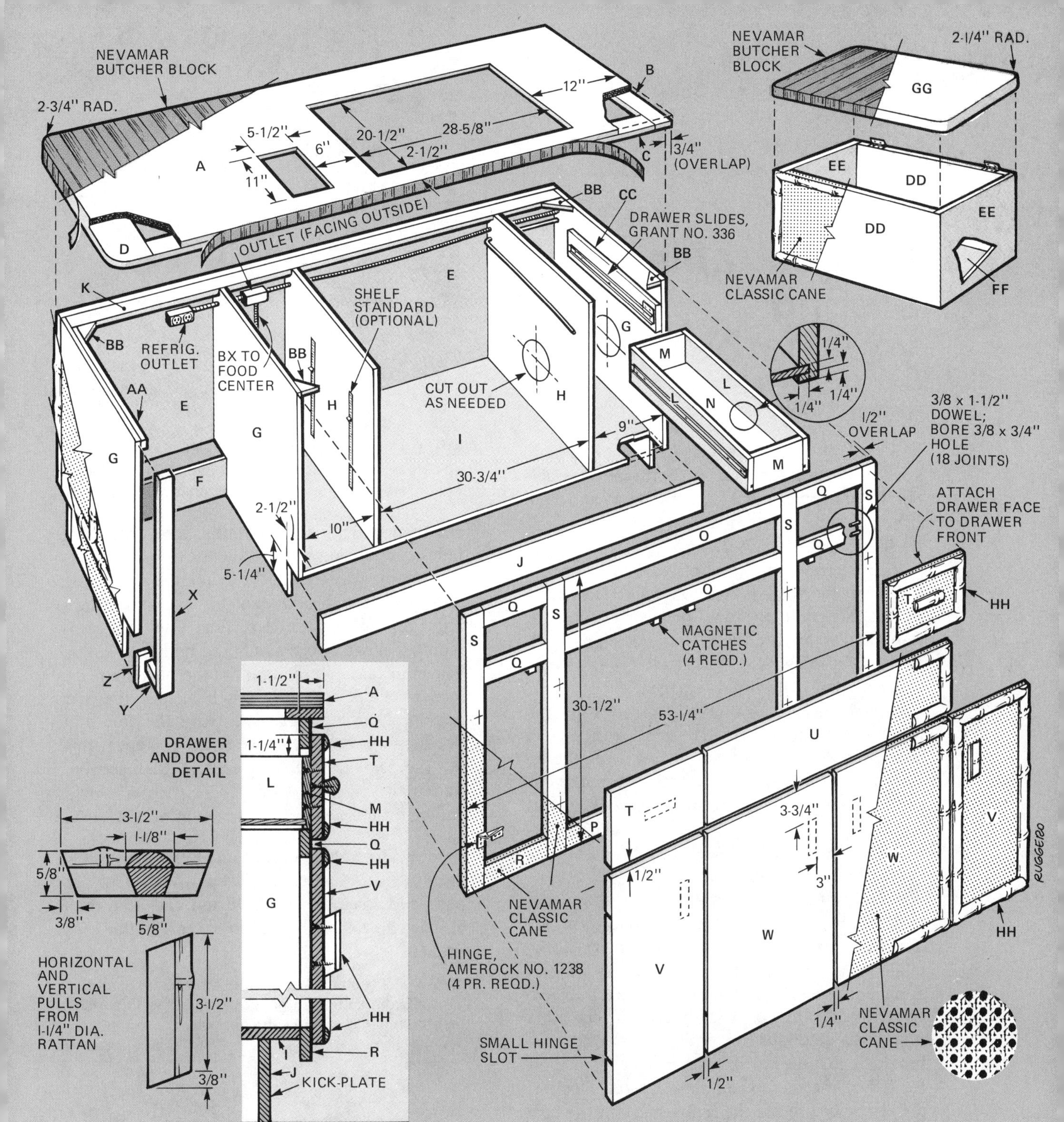

pieces. Next, lay the cabinet carefully on its face. Trim back corner with two rattan pieces. Plane the edge of the second piece for a tight fit. Add all rattan trim on the back.

Cut and install laminate facing on the refrigerator front. Add shelving if desired. Varnish the interior.

Cut countertop **A** to size. Cut reinforcing pieces **D** and **B,** glue and nail in place. Then cut and add strips **C.** Cut the corner radius with a sabre saw and sand smooth, keeping top edge square. Cut laminate self-edge slightly oversize, bond it in place and rout the overhang flush with a straight carbide cutter in the router. File it even with the top surface. Then cut the top laminate oversize, bond it in place and dress its edges.

Bore starter holes into cutouts and complete cutouts with a hacksaw blade in your sabre saw. Rout and file all edges as needed.

Cut handles, shellac their ends and attach with 1½-in. No. 8 fh wood screws. Position barbecue bar, then cut and cement laminate to the kick-plate.

The coffee-table construction is similar.

ADD-ON BARBECUE TABLE comes in handy for holding cooking gear and food ready to put on the fire. It also makes serving and cleanup easier.

Wrap a table around your barbecue

By ROSARIO CAPOTOSTO

■ BY ADDING this redwood barbecue table to your back-yard cook center, barbecues are certain to be happier times for both guests and chef. It wraps around a standard-size 23-in.-dia. kettle-shape brazier that's 29-in. high.

You'll need about 98 ft. of 2 x 3-in. construction heart redwood. Other materials used are ⅜-in. exterior-grade plywood for gussets, epoxy or resorcinol waterproof glue, 3-in. hot-dipped galvanized finishing nails, 3-in. and 1¼-in. galvanized common nails and wax paper.

Begin by using a 30°/60° triangle to sketch the full-size pattern of half the frame section. Cut mitered ends for the six hub pieces using the jig shown and sabre saw. Use this jig to make left and righthand miters by turning the stock over as required. Also use it to make ¾-in. partial cuts parallel to the miter cut. Make the 1¼-in. middle cut freehand to cut off waste.

A fast-setting epoxy is good for joining the parts of the hexagonal hub. Just position two *alternate* pieces and tack-nail them onto the worktable. Insert wax paper under the joints, then apply epoxy and push the middle piece in place. Leave this first half of the hub tacked to the table to use as a guide for assembling the second half, but don't glue the halves together as yet. Position the halves together. Then place a scrap block in the center and locate the center mark of the hub by intersecting each joint with a straightedge.

Use a beam compass set at 12½ in. to draw the center circle. Cut along the curve with a sabre saw, then epoxy the two hub halves together.

Cut spoke pieces to length and use two 3-in. finishing nails to join each to the hub. Cut five rim sections with notched ends, bore small pilot holes and nail rims to the spokes.

A simple way to add the decking is by cutting only one set with both ends mitered and installing it on the rear center section. Use 3-in. common nails, two at each end, and bore pilot holes. Then cut one mitered end for the next six-piece section of decking and butt it against the first section. Nail it in place, leaving the free end overlapping the next spoke slightly. Repeat this for the remaining four pieces in that section. Tack-nail a straight strip of wood to serve as a guide and use a circular saw to cut off the waste ends.

Turn the table over and make the reinforcing gussets from ⅜-in. exterior plywood. Cut leg parts and assemble with glue and nails to form a T. Then glue and nail the top of the T to the table frame.

USE A JIG such as that shown below to cut mitered ends. Two 2 x 4s on edge make a good work surface. Set-tooth blade assures straight cuts.

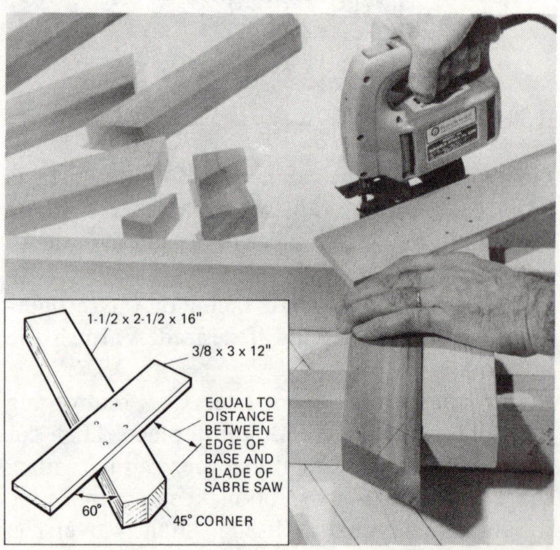

SEE ALSO
Barbecues . . . Benches, deck . . .
Carpeting, outdoor . . . Cookout bars . . .
Firepits . . . Grills . . . Insect traps . . .
Kitchens, outdoor . . . Outdoor tables . . . Patios . . .
Picnic tables . . . Planters

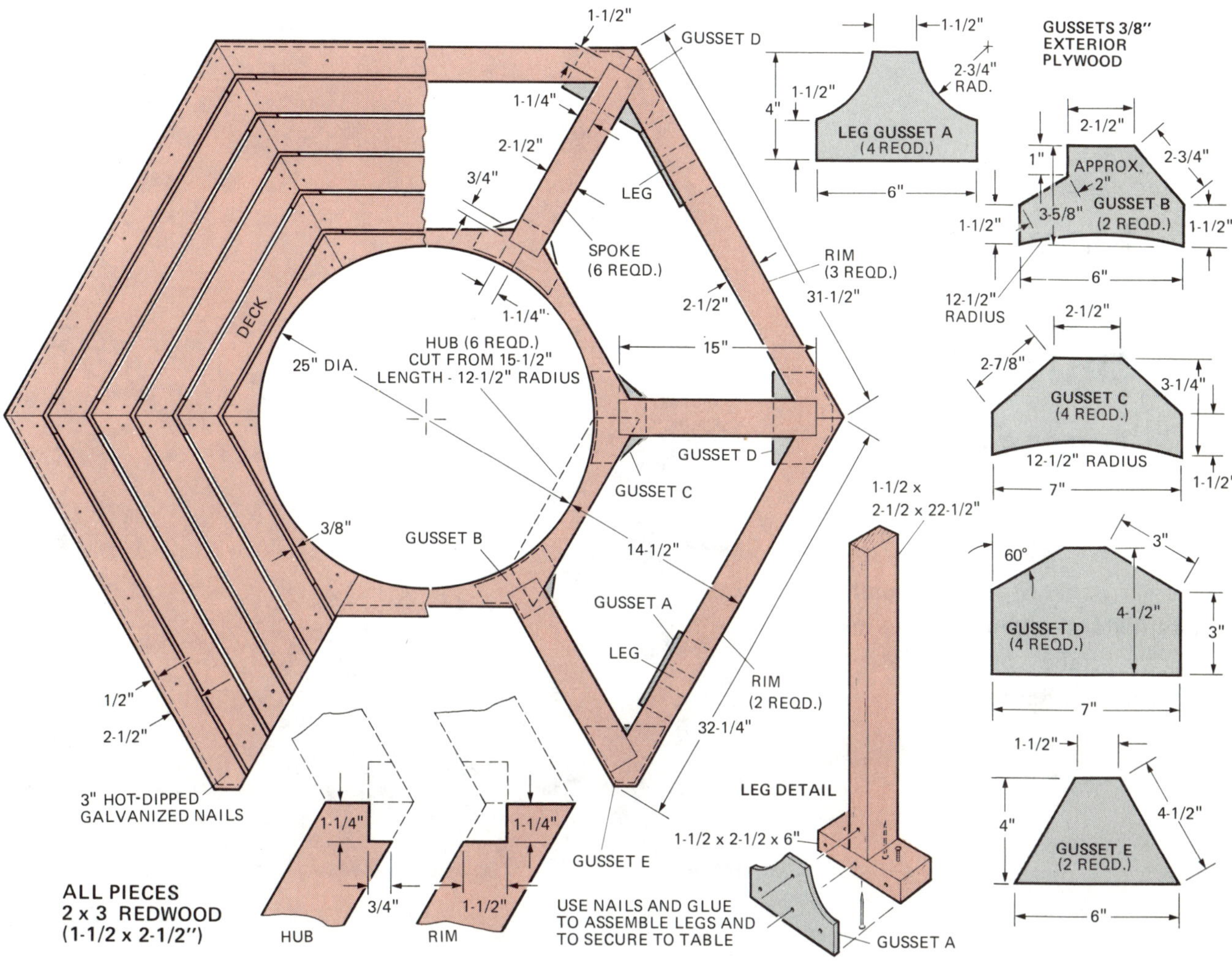

A BEAM COMPASS set at 12½ in. pivots at the center-marked block and marks a curve to be cut to accommodate the brazier.

CIRCULAR SAW shoe rides against a tacked-on guide strip to cut the diagonal joints. Set blade so that it won't cut the frame below.

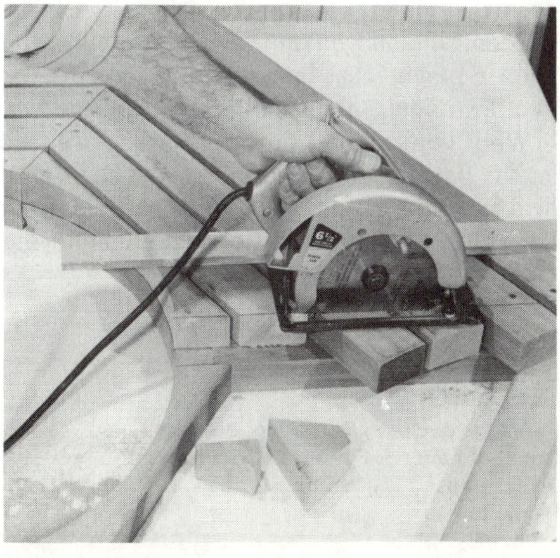

How to install a gas-fired barbecue

By WAYNE C. LECKEY

A gas-fired unit starts instantly and eliminates the messy ashes of charcoal (but not its flavor)

■ IF THE CHORE of starting and cleaning up the mess of a charcoal barbecue is getting you down, let me tell you what a pleasure it is to play head chef with a gas-fired outdoor barbecue.

Nothing could be easier to start. You merely open the cover, light a match, insert it in the ignition hole and turn the temperature control knob to "high." The burner ignites instantly and in a few minutes your barbecue is ready.

When you're through, you close the cover and let the flame burn for 20 minutes. The intense heat burns off the grease and food particles from the grates and the ceramic briquets and your barbecue is clean for next time.

SEE ALSO

Benches, deck . . . Carpeting, outdoor . . . Cookout bars . . . Firepits . . . Grills . . . Insect traps . . . Kitchens, outdoor . . . Patios . . . Picnic tables

Contrary to popular belief, you don't need charcoal to add charcoal flavor. The outdoor barbecue flavor you get is a result of charring and searing. The flavor and aroma actually come from the smoke of natural juices dripping on the hot ceramic (glass rock) briquets.

I had to see for myself and I can truthfully say that barbecuing with gas is having a cookout the "in" way—with the dependability of a kitchen range. I found that even the more economical cuts of meat can be transformed into mouth-watering delicacies—and fast. A one-inch thick steak can be grilled, well done, both sides, in about 11 minutes.

The gas-fired barbecue you see here is the Master Chef, manufactured by Charmglow Products, Inc. Antioch, Ill. 60002. It's a heavy cast-aluminum affair, which means it won't rust, and it can be mounted either on a fixed post or a pedestal base. It has a king-size, stainless-steel grill (375 sq. in. of cooking surface) and comes with an all-purpose rack for additional cooking

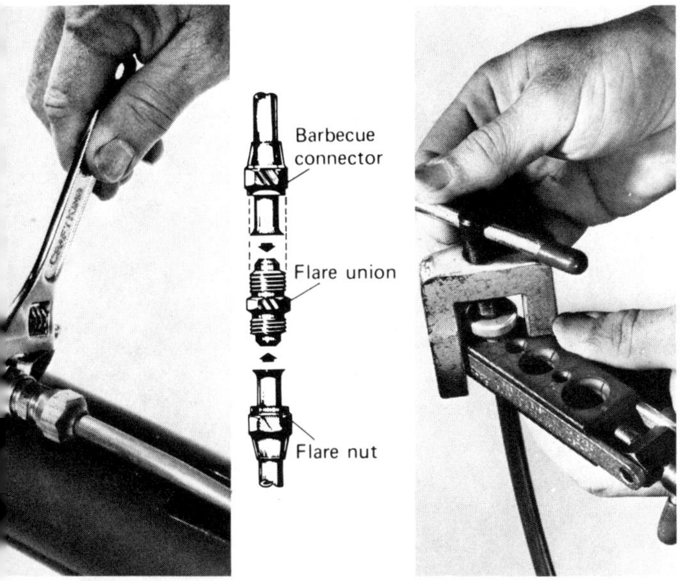

A FLARE-UNION FITTING is used to connect the supply line after the end of the ⅜-in. copper tubing has been flared with a flaring tool.

AFTER CONNECTING the supply line, center the post in a 2-ft.-deep hole and brace it plumb.

THE HOLE is filled with concrete to 1 in. below the gas-line connection, then with dirt.

ALUMINUM PIT is placed over post and locked by wingnut. Its front should face the same way as valve knob.

and warming. A full line of accessories includes a battery-operated rotisserie, a rotisserie basket, a wiener wheel, plus a handy "up front" shelf. You have to provide the ⅜-in. copper tubing for the gas line to the house and the necessary fittings. The series of pictures on these pages shows how I installed it.

How you tie-in to your existing household gas line will vary with each installation. I brought the tubing into the basement through a hole in the block wall and connected it at a point where a line branched off to the kitchen stove. This required shutting off the gas at the meter, backing out the stove-line connection, installing a ½-in. pipe-tee fitting as shown in the drawing on page 232 and reconnecting the stove line. A gas cock lets me shut off the gas to the barbecue during the winter. Your local gas company will make the actual connection if you prefer. If you do the job yourself, use pipe-joint compound on the fittings.

A word about using your gas-fired barbecue:

- Be sure the glass briquets are distributed evenly, one layer thick, over the entire surface of your grate. Under normal use, the briquets should last for years.
- If it's windy, swivel your barbecue with its "back" to the wind before you light it. This is done by loosening the thumbscrew just below the pit.
- Always light your barbecue with the cover wide open. Keep the cover open and leave the

BURNER IS PLACED in bottom of pit and air mixer lowered into hole until it fits over the orifice cap.

TO TURN ON GAS, valve is pressed inward, turned counterclockwise. *Never light gas with cover closed.*

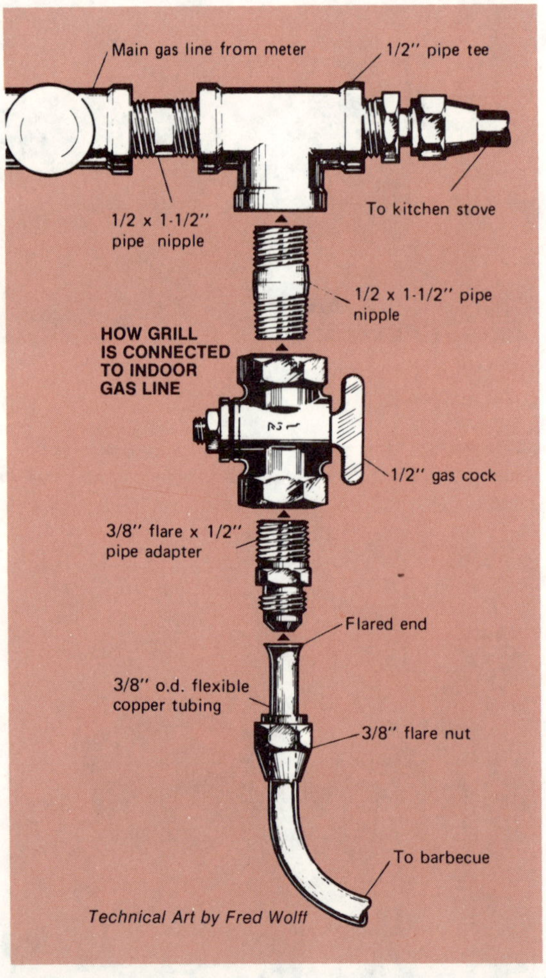

control on "high" for about 10 min. to heat the glass briquets thoroughly before you begin cooking. The briquets will not turn color when heated, so allow ample warm-up time.

- For broiling and most grilling you will want to leave the cover open. But for roasting, with or without a rotisserie, the cover should be closed. When it's closed, "low" heat will hold the temperature at about 300°, "high" heat will hold the temperature at about 500°.
- Some "flare up" of meat juices dripping onto the heated glass briquets contributes to the outdoor flavor, but excessive flaming can burn meat. Fortunately, flare-up is minimized with a gas barbecue because you can control the heat. If you trim excess fat from the meat beforehand, most drippings will be dissipated by the radiant heat of the briquets. If flame persists, just sprinkle a little water on the glass briquets to extinguish the flames.

Occasionally, the glass briquets should be turned over to clean and burn off the excess grease. The stainless-steel cooking grids may develop a "rust" color or stain due to intense heat. To brighten, rub with steel wool. The first time the barbecue is lighted, let it burn at "low" heat for about one hour to burn off the newness.

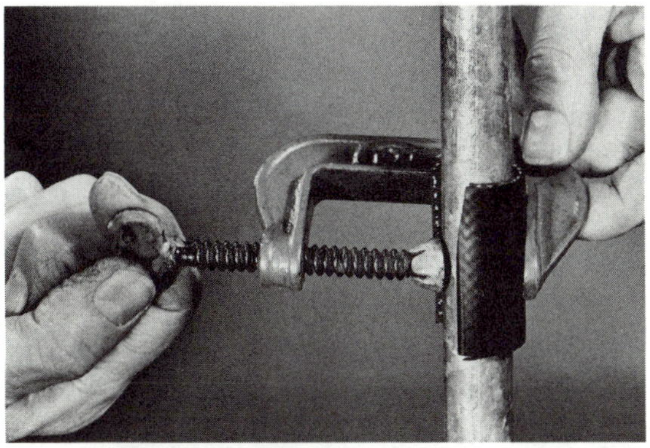

IF A WATER PIPE BREAKS on Sunday, a C-clamp and a piece of garden hose will stop the leak until you can get a plumber. Slit the hose, place it over the hole and clamp it tightly.

A STRIP OF SANDPAPER glued to the handle of your saw will be extra handy when you wish to keep a fine point on your marking pencil. Use double-back tape to simplify renewing the paper.

CUTTING THE OPENING for a switch or receptacle in a plaster wall is less messy if you tape a cardboard box to the wall before you start sawing. It will catch most of the dust.

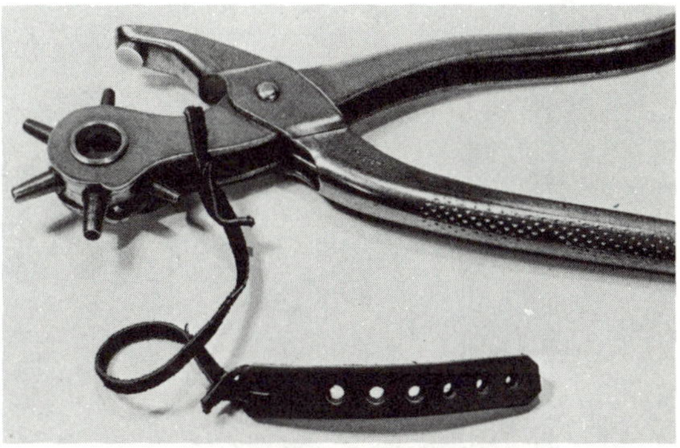

A HOLE SIZER made of scrap leather is a handy gauge to have tied to your punch. It gives you a chance to try out the rivet for size and assures picking the right one before punching the hole.

WHEN YOU'RE FACED with pulling a headless nail with a hammer, remember this time-saving stunt. Clamp your locking pliers on the nail and then hook the hammer claw under the pliers. Out comes the nail in a jiffy.

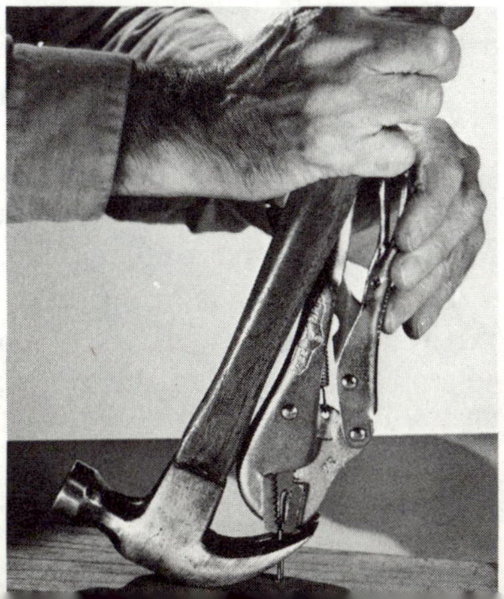

WHEN BORING A ROW OF HOLES to form a mortise, you can prevent the bit from "running out" by inserting a short dowel in the last hole bored. The dowel stops the bit from wandering offcenter and into the previously bored hole.

STARTING A NAIL overhead when it's too high to hold by hand is simple with the help of aluminum foil. Poke the nail through the foil, then wrap the foil around the end of a hammer. Once the nail is started, it will pull free.

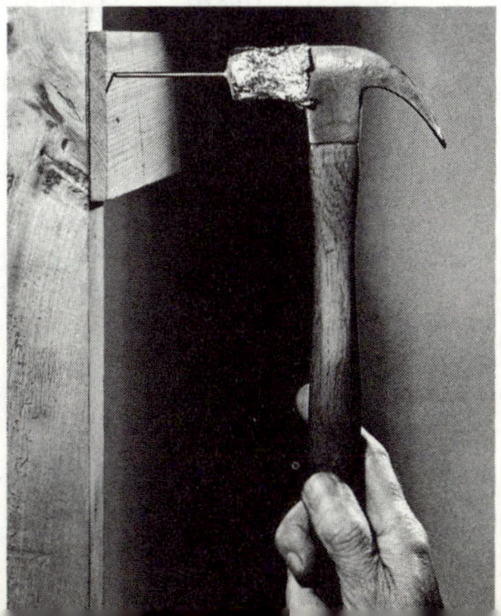

An accurate water barometer

By GERALD ZUHLKE

What does it mean when the water in this acrylic plastic device rises to a high level? Stormy weather's coming!

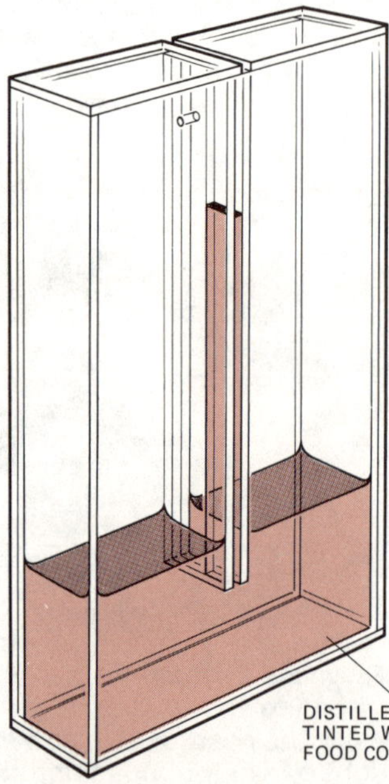

■ BAROMETRIC PRESSURE can be measured by a variety of devices. A most ingenious—and simple—one to make is the water barometer. It is surprisingly accurate in predicting stormy weather by the rise of the water level in its spout.

In this barometer, a high water level in the spout corresponds to a low-pressure system and vice versa. Being sensitive to temperature changes and atmospheric pressure, it should be placed where room temperature is fairly constant—not in direct sunlight.

Except for the walnut mounting panel, it is made almost entirely of ⅛-in. sheet acrylic plastic. The three pieces for the internal U-shaped spout are cut and cemented together first. Here it's best to use a fourth (scrap) piece as a temporary spacer between the two sides to keep them parallel. Hold the four pieces together with one hand and apply the cement to the back edges of the three with the other. See that the cement does not reach the temporary spacer and prevent it from being removed when cement is dry. A 7/64-in. hole must be made in the glued-up assembly to insure equal pressure in both chambers of the barometer.

The spout is centered and cemented, first to the 4 x 7¼-in. back member, then to the front, ⅛-in. from the top. Tabs of masking tape will help you hold the spout in position. See that there are no air leaks along cemented edges. If a leak is found, a drop or two of epoxy glue will seal it.

All other pieces, except the mounting post, are 1 in. wide, and to insure uniformity and a perfect fit, it's best to cut the five parts from a single inch-wide strip of plastic. Sanding and buffing, necessary only where edges are exposed, should be done before the parts are cemented. Start with medium-grit abrasive paper, then use fine and, finally, very fine grit before polishing with a cloth buffing wheel charged with jeweler's rouge. Cement the two 1 x 7¼-in. side pieces to the front and back members first, inserting them between the two and flush with the edges. Then cement the 1 x 4¼-in. bottom piece, using masking tape to hold it, followed by the two top pieces. Top and bottom pieces lap the edges; only the sides fit between.

SEE ALSO
Plexiglass projects . . . Weather instruments

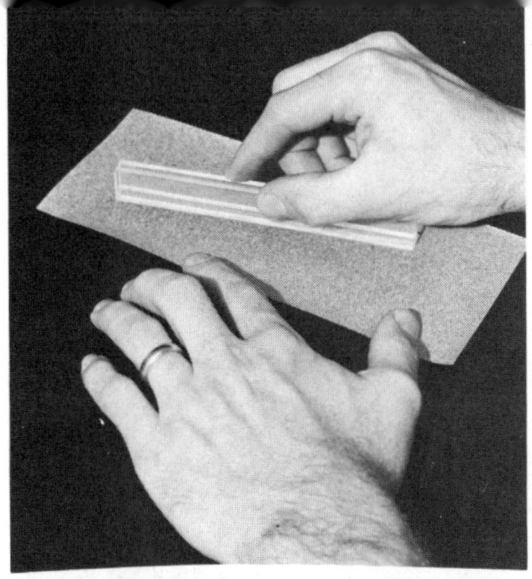

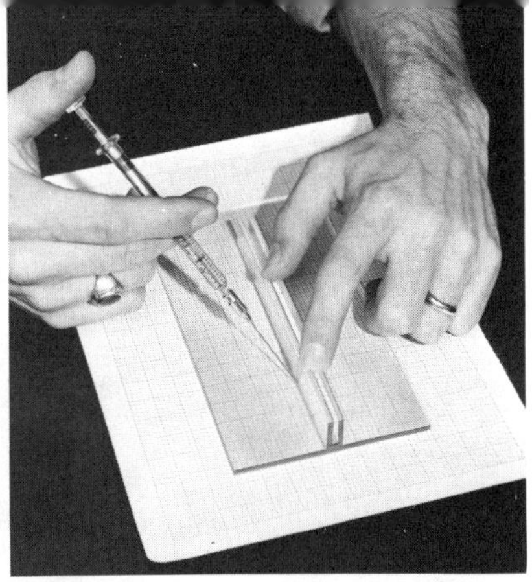

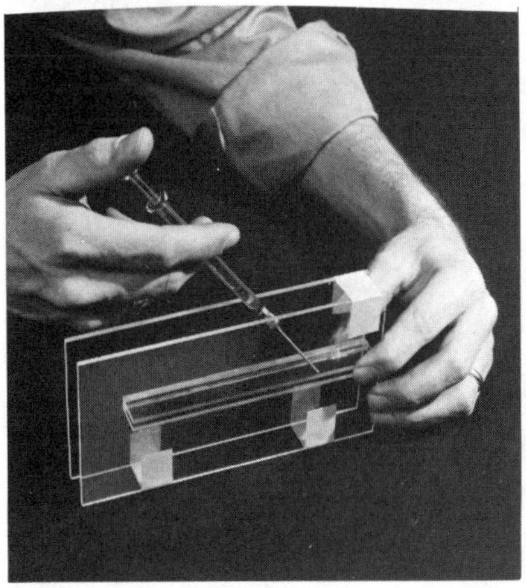

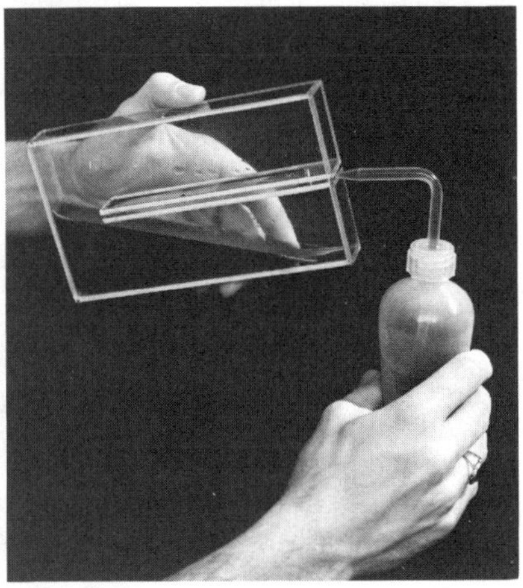

1. SANDING and polishing of the edges is required only when they are exposed. Start with a medium paper and work up to a very fine grade.

2. A SPECIAL cement applicator, or syringe, is used to "weld" parts together by capillary action. Avoid getting cement on the surface.

3. MASKING TAPE is used to hold the parts in alignment while they are being cemented. It's important that the joints do not leak air.

4. FILLING WITH distilled water tinted with food coloring is best done with a chemist's wash bottle or a clean plastic squeeze bottle.

Now check for leaks by filling the barometer with water; use epoxy to seal any holes. A ¼-in.-sq. plastic post is used to mount the barometer to the walnut panel. Before cementing it to the back of the barometer, drill and tap two holes in it for 6-32 x ¼-in. rh machine screws. The section view, at right, shows how screws fit in counterbored holes in the back of the mounting panel.

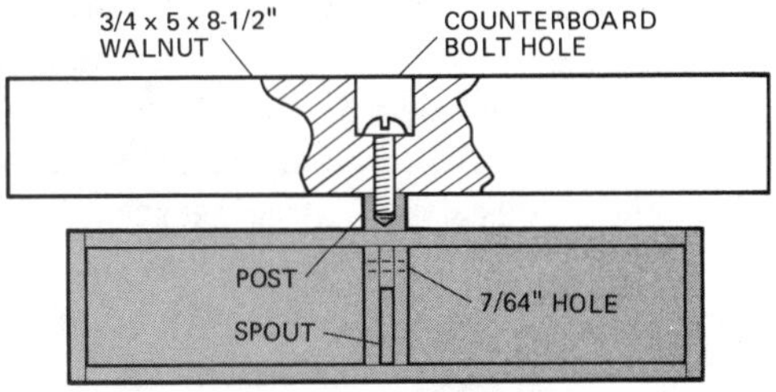

SECTION
(TOP REMOVED)

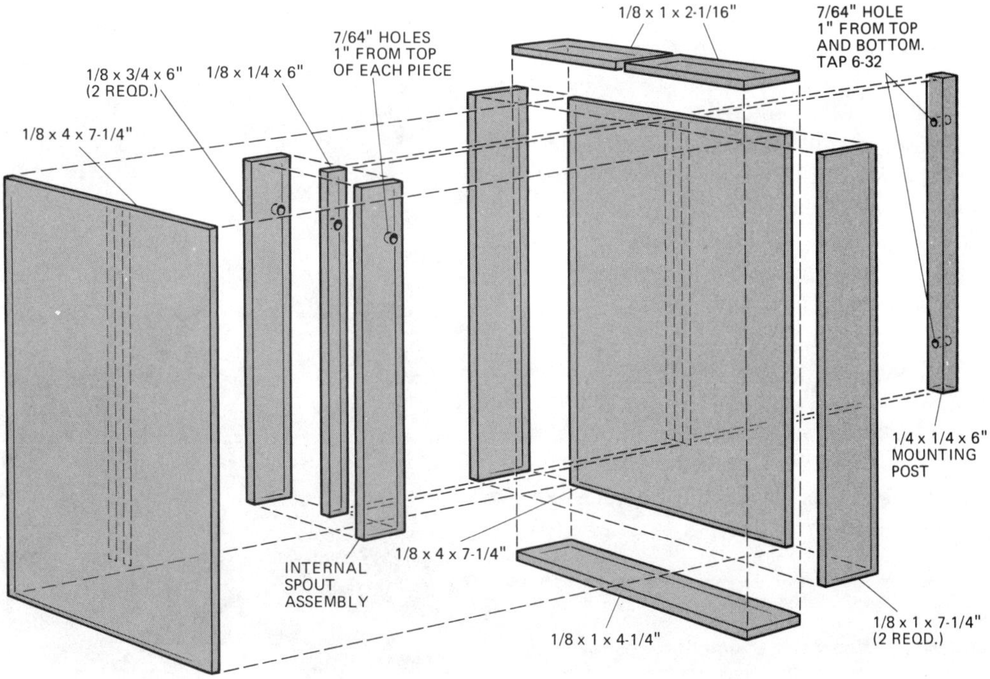

Make this handsome banjo barometer

By W. CLYDE LAMMEY

■ IN EARLIER DAYS householders relied on barometers for daily weather "reports." These instruments were generally of the "banjo" type and many were made both large and ornate. By using less complicated and relatively inexpensive instrumentation, you can make a banjo barometer which is an ornamental and useful replica of the older types.

The barometer illustrated has all the fittings of the old ones except the level, which is unnecessary when an aneroid-type instrument is used. The frame, cap and pediment are of mahogany. Select a choice piece with attractive grain for the frame, enlarge and trace the pattern on it and then saw just outside the pattern lines so that you have a little stock left for sanding to profile.

Before you bore or saw the openings for the barometer and hygrometer, have the instruments at hand and determine from them the size of the openings. Allow a little extra for clearance, about ⅛ in. all around. Be sure also that the holes are located on the center line of the frame. The same will be true of the boxed thermometer, the oval-shaped "shell" inlay and the mirror. Overall dimensions given for the oval-shaped inlay are only approximations; they may vary so have the inlay at hand to lay out the recess.

Screws will be furnished with the fittings for attaching the mirror, the barometer and the hygrometer but not always for the thermometer. Use No. 0 ½-in. roundhead screws to attach the latter. Don't take the inside dimensions of the thermometer box literally. Check the size of the thermometer before you make the box, just to be sure there are no variations.

SEE ALSO
Finishes, wood . . . Weather instruments

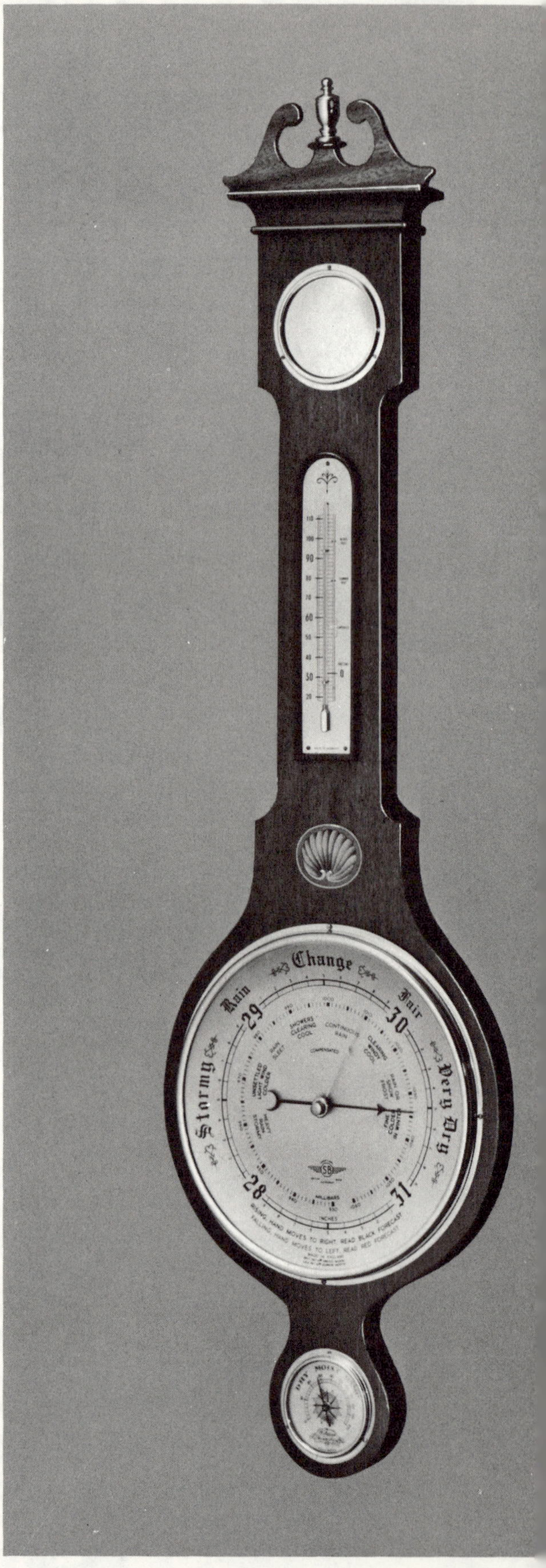

Don't hurry the sanding of the frame, particularly the bandsawed edges. Here you'll want to remove every saw mark by careful and thorough sanding to assure a flawless finish. The corners will require sanding with the paper wrapped around a dowel. Work progressively finer grades, finishing up with 180-grit garnet paper. A cabinet scraper will help remove saw marks fast.

The finish can be anything you like on mahogany, from natural color to dark reddish brown,

THE PEDIMENT PATTERN is traced on ¼-in. mahogany plywood. Place it so grain runs horizontally.

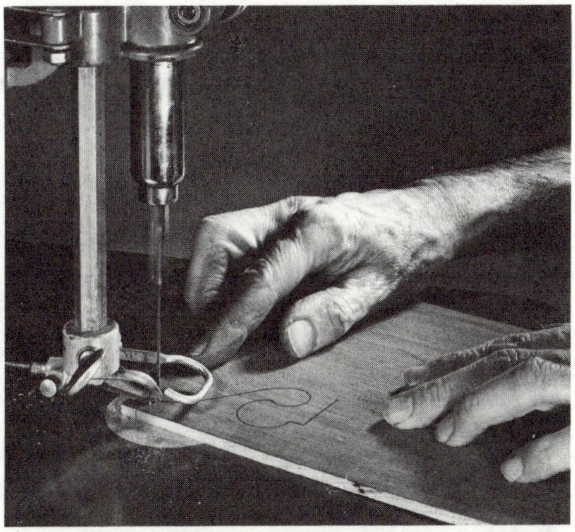

A JIGSAW does the best job of sawing out the pediment. Use a fine blade and follow the line carefully.

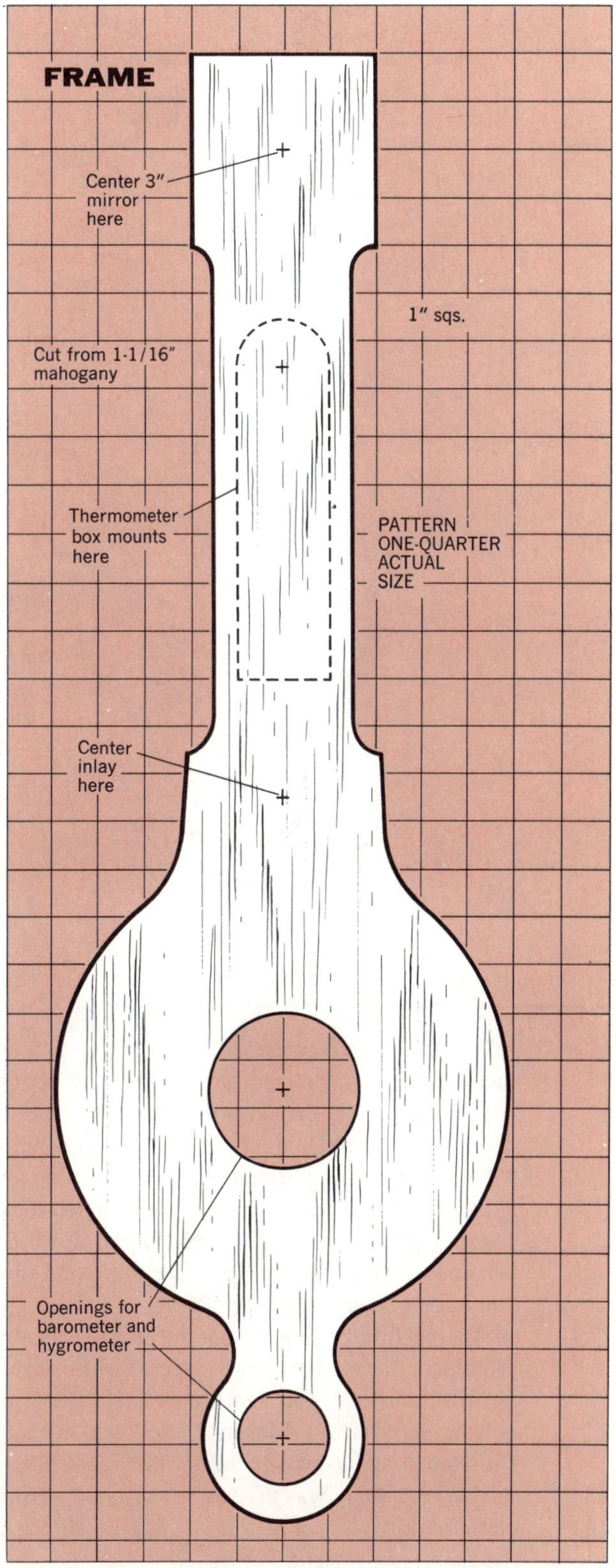

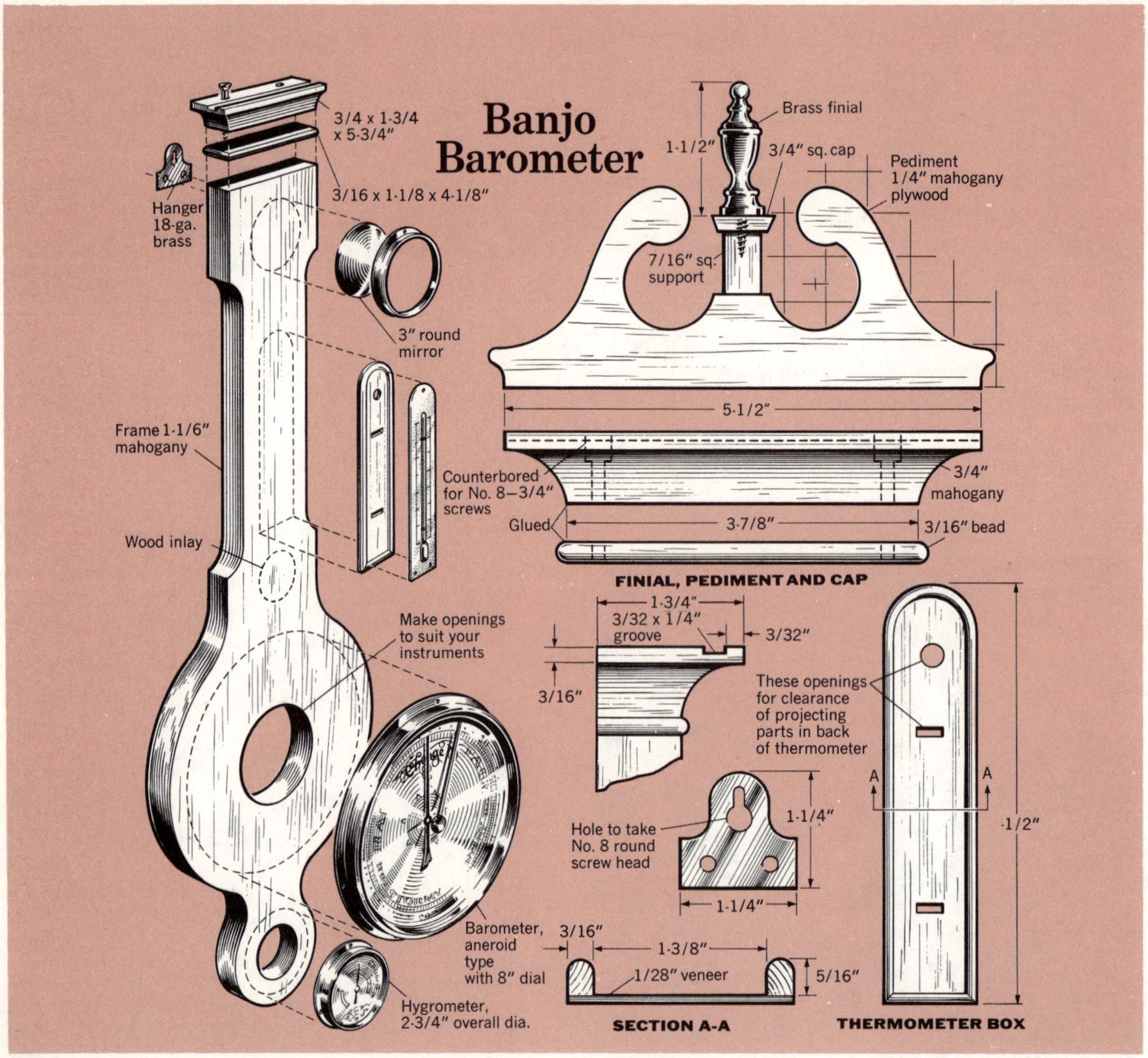

banjo barometer, continued

the latter being achieved by staining. Use a wiping stain so you can control more closely the depth of color. Then apply paste wood filler, wipe off, following directions on the can, and apply sealer when dry. Follow with at least two coats of semigloss finish. Carefully rub down the last coat with very fine (No. 4-0) steel wool until you have a beautiful satiny gloss.

All the fittings (including the barometer, hygrometer, thermometer and mirror) with matching silvered dials, plus the brass finial, are available in a kit from Mason & Sullivan Co., 39 Blossom Ave., Osterville, Mass. 02655. While an oval "shell" inlay was used in the original barometer, the kit includes a round inlay as shown in the photo at the right.

THE KIT includes all the instruments, mirror, finial and round "shell" inlay.

A handsome space-saving bar

By HARRY WICKS

WHEN YOU DECIDE to refinish your basement, the first, and wisest, step you can take is to draw up a floor plan. On it, in addition to the overall room dimensions, indicate floor-to-ceiling height, locations of pipes hanging from joists, meters, electric panels and any other apparatus that might require an access panel.

The Eugene P. Southers of Bellerose, N.Y. approached their basement project in just such a manner. Then, armed with this information,

SEE ALSO
Basement remodeling . . .
Basement waterproofing . . . Family rooms . . .
Game tables . . . Pool tables . . . Remodeling . . .
Shelves . . . Snack tables . . . Storage ideas . . .
Storage walls

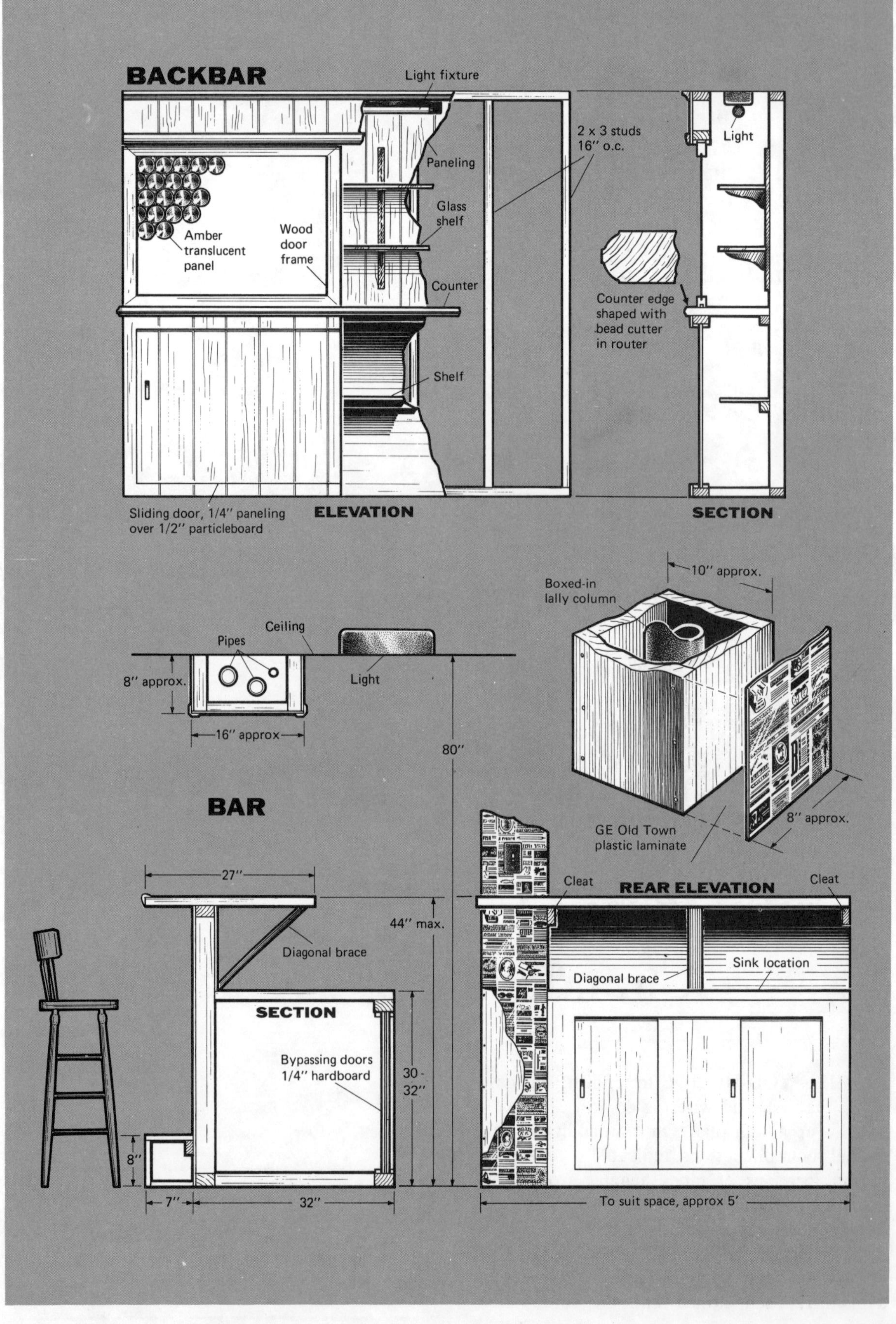
BACKBAR
Light fixture
2 x 3 studs
16" o.c.
Paneling
Glass
shelf
Amber
translucent
panel
Wood
door
frame
Counter
Shelf
Sliding door, 1/4" paneling
over 1/2" particleboard
ELEVATION
Light
Counter edge
shaped with
bead cutter
in router
SECTION
10" approx.
Boxed-in
lally column
Ceiling
Pipes
8" approx.
Light
16" approx
80"
8" approx.
GE Old Town
plastic laminate
BAR
27"
44" max.
Diagonal brace
SECTION
Bypassing doors
1/4" hardboard
30 -
32"
8"
7"
32"
Cleat
REAR ELEVATION
Cleat
Diagonal brace
Sink location
To suit space, approx 5'

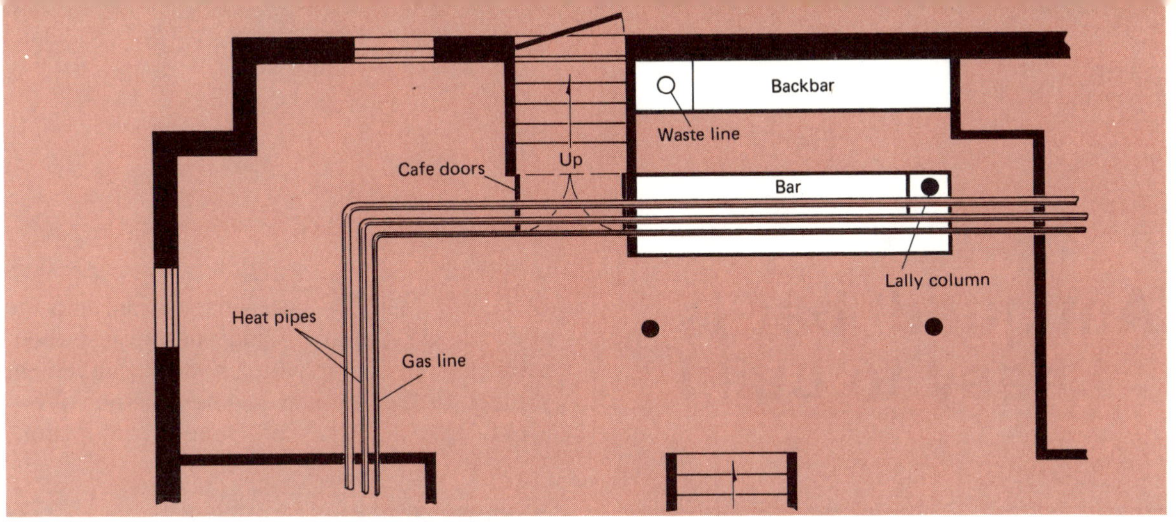

they determined how the entire room would be treated logically and attractively. Since they do considerable entertaining (and the family includes six active youngsters) they viewed the problem from a very practical and convenient viewpoint and wisely decided there was a need for a "wet" bar (a bar with a built-in sink).

There's no arguing that a bar takes an inordinate amount of floor space. So, where to place it is of considerable concern. In their layout (above) they located the bar directly beneath several low-hanging heat pipes. (There is also a water line and shutoff valve in the cluster hanging below the joists but for clarity's sake, they are not shown in the art.) This location is space that would otherwise have been wasted because of the drop ceiling. As can be seen in the drawings and the photograph, there is plenty of headroom for the bartender behind the bar and the guests in front on the barstools.

The bar is built to architectural standards. The dimensions shown give a comfortable working area, and you will notice that most of them are variable. The variables, of course, are for customizing the bar to suit the person who will use it, as every person has his own opinion as to the location of certain items.

The sink was no problem because in this house the drain-waste line exits from the cellar floor. But if your line is hung from the joists, you can install a pump to handle water discharge.

plastic laminate on counter surface

As a matter of convenience and to reduce maintenance, Souther used plastic laminate on the work-counter surface behind the bar. And he went all the way by installing a laminated backsplash. In the final analysis, his decision was a sound one, as it was more durable and made cleaning up an easier job.

The lally column at one end of the bar was slightly out of plumb; thus, as can be seen in the drawings, it took considerable material to box it in. And the appearance was not good, so it was decided to make a strong point out of a weak one by making it decorative. Since the bar top was laminated with Formica's Persimmon (suede finish), the laminate applied to the boxed-in lally was selected to heighten the festive air that a party room should have. GE's Texolite Oldtown 6000 pattern was the choice.

nook in foundation wall

Another factor in selecting this particular location for the bar was the "nook" that existed in the foundation wall. It was a natural for a back bar. Fitted below with sliding doors that can be locked with a standard sliding-door lock, the space behind provides storage for party potables and the like.

For appearance's sake, the deck (the counter separating the upper and lower sections of the cabinet) was made of 5/4-in. (nominal) stock. The top and bottom edges were shaped with a bead cutter in the router to create an architectural shadow-line. The deck was stained to match the paneling and treated with two coats of semi-gloss varnish.

To help eliminate the dark, cavelike look that is common in many finished basements, the upper part of the cabinet was fitted with a pair of sliding doors made of translucent, amber panels of "bottle" design. Then, with a light installed overhead and glass used for shelving, the effect is much the same as if it were a first-floor window.

access to water valve

Though not obvious in the photo on page 185, there is an access panel fitted under the dropped ceiling for quick access to that water shutoff valve mentioned earlier.

All in all, Souther's planning paid off; the room provides an area for the youngsters, another for adult gatherings, and the handsome bar to serve as a focal point.

'Antiqued' bar is easy to build

■ START WITH a little imagination, add the ability to do it yourself and you are just about assured of ending up with a home improvement project full of creative—and inexpensive—ideas. David Noyes of Deephaven, Minn.,

"OLD WORLD" LOOK is achieved through the use of some dark-stained beams, a wine rack and stemware shelving. For convenience, the bar was built near existing sink.

SEE ALSO

Basement remodeling . . . Cabinet furniture . . . Family rooms . . . Game tables . . . Shelves . . . Soda fountains . . . Theaters, home . . . Wall shelves . . . Wine racks

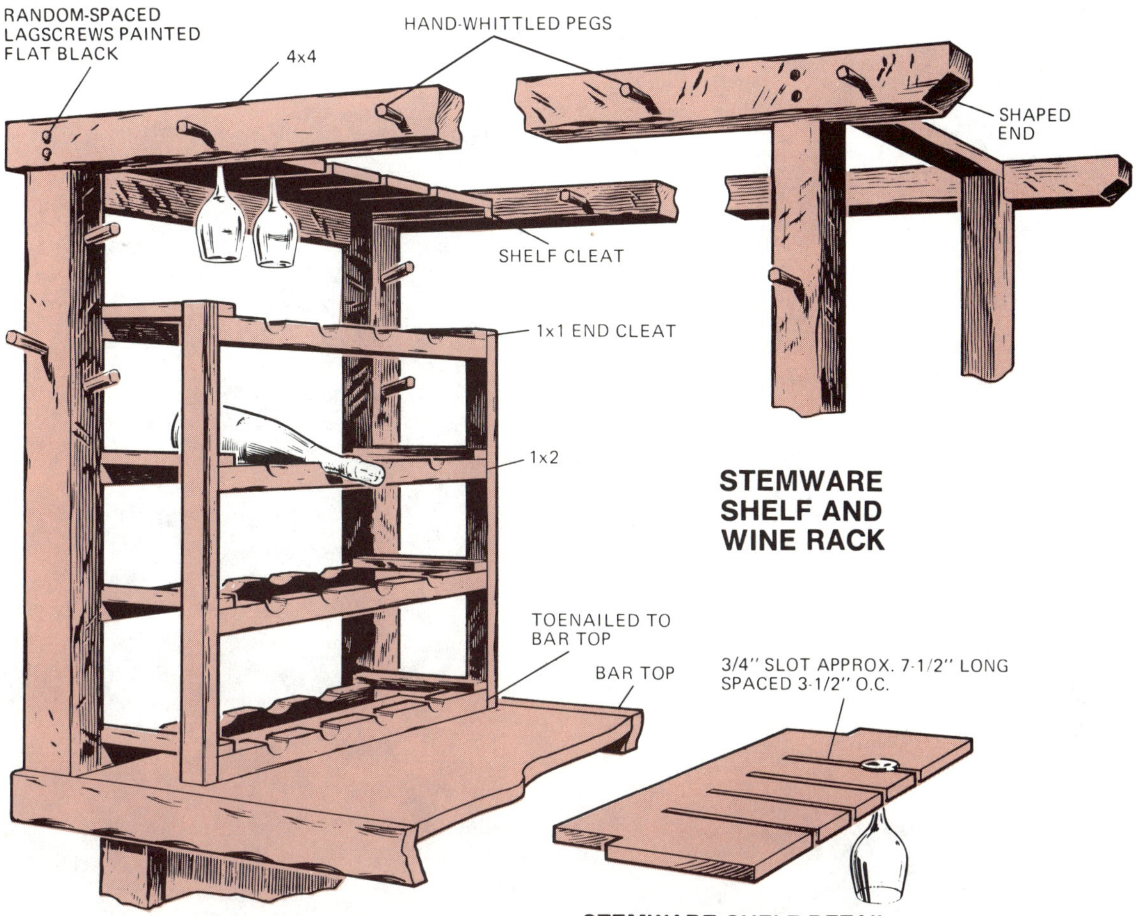

STEMWARE SHELF AND WINE RACK

STEMWARE SHELF DETAIL

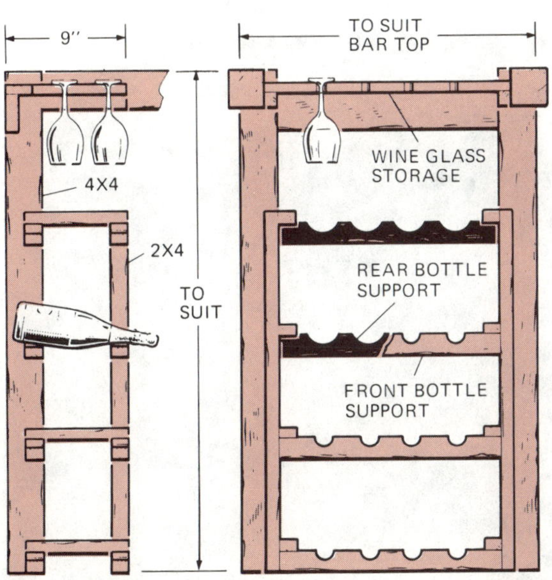

wasn't afraid to tackle the actual work, and for out-of-the-ordinary ideas, he consulted Minneapolis designer Paul Albitz. The resulting warm, informal room proves you don't have to pour thousands into a project to get additional attractive living space.

Strategic placement of the bar enables the "bartender" to make use of appliances and sink in the kitchen that was already in the basement. Two elements that distinguish this bar are distressed beams and the combination wine-rack, stemware-storage shelf. Antiquing the beams is more a matter of time than skill; for effect, use a dark stain and semi-gloss varnish to finish.

THE OAK TEXTURE of the staves (above) is obvious. When closed (right), the bar serves as a table. Potables and glassware (below) are neatly corralled.

You can add a bit of humor to your den or family room by making a novel bar that will be ideal on those occasions when the gang's all there

Roll out the barrel!

By HARRY WICKS

■ A USED WHISKEY BARREL—which a distiller will ship to you for under $30—can be converted into a handsome, masculine bar that will be a focal point for your home entertaining.

The barrel is readily available. (See the "Manufacturers of Materials" list on page 193.) It comes from distillery to you as shown in the photo on the same page.

Before you put a saw to the barrel, securely fasten the hoops to the staves with screws. Also, you should drill through each stave into the barrel top and secure the top with 1½-in. screws.

For the door cutout I chose a spot near the bunghole so that this feature would face the room. Make the cutout with a bayonet-type saw; I used a Sawzall fitted with a hacksaw blade. A sabre saw could be used but it will take more time.

Once the barrel is cut open, you'll know it's authentic. Its inside face is charred and reeks of bourbon. So, cart it outside and use a hand scraper to remove the char. Then, give it a good sanding with a belt sander and about a No. 40-grit paper.

On the bar shown I left some char in the crevices to retain authenticity. Also, I saved the shipping label, glued it inside the barrel and antiqued it with burnt umber. The only further work inside the barrel is to varnish it. To seal in that smell, give it at least three or four coats.

The various shelves and support ribs are all cut from ¾-in. plywood. Their exact radii and dimensions will be determined by where you place them in your barrel. The safest bet is to make either cardboard or ¼-in. hardboard templates first; then, when satisfied with fit, transcribe outline to the plywood and cut.

The bottle base. Though the bottles could stand in a much easier-to-construct, fixed stand, I decided to incorporate a rotating base utilizing a lazy Susan ring purchased at the local hardware store. When laying out the bottle shelf, first decide which whiskies will be held by the shelf; then, depending upon the brand, you can conceivably vary the hole diameter if desired. All openings here were cut to a 4-in. diameter, and the shelf holds seven bottles.

The bottle base (E) is painted flat black and the wells which receive the bottles, made with a router, are lined with adhesive-backed green felt. Part G is laminated as are the tops and the shelves.

The glass shelf. Make certain that you place the glass shelf so that when the glasses are suspended in it, the bottles will clear them when the lazy Susan is rotated. Here again, cutouts will be determined by what glasses you wish to keep in the bar. Dimensions shown are for standard highball glasses.

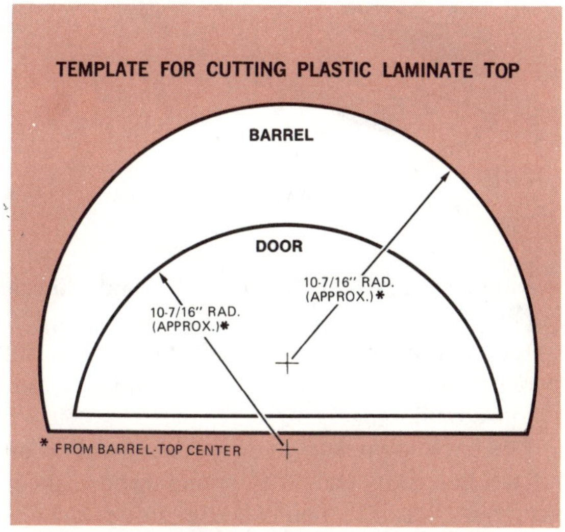

CUTTING LAMINATE for the tops of both the barrel and the door can be somewhat tricky. To save wasting your costly laminate, make the cardboard templates first, using the approximate radii shown. Then fit the cardboard, using scribers. When you're satisfied with the fit, transfer the marks to the laminate, cut them out with a sabre saw, test-fit the pieces and, if necessary, file any rough spots. Before you apply any contact cement, make matching position marks on both the laminate and the barrel.

SEE ALSO

Butler's tables . . . Cabinet furniture . . . Family rooms . . . Mobile furniture . . . Modular furniture . . . Planters . . . Snack tables . . . Storage ideas

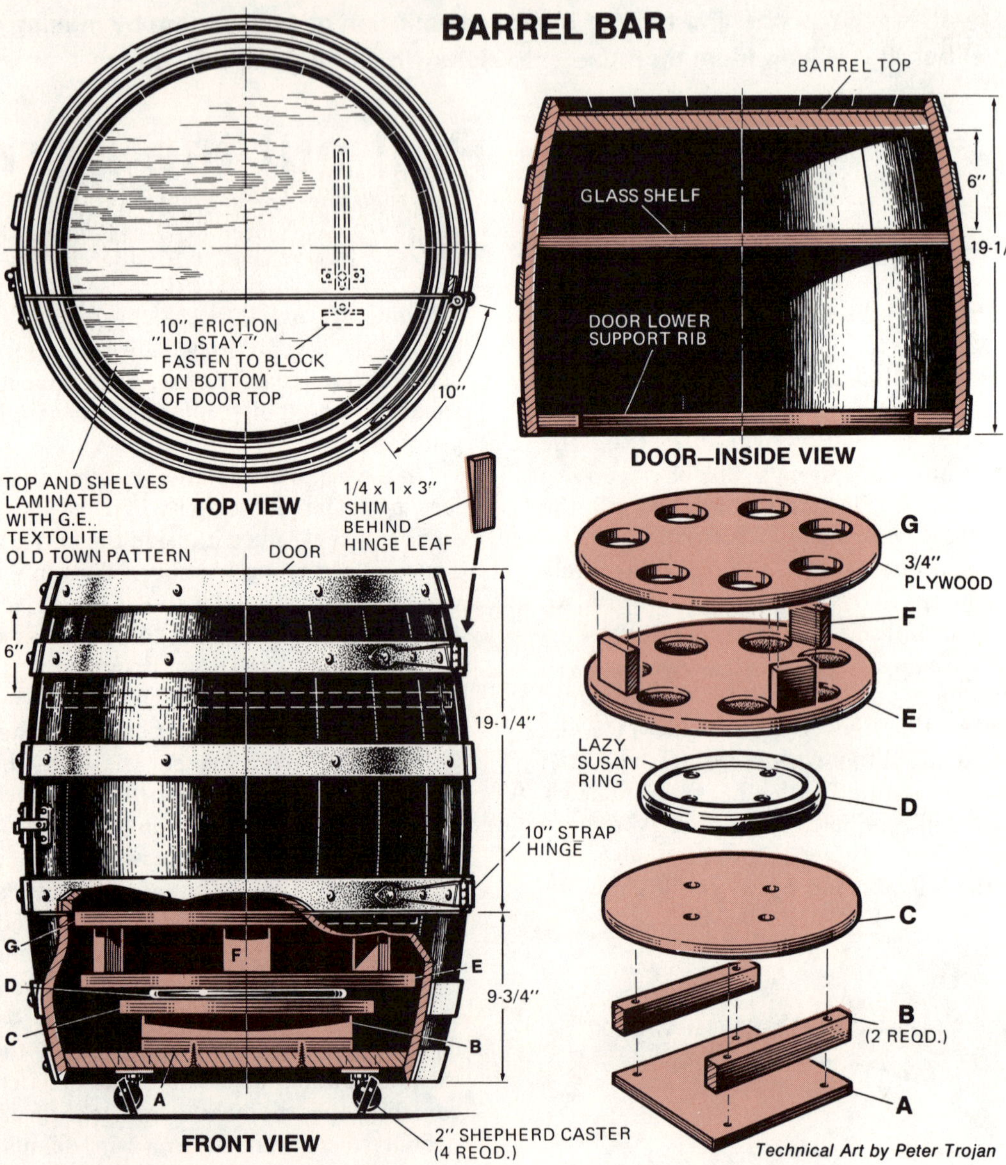

Once the plywood has been fitted where you want it and the glass hole cutouts have been made, the part can be laminated and installed. To fasten it, use counterbored 3-in. screws (one through each stave) and plug the holes with hardwood dowels.

Follow the same procedure for parts that go into the door. Again, cutouts should be determined by the bar accouterments you plan to use. In fact, if desired, the glass shelf on the door can be laid out to provide a cutout for an ice bucket. Swizzle sticks, as shown in the photo, are simply stacked in one of the old-fashioned glasses.

Finishing the outside. Since you'll want to retain an authenticity and that tavern look mentioned earlier, don't oversand the piece. Using a belt sander, start with a No. 40-grit paper, then graduate successively to 60, 80, 100 and 120-grit paper.

If there is excessive rust on the hoops, chuck a wire brush in your drill and remove any rust that is loose or flaking.

The bar shown was given a coat of walnut oil stain followed by walnut filler and three coats of semigloss varnish. You can eliminate the staining and filling if you prefer the oak's weathered-gray look.

If the bar is to stay in a contemporary playroom, paint the barrel hoops and staves to suit the decor. On this one, hoops were simply painted with flat black before the varnish went on. Another look could be achieved by applying aluminum paint to the hoops and dulling them for a pewter-like finish.

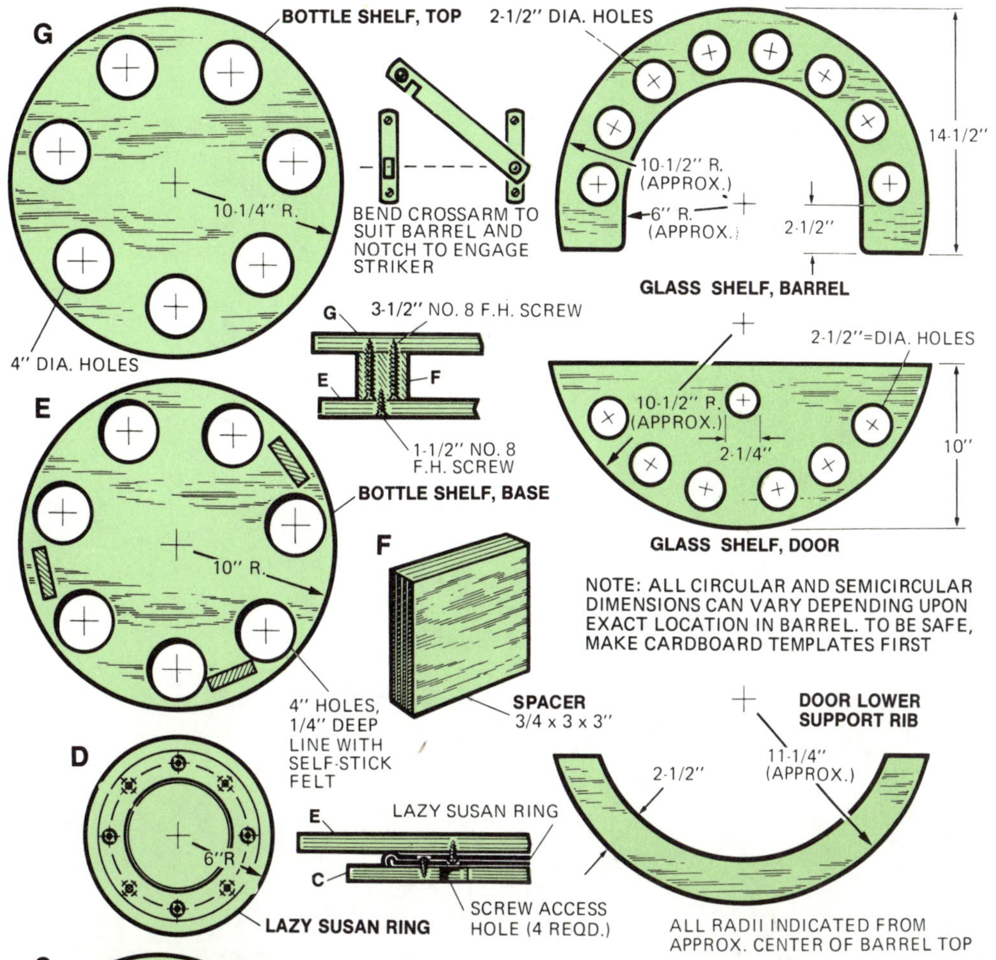

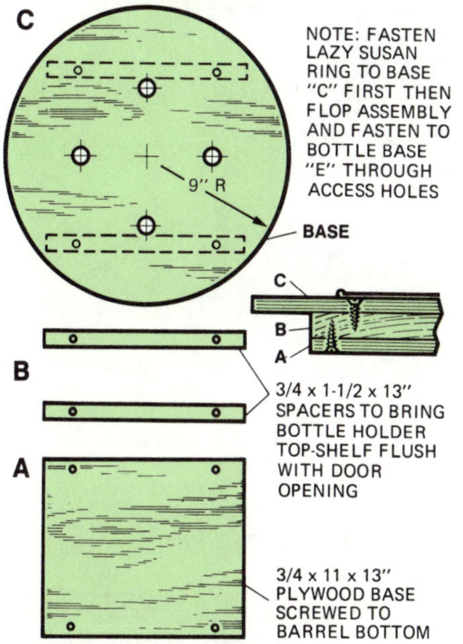

MANUFACTURERS OF MATERIALS

Barrel: G.I. Frazier Co., Box 8275, Louisville, Ky. 40208.
Casters: Shepherd Casters, Inc., St. Joseph, Mich. 49085. Model No. 200 (2" dia.).
Plastic laminate: G.E. Textolite, Old Town pattern. Available at lumberyards and building supply houses.
Finish: McCloskey Varnish Co., 7600 State Rd., Philadelphia, Pa. 19136. Walnut oil stain and Heirloom semigloss varnish.

THE BARREL is rough as shipped and has rusty bands. The best way to handle the 105-lb. container is to roll it along.

WHEN IT'S CLOSED, no one would guess this handsome cabinet is a home bar in disguise. You'd be more apt to think it a stereo console with speakers behind the doors. When open, it's a party center with all you need to add cheer to your entertaining.

This bar offers everything

By WAYNE C. LECKEY

■ OPEN OR CLOSED it's a beauty. It's a bar your guests will admire every time the drinks are on the house.

True, you'll have to be able to tie the sink into a drain pipe and connect it to hot and cold-water lines, but you'll have the ultimate in a home bar. It offers a roomy storage compartment for beverages; a handy drawer for napkins, stirrers and jiggers; a colorful bar-type sink; and a built-in mini-size refrigerator.

Its cost depends on materials used. We built ours from lumbercore plywood—better plywood than common fir but more expensive. We covered the plywood with plastic laminate to add a handsome, durable finish. It, too, added to cost. We used piano-type hinges for the drop-down counter and the flip-back top. Again plain butts would cost less.

If you skip the laminate and finish your cabinet with stain and varnish, you can't get by with less than cabinet-grade, veneer-face plywood for it to have a furniture-store finish. However, if a simulated wood-grain finish will do, you can build your bar from less expensive fir plywood.

building the cabinet

The basic cabinet is a simple structure. A ⅜-in. plywood back sits in a rabbet; shelves A, B and C, plus partition D, rest in rabbets and dadoes. Note that the ¼ x ¾-in. blind dadoes for shelf A and partition D are cut to full panel width and later filled at the front with filler blocks. A 13¾-in.-sq. cutout is made for the sink with a sabre saw before shelf A is installed.

If you cover the plywood with laminate, it's best, and easiest, to apply it to the interior surfaces before the parts are glued and nailed. We lined the three sink-compartment walls with Chinese red and faced the counter with black slate.

To assemble your cabinet, first glue shelf C to partition D, then the partition to shelf B. Add shelf A, then the ends and the back last. Add the back temporarily for now to help brace and square-up the assembly.

build kickboard separately

The three-piece, butt-joined kickboard is assembled separately, covered with laminate, glued to the bottom of shelf B and nailed from the top. We picked carpathian burl laminate and used it for a rich look on kickboard, ends, doors and top.

Rip the 2½-in.-wide skirt from ¾-in. hardwood, rabbet the back and run a cove along the top edge. Miter the front corners and glue it in place. The skirt is later antiqued and varnished, as is the door molding.

add laminate before hinges

To laminate exterior surfaces: First, edge-band top and front edges of end panels before the two-piece hinged top is in place. Then face the ends. As when edge-banding, cut the laminate ⅛ in. oversize and later trim it flush with your router and a special laminate cutter or by plane and file. In positioning laminate, butt the lower edge against the skirt and place the laminate just where you want it; once the cement-coated surfaces touch, you can't shift it. Contact cement bonds instantly. The edges of partition D and shelf C are painted along with the rest of the interior.

Next comes the two-piece hinged top: The front half has a cove around three edges; the rear half has one on outside edges only. A ⅜ x 7/16-in. blind rabbet is cut along the back edge for the cabinet back. Band the edges with laminate first. Keep the strips even with the cove and trim them flush at the bottom. Cover top and bottom surfaces with laminate, but do not face the top of the rear half until it has been installed with finishing nails driven through the top into top edges of the end members. The nails will go through the banding previously cemented to the edges.

You now can cover the top surface. Try to buy a 1½-in.-wide piano hinge to join the two halves; the hinge leaves will cover the full thickness of the plywood. If you have to settle for a ¾-in. hinge, you'll need to stain the exposed wood.

SEE ALSO
**Butler's tables . . . Family rooms . . .
Game tables . . . Hutch tables . . .
Nesting tables . . . Party tables . . .
Serving carts . . . Trays, folding . . . Wine racks**

doors are like picture frames

Doors and the drop counter are ⅜-in. plywood, covered both sides with carpathian burl laminate and framed like pictures. The 1⅛-in.-thick pine molding is stocked at lumberyards as solid crown. You have to rabbet it and miter the corners. Cut the rabbet 7/16 in. deep to take the added 1/16-in. laminate thickness. Make your frames first, insert the covered panels in the rabbets and then apply laminate to the entire backs.

The drop counter is built up quite similarly; while the frames start as two separate assemblies with inserts, they become one when glued and butted end to end. Install a drop pull in the center of each frame, with bolt heads set flush. Then cover the backs of the two frames with one piece of black slate laminate so the drop-pull screws are concealed below the surface. The counter is hinged to shelf A with a brass piano hinge, and an 18-in.-long brass support chain is attached at each end with screws. Magnetic door catches keep the counter and doors closed. The doors are hinged with 3-in. brass butts and fitted with Amerock's T-871 drop pulls in antique brass. The drawer rides smoothly on two ¾-in.-wide strips of scrap laminate cemented to the bottom of the compartment along the sides.

The refrigerator compartment accommodates an RV unit which requires a 2-in. air space in back and 4 in. above. The cabinet back is permanently attached after boring holes for water and drain lines and the refrigerator cord.

We used an antiquing kit to add a chateau-walnut finish to the pine skirt and door molding.

Here's how it's applied: Prime the bare wood with an enamel undercoater. When dry, brush on base latex (first coat in kit) and let this dry about 3 hours. Following the kit's instructions, wipe on sparingly a finish glaze with a lint-free cloth. For a realistic wood-grain effect, stroke the wet glaze lightly with cheesecloth. When glaze is thoroughly dry, you can apply clear urethane for a more durable finish.

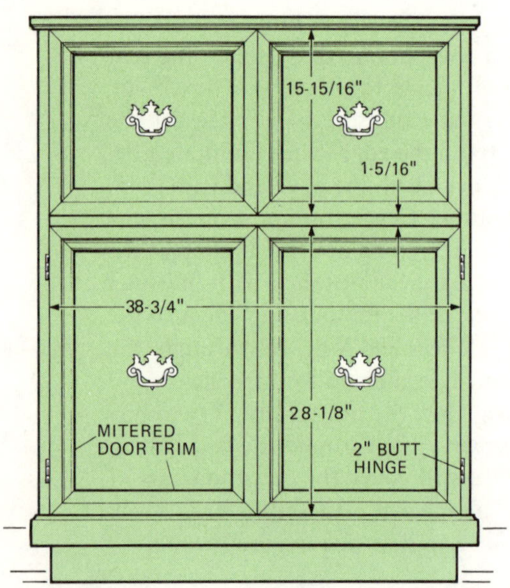

FRONT VIEW

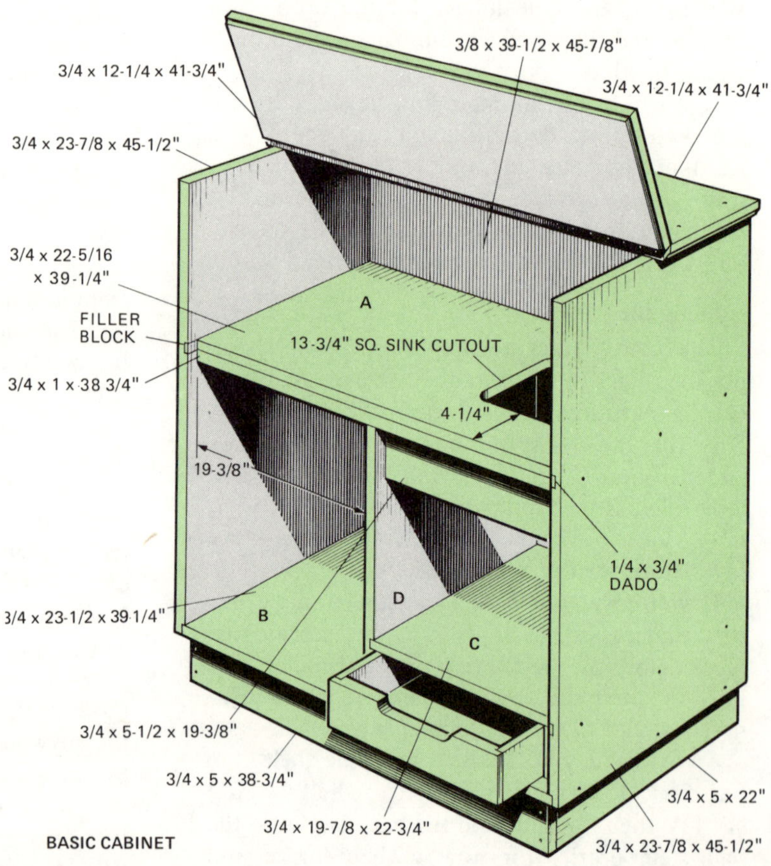

BASIC CABINET

RECESSED SHELF between counter and doors lets you lower counter without opening doors first. The recess depth should equal the thickness of the counter plus 1/16-in. clearance. A similar clearance is allowed at top of the counter and bottom of the doors.

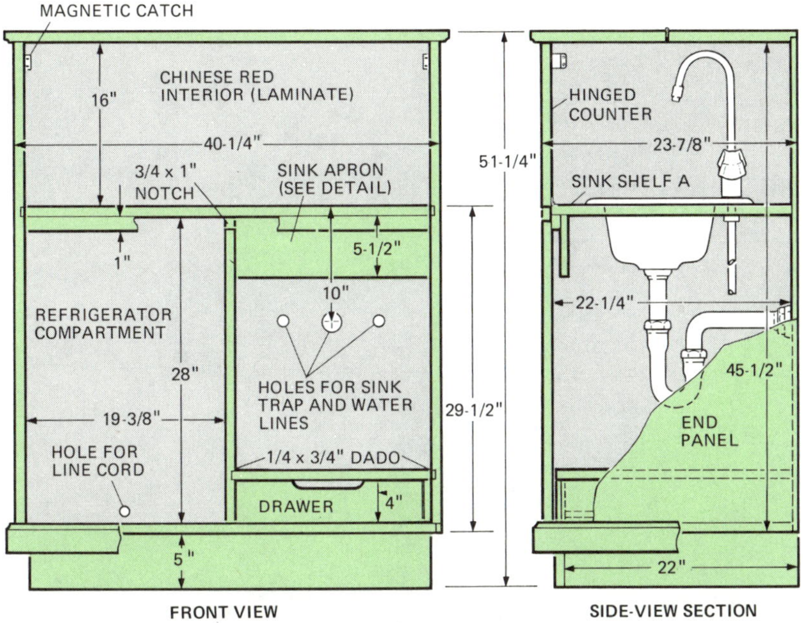

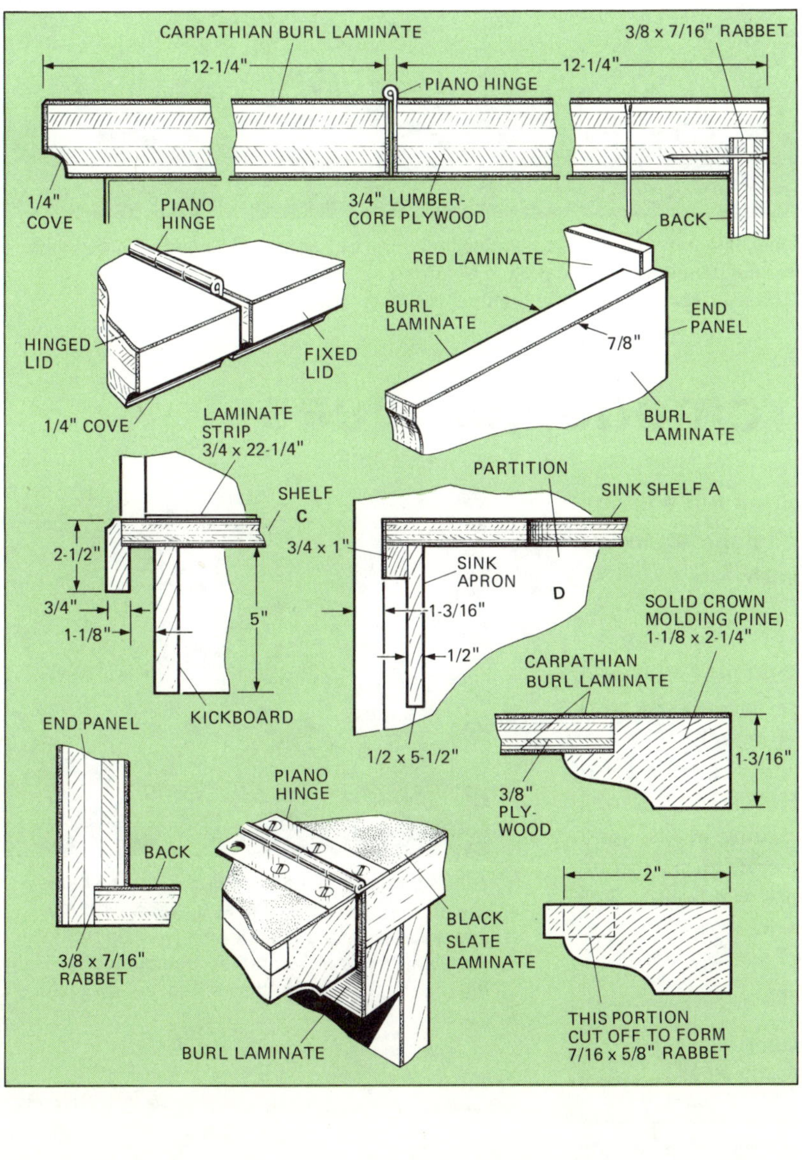

BAR'S REFRIGERATOR compartment is dimensioned to accept this Norcold RV unit. The refrigerator has walnut-finish door and runs on a battery or 110-v. current.

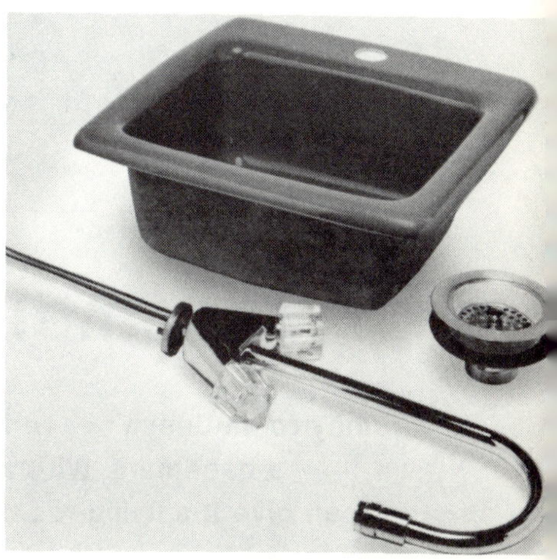

ACRYLIC BAR sink called Gimlet comes in red, black and sunflower colors with gold or chrome faucets, measures 15 x 15 in., is easy to install. From Kohler Co., Kohler, WI.

This view, taken from the same point as the photo below, was taken after remodeling. Rich walnut paneling was installed over furring strips nailed to the old wall. The handsome library wall features recessed lighting

Basement remodeling ideas

A family room doesn't have to look as if it's in a basement. With a little imagination you can give it a living-room warmth

■ THE DRAMATIC TRANSFORMATION of a family room shown on these pages is the work of interior designer Virginia Frankel, AID. Her client, a resident of Long Island, is a collector of rare books and lithographs. He wanted the room renovated to fulfill several specific needs. First, it had to house his rare-book collection. Second, he wanted to use it occasionally as a home office.

SEE ALSO

Bars . . . Basement waterproofing . . . Family rooms . . . Game tables . . . Mobile furniture . . . Paneling, wood . . . Remodeling . . . Shelves . . . Storage ideas . . . Storage walls

This is the view that greeted Ms Frankel when she arrived. Note the almost-useless window and wood paneling installed halfway up the wall, which magnifies, rather than camouflages, the foundation wall in this split-level basement

And, if needed, it had to be able to do double duty as a guest room.

The family room was dramatically changed from uninteresting to elegant and vibrant mainly by using rich, luxurious walnut paneling from U. S. Plywood's Weldwood collection. Ms Frankel was so successful in her efforts that the owners now confess to "almost full-time living in the room."

The conspicuous foundation-wall ledge typical of split-levels, was hidden by paneling fastened to furring strips installed over the existing wall. Cleverly arranged cafe curtains and drapes are used to hide the ledge behind the sleep-in sofa shown below.

The almost-useless window to the left of the triple mullion was closed in and concealed by installing bookshelves over the ledge; cabinets below this bookcase are fake. They are intended to carry out the library wall theme. The finished room suits this family's needs perfectly. More important, there are many features shown here that could be incorporated into the family room in almost any house.

These before and after pictures show what was done with the offcenter triple-mullion and half-wood wall. Creative use of paneling, a cafe-curtain arrangement and fake cabinets under the bookshelves mask the foundation ledge which had been obvious. Window shades are covered to match the curtains

How to frame a basement partition

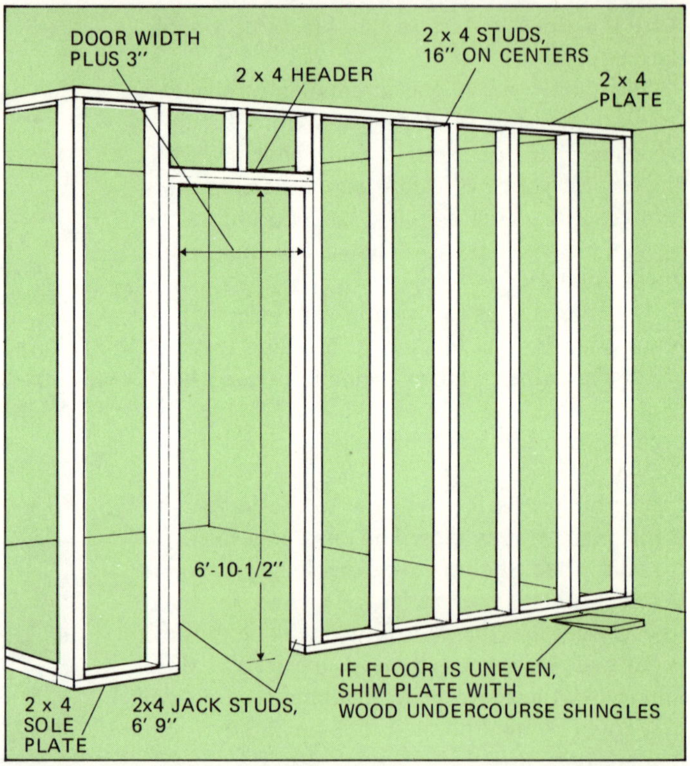

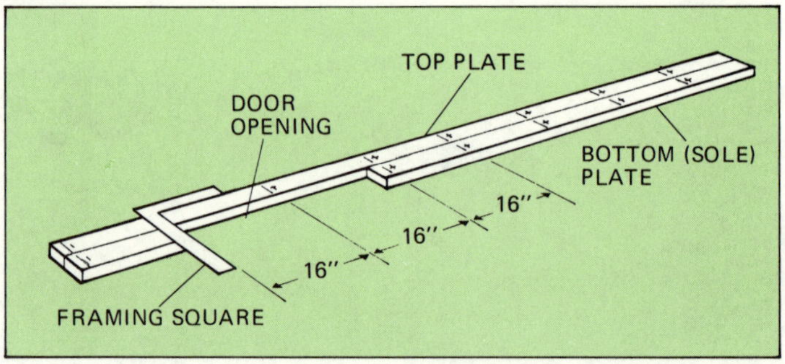

LAYING OUT STUDS

PARTITION WALLS can be erected by using single plates at bottom and top. Use long stock (at least 10-footers) for this chore, making certain that it's free of twist and bow. After cutting the plates to the required length, lay them side by side and mark off the stud locations (16 in. on center). Cut away portions for the door openings on the bottom plates only.

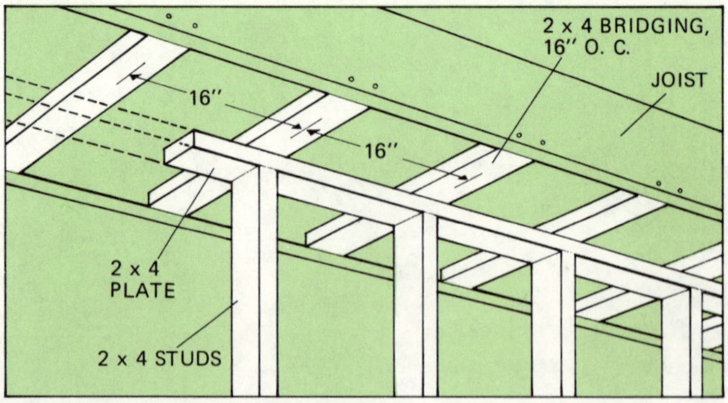

PROVIDING SOLID NAILING

IF YOUR PARTITION wall will be parallel with and between joists, you'll have to install nailers (often called cats) between—and flush with bottom of—the joists. The minimum number of nailers should be three in a 10-ft. plate-run—put one near each end and a third at the center. Cut the nailers for a force-fit between joists and install each of them with two 10-penny (10d) common nails.

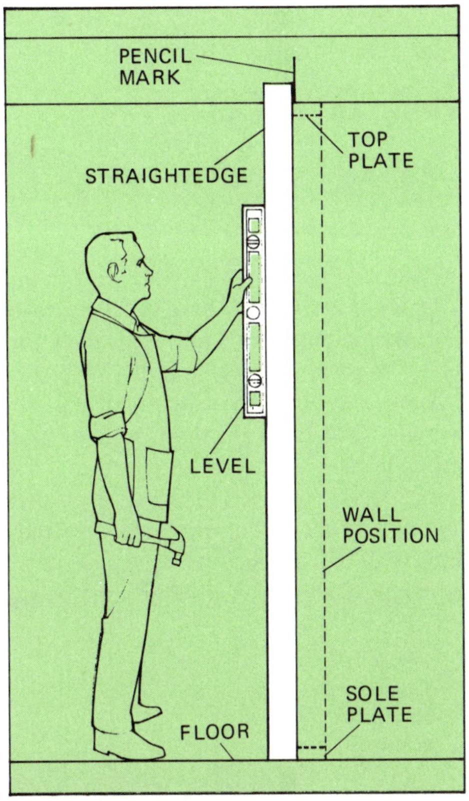

LOCATING TOP PLATE

TO SET THE WALL, snap a chalkline on the floor to mark the partition location. Then fasten the bottom plate in position, using either fluted masonry nails (wear safety goggles), lead anchors or masonry pins. To locate the top plate directly over the sole plate, use a straightedge (length of 2 x 3) and level as shown above. Plumb the straightedge and make several marks on the joists for the top plate at several points along the plate run.

BUILDING THE WALL

IF YOUR CONCRETE FLOOR is in good shape—that is, relatively level—you can assemble the studs to the top plate on the floor, then tilt the wall up into position as a unit. Check studs with your level (both vertical planes must be plumb) and fasten the top plate to joists with 10d nails spaced 16 in. o.c. But if your floor is not level, fasten the top plate only to those points marked on the joists and cut and install the studs one at a time. Stand on the sole plate to mark a stud for length, then cut the stud full (i.e., leave the line). Such a force-fit bears against the plates for rigidity; when you remove your weight, the plate springs up. You may find an assistant helpful for this part of the work.

NAILING A STUD

TO TOENAIL A STUD, place the stud on the line on the bottom plate and about an inch or so above the plate, then drive two 8d nails at about a 60° angle. Even though you buck the board (brace it with your shoe) it will move slightly off the line; bring it back to the line by driving a third 8d nail on the opposite side. Finally, to fix the stud, drive in a fourth nail on the face, or narrow, side. Repeat the toenailing at the top if installing the studs individually as mentioned under the heading *Building the wall* in the column at the right.

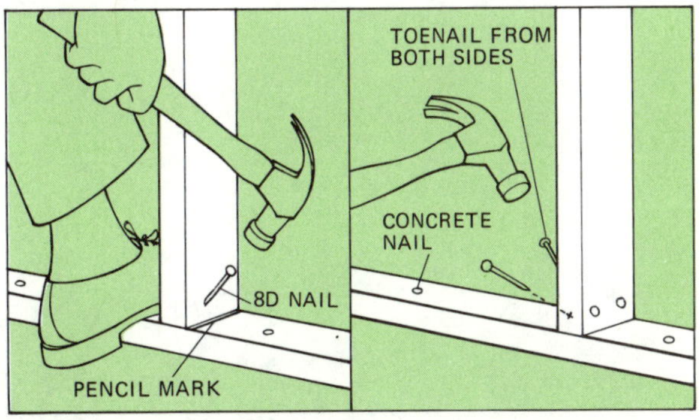

SEE ALSO

Basement stairwell . . . Bearing walls, removing . . . Family rooms . . . Fasteners . . . Hardboard . . . Home improvement . . . Lumber . . . Measurements . . . Moldings . . . Nails . . . Paneling, hardboard . . . Paneling, plywood . . . Paneling, wood . . . Plasterboard . . . Remodeling

Finish your basement like a pro

By JOHN GAYNOR and HARRY WICKS

THOUGH MANY do-it-yourself magazine articles make it seem that finishing a basement is a snap, it's not all that easy. It takes hard work and, more important, thorough planning before the job even starts. Framing and paneling the walls are probably the easiest parts of the job; how to handle finish details attractively is what usually stumps the average man remodeling his first basement.

In most basements (particularly in older homes), many access doors and some intricate framing around pipes and stairs are called for. This sets up a good rule of thumb: Wherever possible, keep eye and dust-catching hardware to a minimum. The ideas on these pages—used by the professionals—accomplish just that.

The three "door" treatments shown can solve just about any concealment problem, yet they boast a flexibility that lets you adapt to suit a particular problem. There are two important points

WATER SHUTOFF is hidden by a panel that is practically invisible because there is no hardware. The "door" removes quickly—a feature that is a must in an emergency; two magnetic catches hold it in place and cost only pennies. To minimize the chance of ½-in. panel warping, use contact cement to glue cutout before fitting magnetic catches.

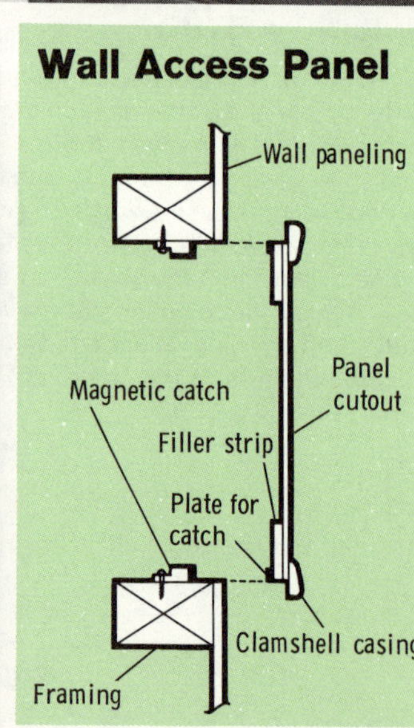

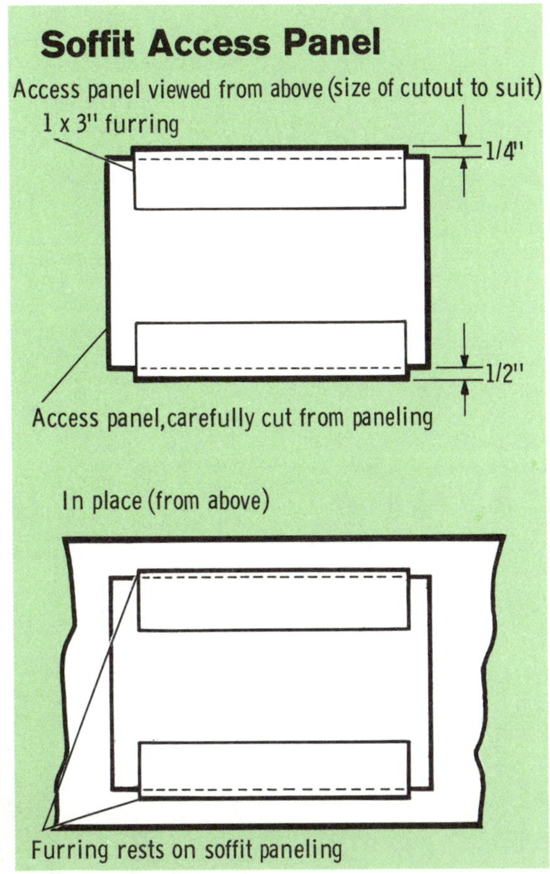

HARD-TO-SPOT access panel in box around pipes is pushed up, then lowered for removal. Here, since the joint is not concealed by molding, the panel should be cut from the drop ceiling to insure a splinterfree straightedge. Furring strips are fastened with glue and brads. Access panels shown are cut to insure a V-groove alignment between the panel and the cutout. Size depends on the opening.

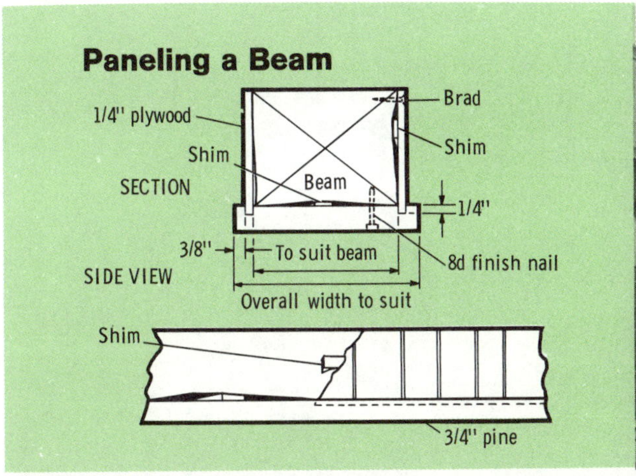

GOOD-LOOKING WAY to box in a beam eliminates time-consuming framing, costs less to do. Tack the clear pine temporarily to the beam's underside, level it with shims and drop the plywood panels into the grooves. Then, using undercourse shingles as shims, plumb the paneling, tack it at the top and nail the pine in place. Panel both sides completely before you drive the nails.

Backbar Access Panel

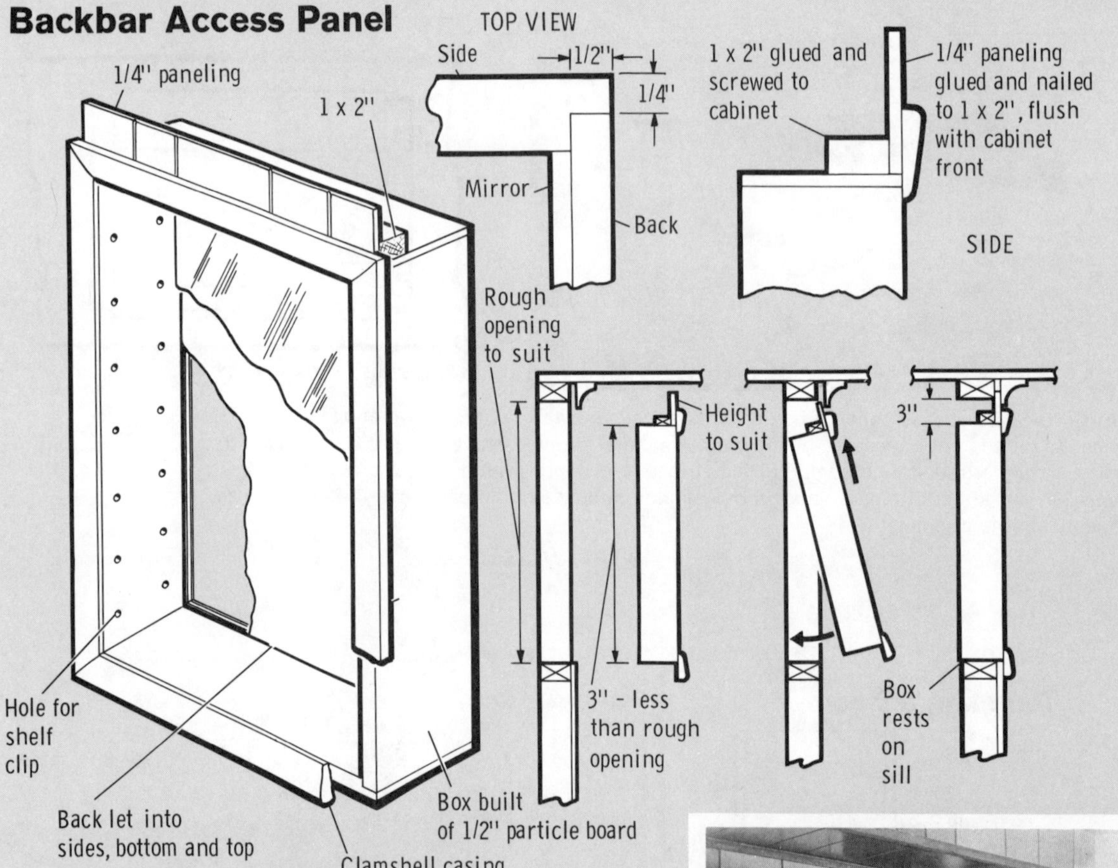

Access to crawlspace and cleanout plug in waste line doesn't have to be an ordinary hinged door. Handsome backbar at top left holds bar supplies, stands double duty. No tools are needed to remove or replace this boxlike built-in. Once it's removed, the rough opening remaining (right) affords ample clearance for swinging a wrench or manipulating a snake to clean out a waste line. Use this method of construction where fast or frequent removal is not of prime concern. Though a mirror was installed on the cabinet back here, you could use paneling or, for a touch of decorator color, a painted hardboard. If a larger opening is called for, you could build the backbar in sections

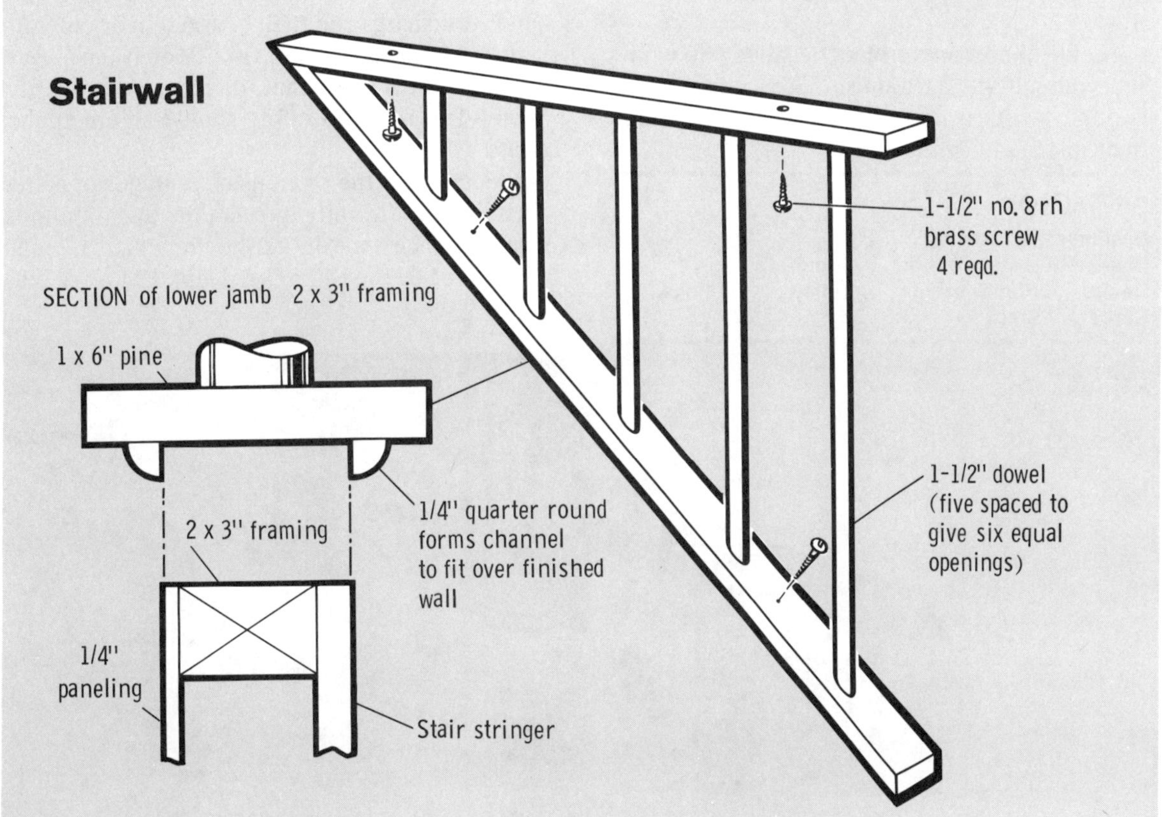

Dowel treatment permits light to enter from above, eliminates cavelike look found in many basements. To remove the "wall," the lowest screw through the pine frame into the stringer is last removed (above right). Stairwall should be framed and paneled first, then removable section built to fit. Quarter-round molding (above) brackets the stringer to guide the unit

to remember: First, make sure that all access openings are framed large enough so that it will not be necessary to rip out a wall if plumbing or electrical repairs are ever needed. Second, after the framing in front of foundation walls is up, walk around the room and double-check to insure that all valves, cutoffs and the like have been provided with an adequate opening.

Though there are several methods for boxing-in a girder (ladderlike framing is perhaps the most common), the technique on page 203 is far simpler and saves materials. To insure a good-looking job, the pine on the underside should be clear.

Finally, it's a mistake to close-in both sides of the basement stairs permanently, since this restricts the size of furniture you can move in or out. Instead, finish the room side up to the top of the stringer only and build a removable frame with four or five heavy dowels (such as closet poles). If your basement has a center stairway, consider making both sides removable.

If you want the convenience of outside access to the space beneath your house, here's a system that's watertight, burglarproof and maintenance-free

Install a stairwell to your basement

By HARRY WICKS

■ ANY MAN with a basement workshop can quickly count off the advantages to be gained by installing an outside—direct-access—basement entry such as the one shown below. By adding this convenience to your basement you can:

• Haul lumber down to your shop effortlessly, even when the materials include 4 x 8 sheets of plywood.

• Tackle almost any project because you won't find yourself—as cartoonists like to depict, for example—with a completed boat in the basement instead of in the water.

SEE ALSO

Basement remodeling . . .
Basement waterproofing . . . Concrete . . .
Decks . . . Family rooms . . . Patios . . . Railings . . .
Stairs . . . Steps

• Quickly store large items such as patio furniture and storm windows in the basement where you can work on them in comfort during the off-season.

From the family viewpoint, direct access is especially important if you have a swimming pool or basement playroom. Related equipment and furnishings can then be toted in or out without any traffic through first-floor rooms. And, perhaps most important, direct-access will give you a fast route to safety should an emergency arise.

Aside from the obvious advantages of a steel installation (termite protection and minimum maintenance), the doors shown, which are manufactured by the Bilco Co., Dept. PM, Box 1203,

AFTER THE DOOR FRAME is placed in position, the siding is marked along the top to determine where to cut.

THE ENTRY IS positioned and fastened to the new foundation; the joint is dressed with mortar.

THE CONCRETE is allowed to set before you engage torsion bars in clips attached to the entry sidepieces.

THE PITCHED CONCRETE ledge gives positive water run-off and makes lawn-trimming a lot easier.

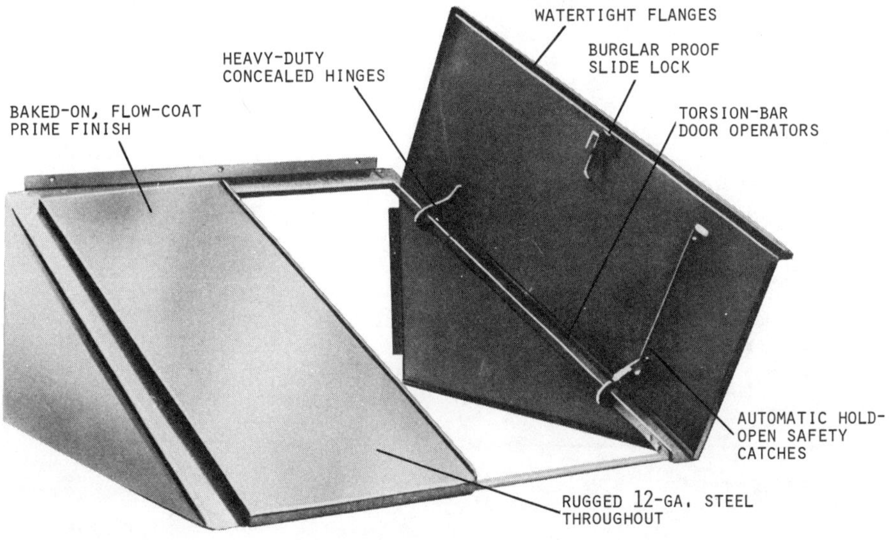

New Haven, Conn. 06505, offer an additional good feature: When a particularly heavy, or bulky, item must be moved in or out of the basement, treads can be quickly removed so the object can be passed through easily.

Location of the entrance is important. If possible, it should go where the outside grade is lowest. This cuts down on the materials needed as well as the number of steps you will have to climb. And, of course, make certain that the finished grade slopes away for proper drainage. Dig the hole large enough to take the new foundation plus an extra foot all around to allow for waterproofing and the footing. It is best to do the digging in stages, cutting the foundation as you go. This permits safer and easier handling of the cutting tool.

Electrical tools for cutting through a poured foundation can be rented from a local mason supply house or tool-rental outlet to speed up this step. A good tool for the job is Skil's Roto-Hammer which both rotates and hammers, and comes with a variety of bits. The chisel attachment, for example, will remove large sections with less rubble. If you have a concrete block foundation, cutting will be easier.

After excavating and breaking through the foundation, a 12-in. concrete footing goes in to provide a firm, level base for the first course of block. Simply dig a 12-in.-wide trench 4 in. deep

a basement stairwell, continued

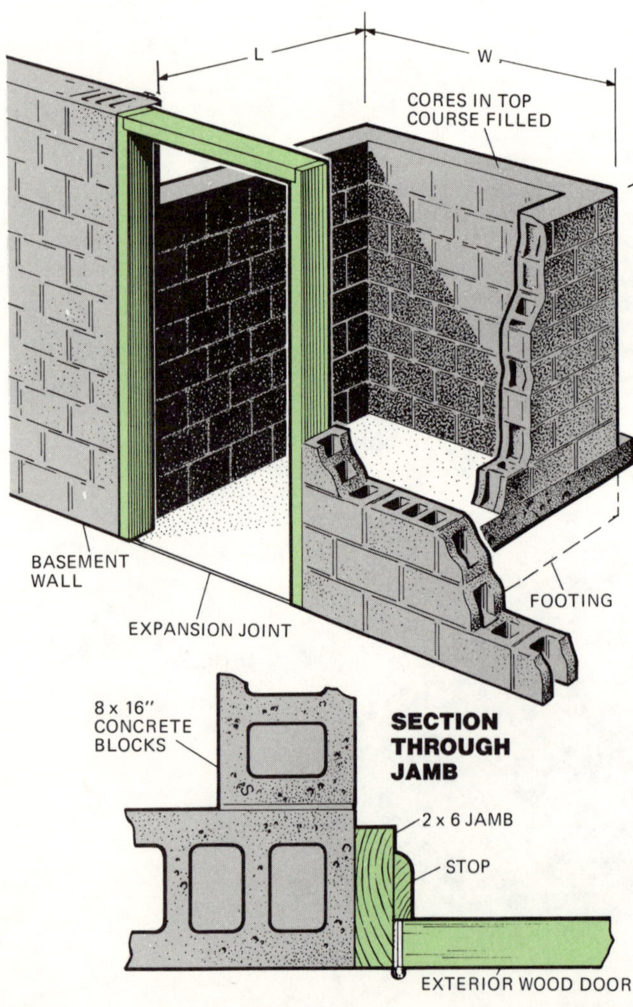

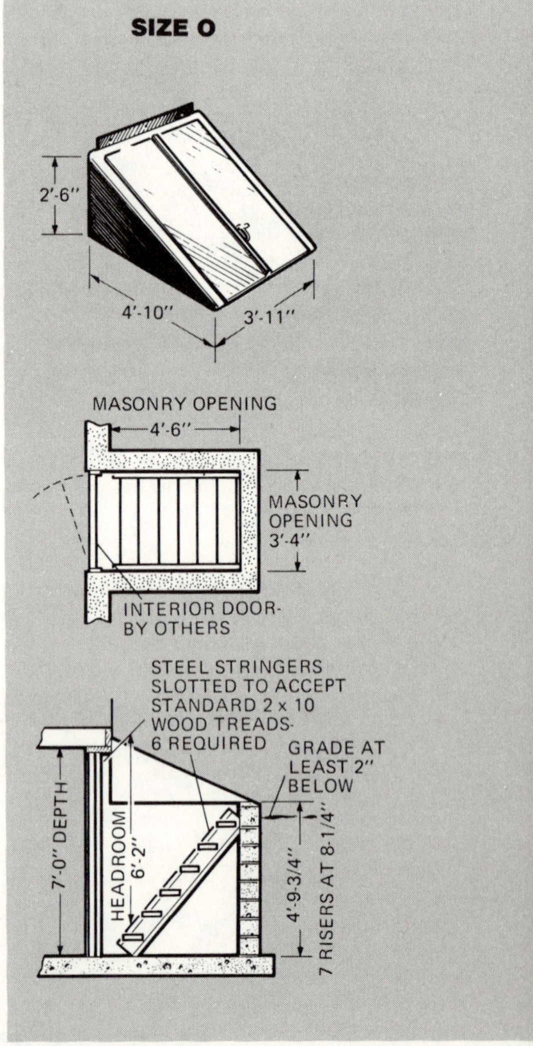

and pour the footing without forms. The top course of block should be about 4 in. above ground. After stuffing the hollow-block cores with heavy paper, trowel on a concrete cap and insert anchors as required.

Assembling the doors in place will save work. Here, make certain that the caulking strips provided are inserted between the header and sidepieces. Installation is not difficult if you read and follow the instructions packed with the doors. It's a must to follow them closely in order to validate the maker's guarantee of a weathertight door.

ALL HARDWARE, including steel step-stringers, comes with the doors. The owner supplies 2x10s for the treads.

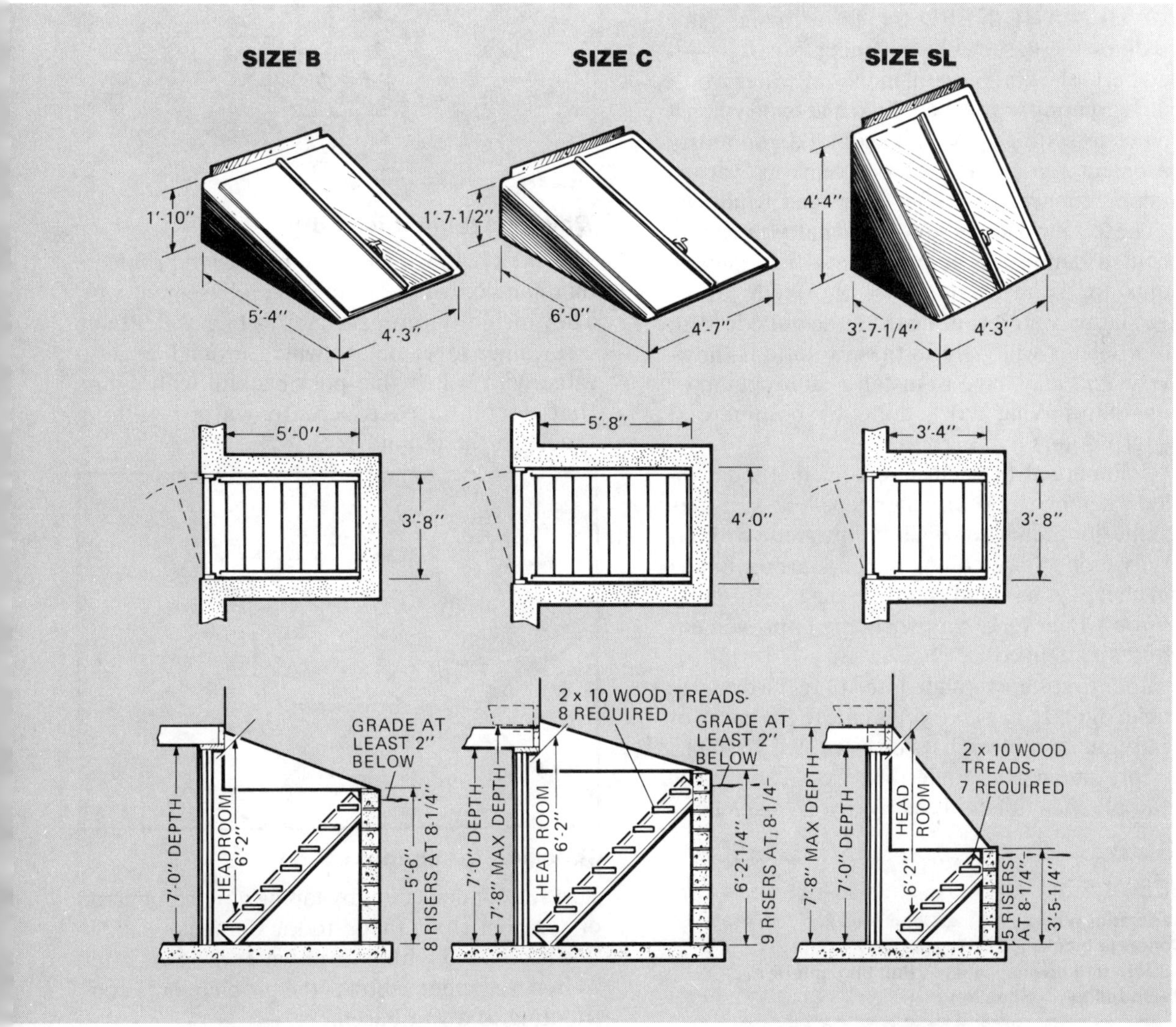

How to waterproof your basement

If your problem is dampness or wetness, here are some solutions that you can try yourself—from simple cures for condensation to a thorough job of foundation waterproofing from the outside.

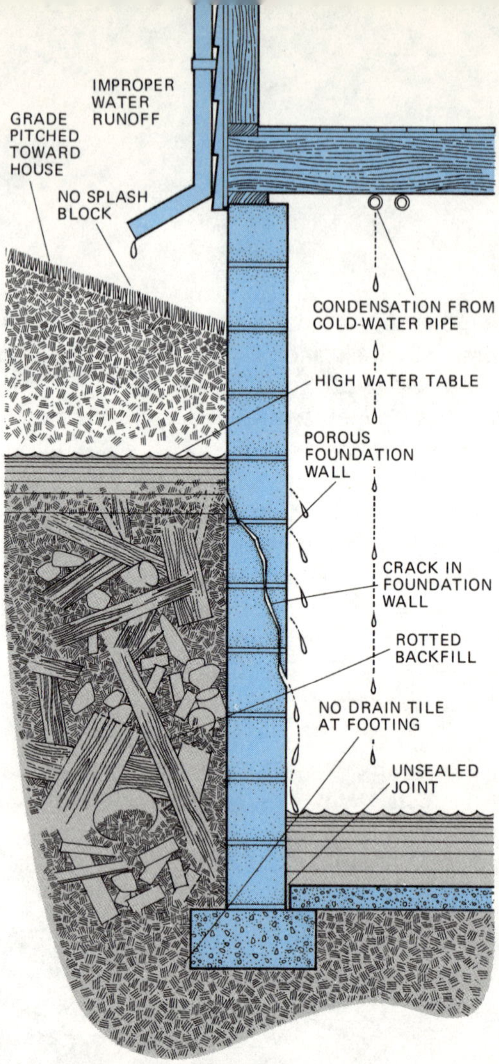

Why a basement isn't dry

The sketch above shows a number of problems that can contribute to making a basement wet. They include improper runoff, a high water table (prevailing level below which ground is saturated with water) and poor backfill with debris that decomposes to create water-retaining spaces in the ground.

WHEN THE NEED for extra living space involves the basement, one thing is certain—it had better be dry. Several inches of water won't help carpeting or wall paneling, and even when it comes to setting up a workshop, a damp musty basement can cause such problems as warped lumber, tool rust, sticking doors and windows.

These four pages show you what you can do about a damp or wet basement—from simple cures for condensation to a thorough job of foundation waterproofing from the outside. Not all problems will yield to these solutions, however. You may have to install a sump pump or consider having work done by commercial waterproofers.

Commercial firms use several methods, including application of water-repellent silicones to exterior foundation walls below grade without excavation. Since commercial waterproofing is not cheap, you should shop for it just as carefully as you would for any other home improvement of comparable cost.

Your first step, though, is to study the drawing above right. It may give you a clue to the cause of a basement problem that you can solve yourself. Simply pitching the grade away from a house, for example, has dried out many a wet basement.

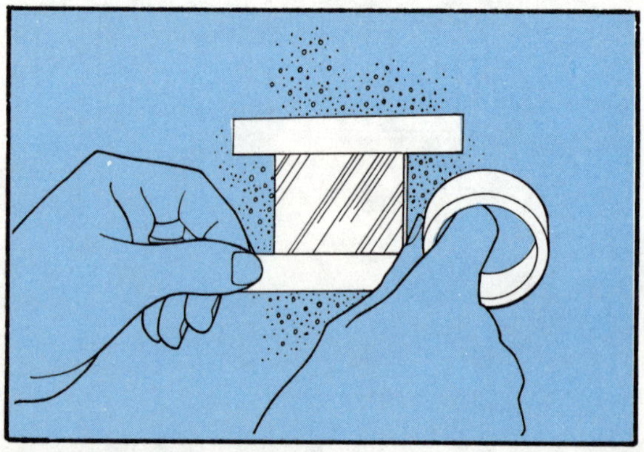

Checking for condensation

Test for condensation by taping a pocket mirror or scrap of shiny metal to the dampest wall. If this is covered with mist or water droplets after 24 hours, condensation is the problem or is contributing to a wet basement.

SEE ALSO

Basement remodeling . . . Concrete . . . Concrete blocks . . . Drainage, downspout . . . Gutters and downspouts . . . Painting, interior . . . Remodeling . . . Sheathing

What to do about condensation

Insulate all exposed cold-water pipes with a good quality wrapping—fiberglass insulation (near right) or foam plastic sleeves (far right), closing slits with tape. Replace any leaking plumbing. Ventilate the basement well: Keep windows open day and night in fair weather, close them when outside air is moist. Prune or thin plantings to let a maximum of sunlight into the basement. Other steps: Do not dry clothes on a line in the basement. Make sure the clothes dryer is vented to the outside. A window airconditioner will remove some moisture from the air; some have dehumidifying cycles. Separate dehumidifiers are also available.

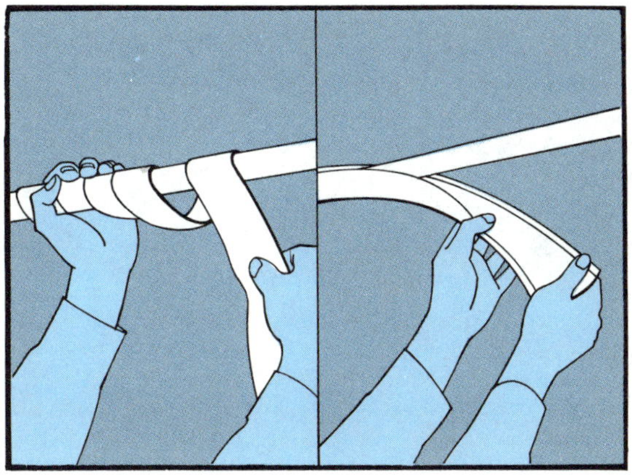

Repairing foundation cracks

Cracks in foundation walls most often occur along masonry-block joints, owing to settling. When inspecting for cracks, start at places where the foundation receives most stress—around windows, doors, and pipe and cable entries. A crack inside may mean a crack outside as well, but interior cracks should be repaired in any case, and in many instances this will complete the repair. Using a masonry or cold chisel, begin the repair by chipping out the crack, undercutting so that the crack is wider at the bottom than it is at the surface. Then rub briskly with a stiff wire brush to remove all loose particles of concrete and mortar.

With the crack prepared, it can be patched with mortar or cement. Wet the crack first; this will retard hydration and assure a strong bond between the patch and the original material. Butter the crack with patch mix, making certain that the patch is forced into every crevice. Allow the patch to cure for 2 to 3 weeks; keep it damp for at least the first 24 hours. Where water is flowing from a crack or hole, patching with quick-setting mortar may be possible; it is held tightly in place against the leak, and sets in a few minutes. Epoxy patches, applied without moistening the wall, cure in about 24 hours. With all patch mixes, follow instructions.

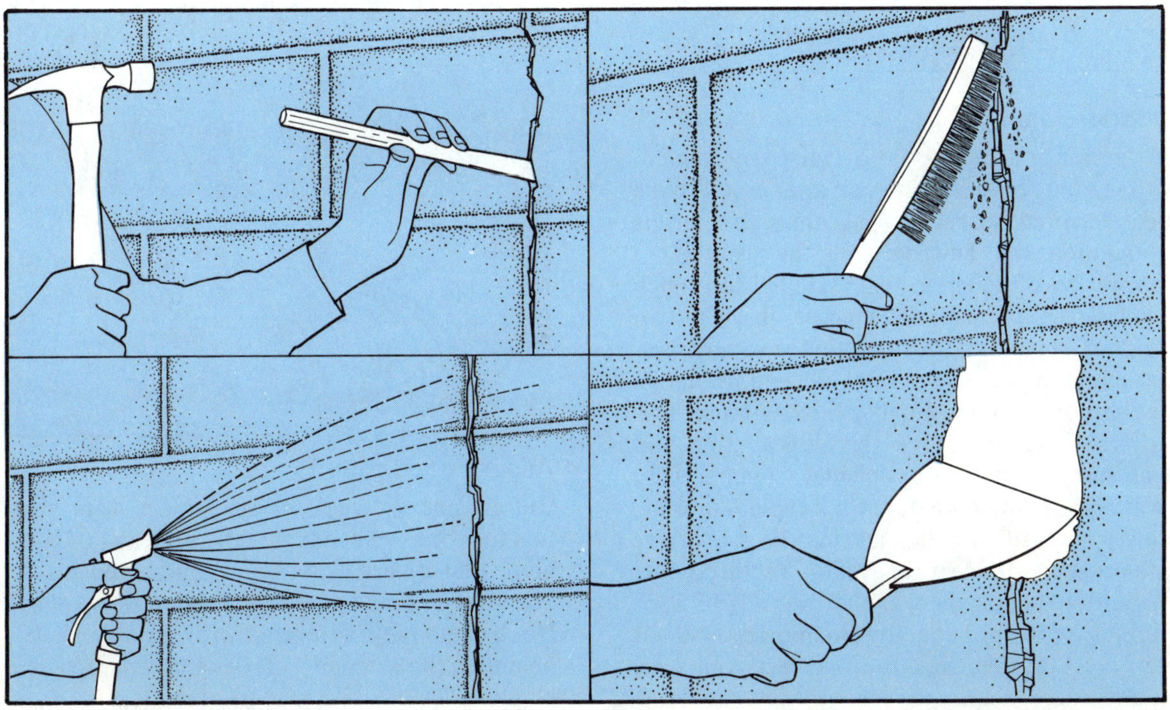

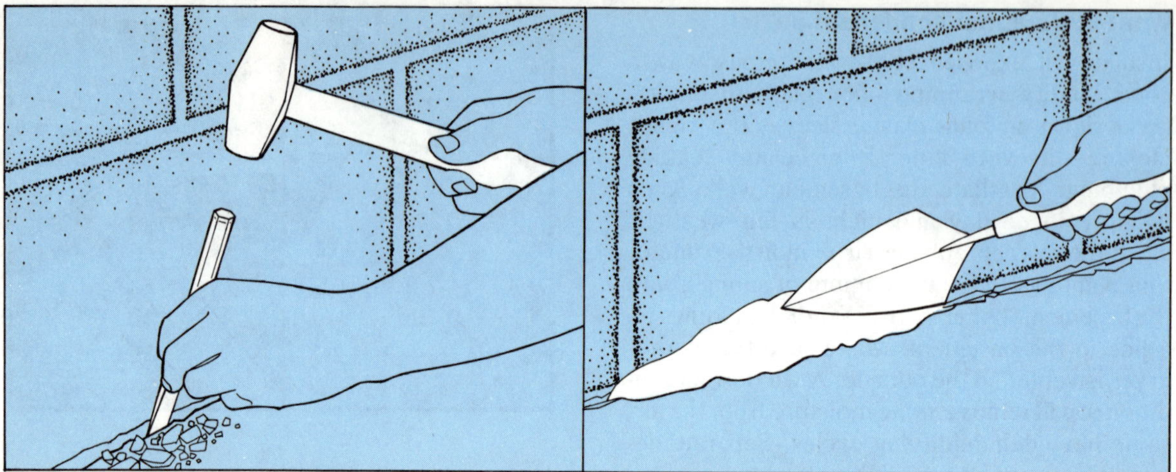

Check the wall-floor joint too

If an unsealed or cracked joint between wall and floor is a source of water, it can be sealed with epoxy mortar. Here, too, the area to be patched or sealed is chiseled out with undercut to key the mortar in place. Loose particles, dirt and chips should be completely removed—use a whisk broom or vacuum-cleaner exhaust. Epoxy mortar is troweled on, smoothed with the oiled bowl of a cheap spoon. Hot tar is generally used to seal this joint in new construction, but it is extremely dangerous for the homeowner to attempt this indoors and is not recommended for a novice.

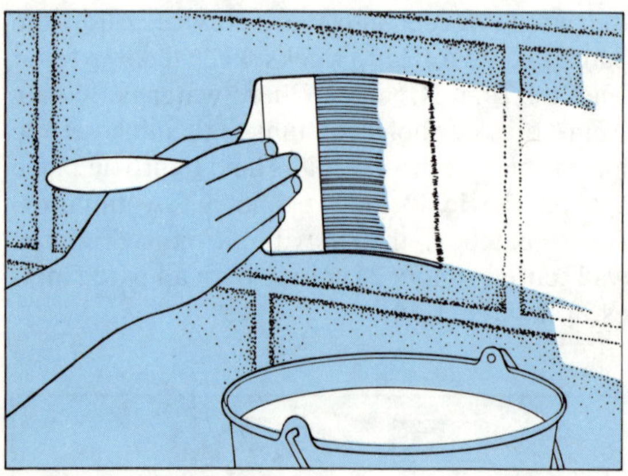

Interior coatings

If wetness or dampness is not caused by condensation, and remains a problem after cracks have been repaired, suspect seepage through a porous foundation wall. This is usually the result of deterioration of concrete that included too much sand in the original mix. One or—better—two coats of an interior dampproofing or waterproofing material may arrest seepage, and, although applying it is not a small job, it is much less difficult and expensive than excavating and waterproofing from the outside. Commercially available coatings are of several types—mortar, epoxy, emulsified latex—and may be sold dry or premixed. Surface preparation requirements vary. Roughening the wall may be called for, or etching with muriatic (hydrochloric) acid—if you must do this, be sure to protect your eyes and skin.

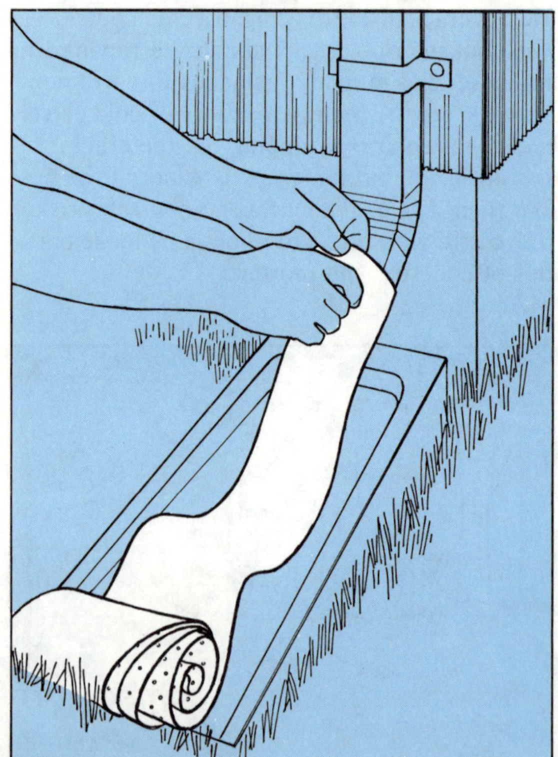

Assure good runoff

Gutters and downspouts are important protection for your basement as well as the rest of your home. To divert water from foundation walls, use a commercial plastic extension or a splash block as above. Perforated with sprinkler holes near end, the extension carries the water to lawn or plantings where it will be absorbed.

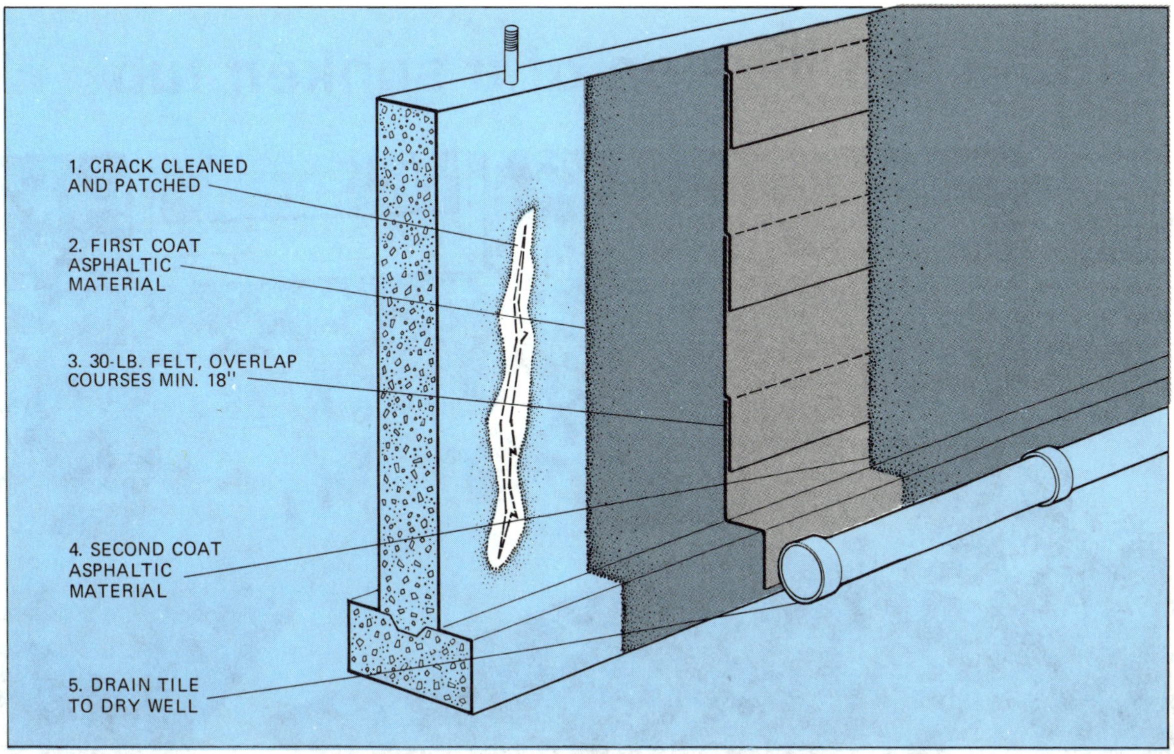

How to do exterior waterproofing

Most drastic but sometimes unavoidable is a complete exterior waterproofing job. Since this project requires excavation to the base of the wall footings, it's a lot of work, but it may be the only effective way to correct wetness.

After excavation, all visible cracks must be cleaned out and patched. Masonry-block walls that do not already have such a coating are then "parged"—given two ¼ or ⅜-in. coats of a mortar made of 1 part portland cement, 2½ parts sand. Masonry should be cleaned and moistened before parging. The first coat (often called scratch coat) is lightly roughened with a stiff brush and should not yet be firmly set when the second is applied. The second coat is steel-troweled to a smooth finish. Poured-concrete walls, like the one shown above, do not require parging.

Next, a coat of hot tar is mopped onto the wall and footing, followed by lengths of 30-lb. felt laid horizontally, each course overlapping the preceding one by a minimum of 18 in. A second coat of hot tar is then mopped on.

Drain tile should be laid along the footing, below the level of the bottom of the floor slab. Pitch the run toward a dry well, outfall or storm sewer. Bell-end tiles shown above are used where water table is high to conduct water from downspouts away from house. Where water table is low, drain tile collects water from base of foundation and carries it off. For this purpose, short sections of tile are used, with ¼-in. gaps between sections covered with 30-lb. felt. Open tile laid this way will, over its run, lose some water to the ground.

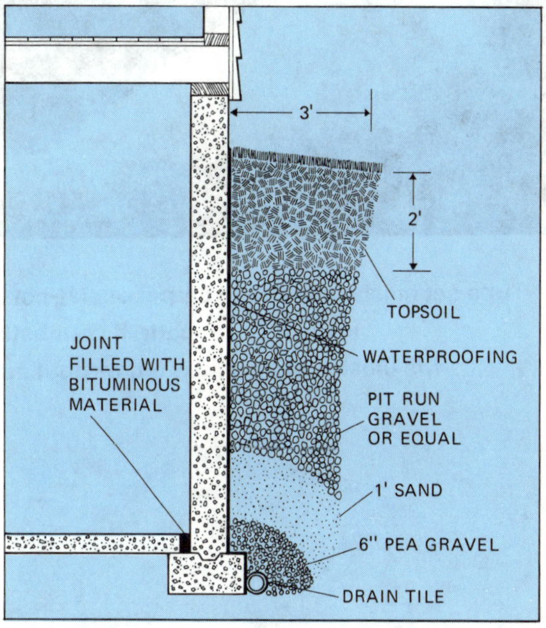

Backfill (replacement for excavated material) should be as shown above. Grade topsoil away from house, with a minimum of 8 in. between highest grade and top of foundation. Tamp fill at each stage to minimize later settling.

Create the illusion of a sunken tub

Tubs set in islands of shag carpet or slat-covered platforms add a bold new look to the modern bath. If your bathroom is large enough you can create the illusion of a sunken tub without making structural modifications

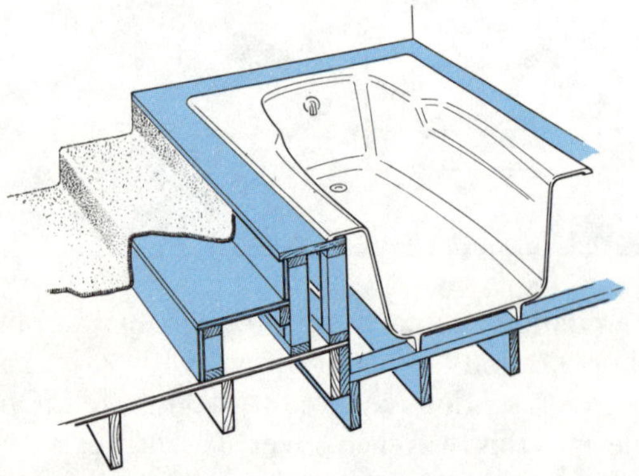

SEE ALSO

Bathtubs . . . Drains . . . Plastic pipe . . . Plumbing . . . Remodeling . . . Shaving cabinets . . . Tile, wall . . . Towel racks . . . Wall tile

By WAYNE C. LECKEY

■ WHEN MODERNIZING a bathroom, you probably think you're limited to replacing old fixtures with new ones and possibly adding tile or carpeting. You're stuck with the original layout, and your new fixtures have to stay in the same old spots.

But when an adjoining room makes it possible to move a wall back a few feet, no longer are you limited to a 5 x 7-ft. floor plan. With an enlarged area, you can start thinking "sunken tub"—the

latest innovation in modern bathroom planning.

A true sunken tub, of course, requires extensive structural modifications. A raised platform, however, can actually create the illusion of a sunken tub that's just as dramatic and attractive as a real one. The examples here by Kohler Co. show how a rim tub can be set in a wood-framed platform surrounded by steps and covered with shag carpet. In one (left), a 20-in.-high tub is in a well a little below floor level; in the other (above), a 14-in.-high apron tub sits on the floor and wood-slatted, split-level platforms are built around it.

Make your bathroom more convenient

NUMEROUS PROBLEMS designed into the original bath in this 20-year-old home are what triggered its total renovation by owner John Gaynor, Seaford, Long Island, N.Y. One of the most annoying problems proved to be the lack of adequate storage cabinets for towels, linens and toiletries. Of even greater and more serious concern was the location of a window which was placed squarely over the bathtub. It eventually permitted water seepage behind the wall covering. Before long the plasterboard beneath the window was severely damaged.

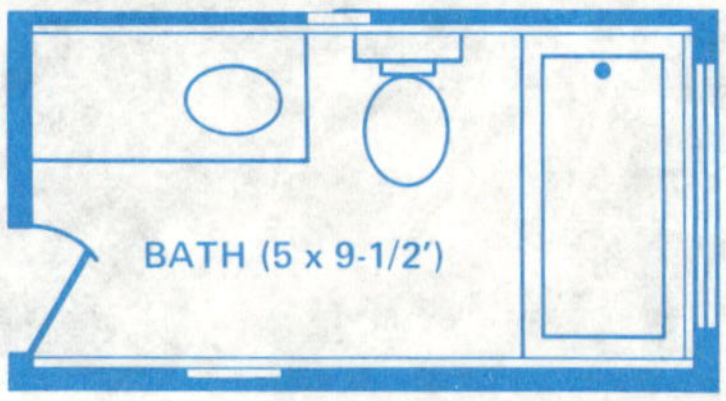

ORIGINAL DESIGNS, and plastic material that looks like marble, fill this bath with ideas you can duplicate in full or in part in your own bathroom. Photo (above left) shows tub enclosure and factory-made, one-piece vanity top with bowl. Towel closet (below left) is shop-built as is the plastic-laminated medicine cabinet below. Owner altered the vanity so that a clothes hamper is behind the doors at the far end.

SEE ALSO

Bathtubs . . . Closets . . . Drains . . . Fasteners . . . Home improvement . . . Mirrors . . . Plumbing . . . Remodeling . . . Shaving cabinets . . . Storage ideas . . . Tile, wall . . . Towel racks . . . Wall tile

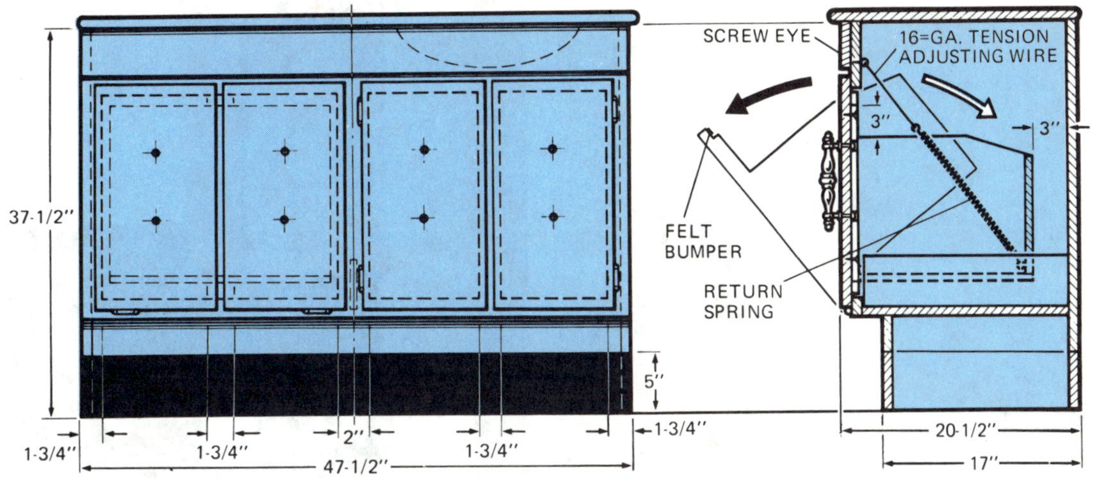

VANITY HAMPER DETAILS

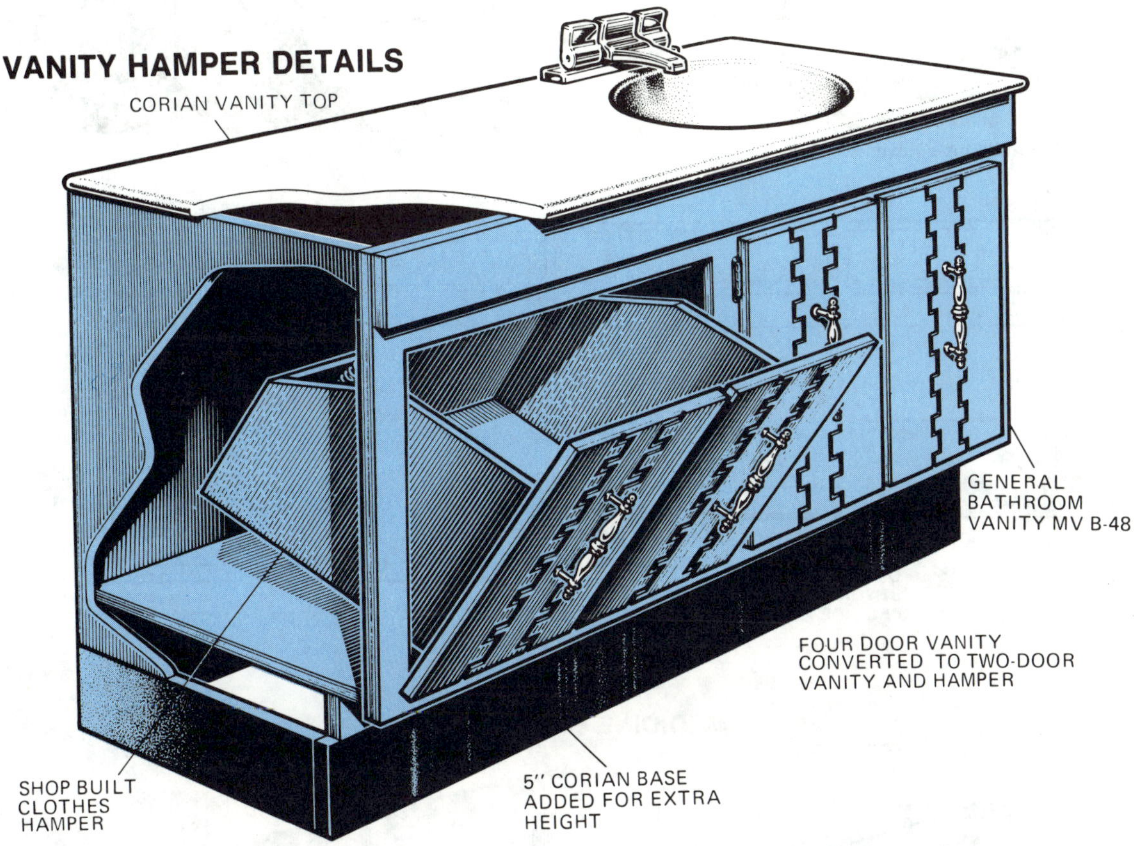

Gaynor began by closing that drafty window. It was necessary to install an exhaust fan in its place to take care of humidity. The fan (with heat lamp) was wired to turn on automatically with the overhead light. To conceal the ductwork leading from the exhaust fan, a suspended ceiling was installed. After replacing rotted studs and plasterboard, Gaynor used ¼-in. Corian to cover the walls. That's a man-made plastic material that looks and feels like marble but there's an important difference: It can be worked with carpentry tools so the do-it-yourselfer can easily install it. It provides a maintenance-free, waterproof room for years to come.

As you look at these photos and diagrams you will see that the bath is completely rebuilt from top to bottom. The only fixture remaining from the original room is the tub. The new toilet, as well as the ceramic floor tile, was purchased at Sears, Roebuck. The one-piece vanity top with

PARTITIONED CERAMIC tub-shower enclosure solves the moisture problem, contrasts nicely with wood paneling.

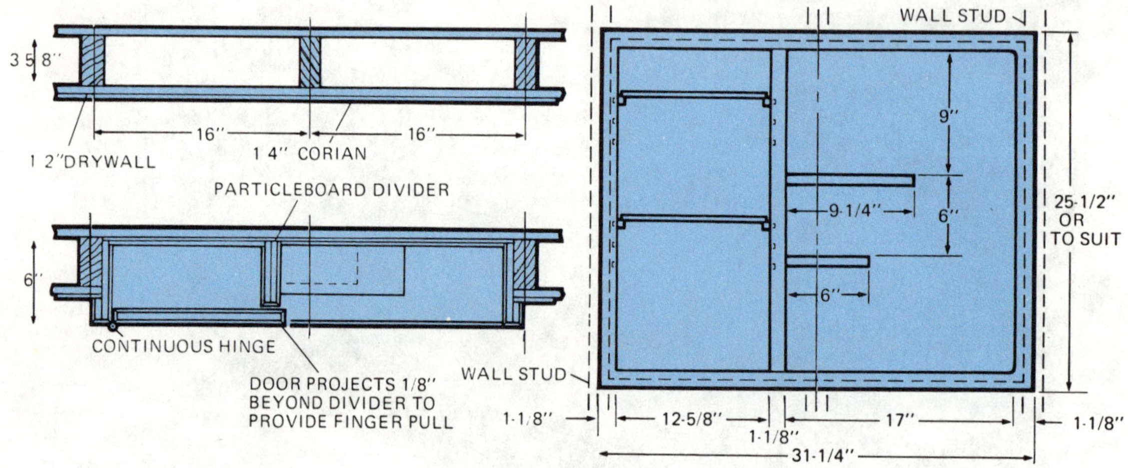

MEDICINE CABINET

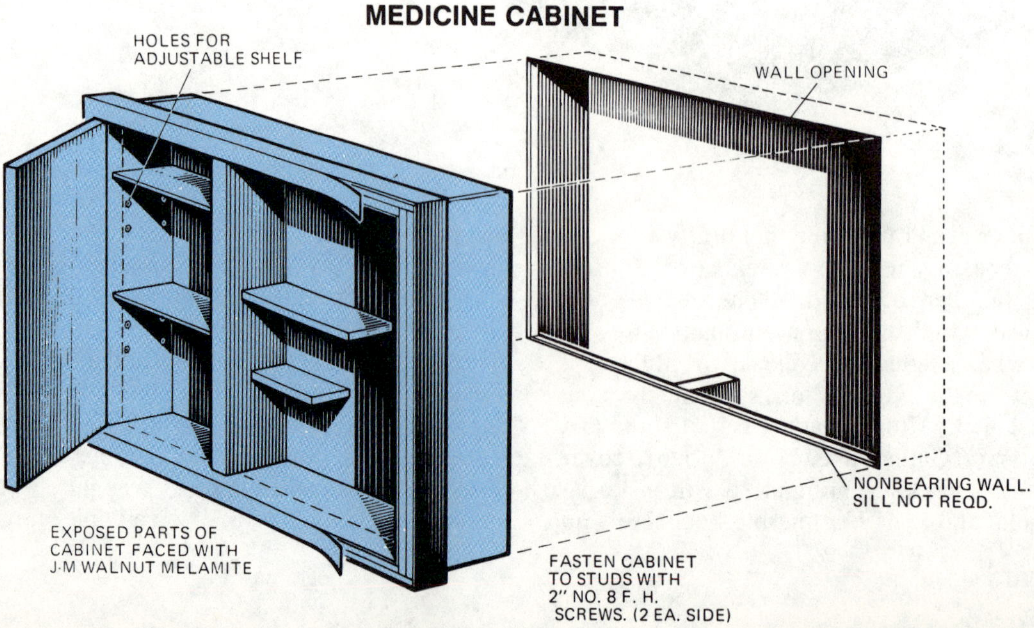

EVEN THE SMALLEST bathroom can be modernized into a glamor spot. You can build this vanity top yourself, and also apply plastic laminate to the wall after cutting three holes for the dispensing fixtures. This is a similar, though somewhat different, vanity from the one shown on page 292.

bowl comes as it appears in the photos on page 216. The prefinished vanity was altered slightly to provide an out-of-sight clothes hamper (see drawing) because there was insufficient space for a freestanding one. The original dated vanity was completely removed to make way for the new one.

The two wall cabinets were built in Gaynor's shop. The towel closet is built of Corian and Plexiglas and the medicine cabinet is skinned with walnut laminate. By carefully studying the drawings you can see how Gaynor built them and how he altered the vanity.

Now that you have seen how Gaynor remodeled his bathroom, how about yours? Study the problem, work up a plan and perhaps you can use some of the modern materials and ideas shown here to modernize your own bathroom.

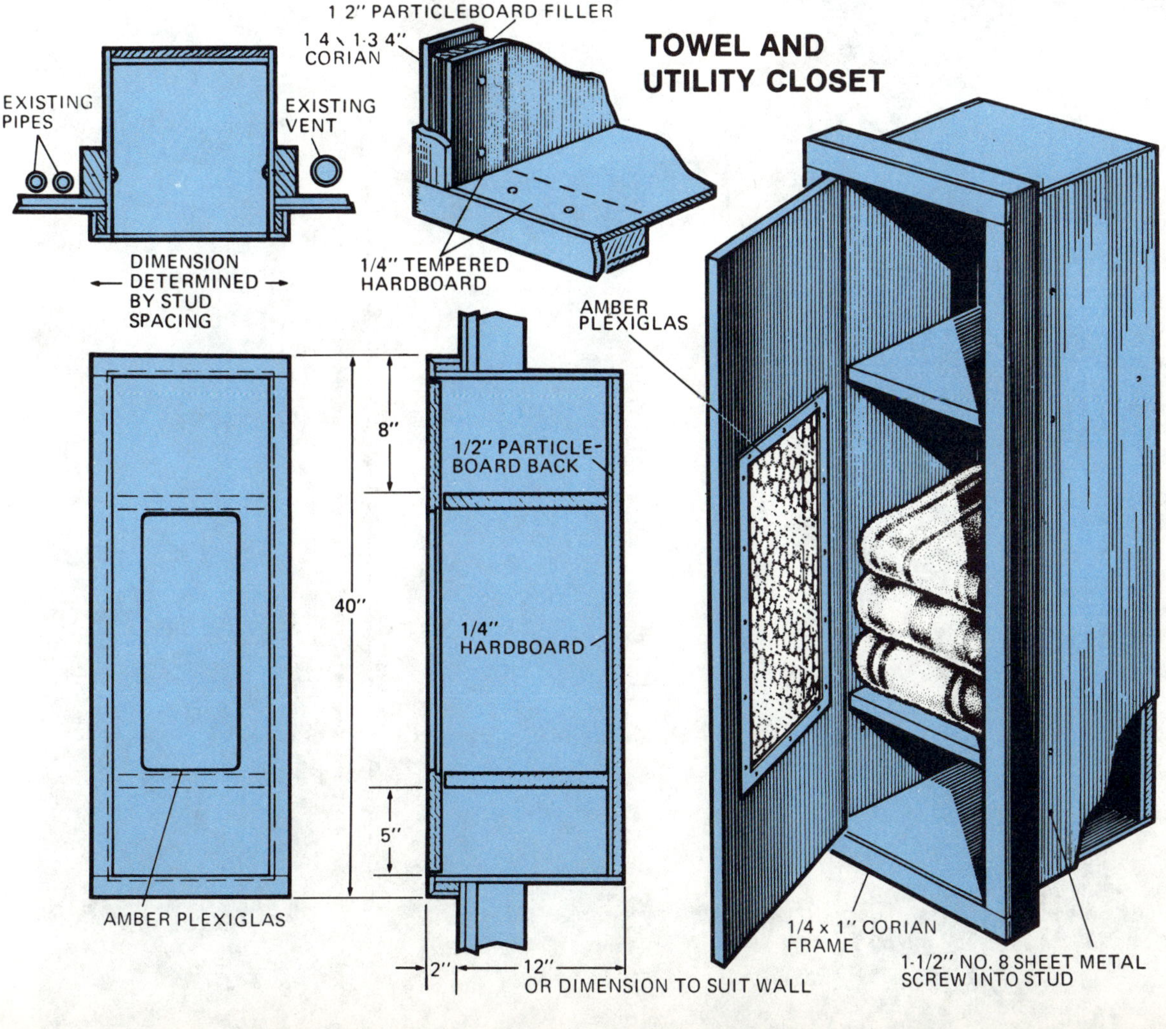

Prefab baths are easy to install

CERAMIC TILE surrounding a bathtub looks nice, but it presents two problems for homeowners: All those grout lines between the tile are hard to clean, and as the house settles, there's the periodic job of recaulking the crack that invariably develops where the tub and tile meet.

Happily, several makers of tub/showers have done something about it and are offering sectional and unitized bath units in reinforced fiberglass. Interlocking sections become a single leakproof assembly, making cleaning easier than ever before and ending crack filling for good.

From a remodeling and modernizing standpoint, these new no-tile tub/showers are made to order for the do-it-yourselfer. Being molded of

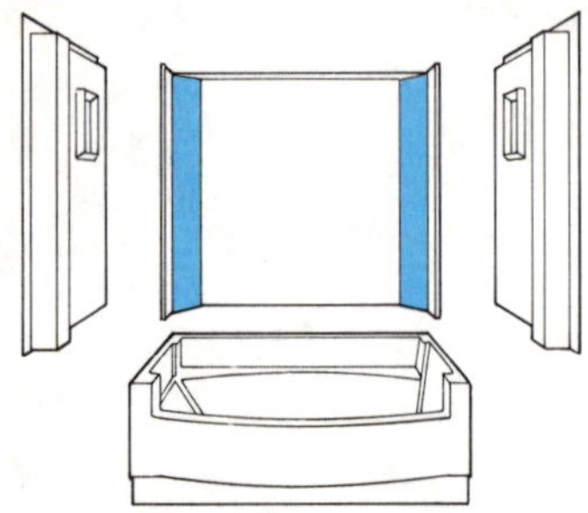

FEATURING COLOR-COORDINATED accessory panels to complement other bathroom features, this four-piece tub-shower has sculptured shelves, a wide rim seat and a slip-resistant bottom. By Owens-Corning.

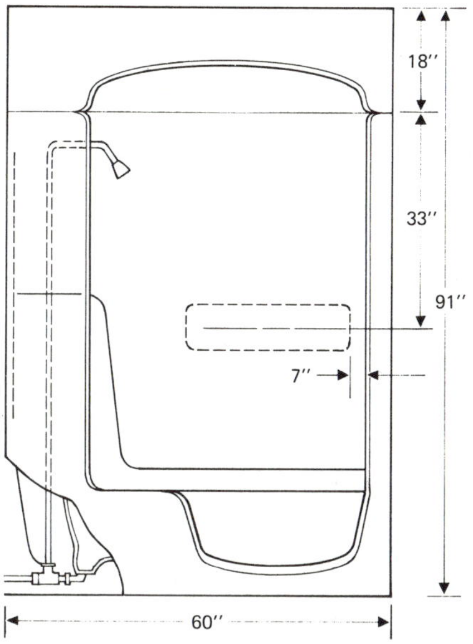

RIGHT, PRIMARILY FOR new construction, the Concept III is a one-piece tub/shower that offers an optional cap to finish off walls and ceiling.

BELOW RIGHT, ideal for modernizing existing bathrooms, the Versa-Bath will fit through doorways as narrow as 26 in. Strong, rigid and leakproof.

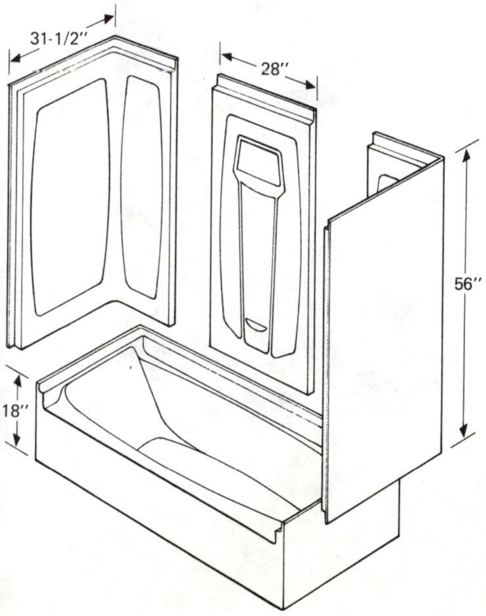

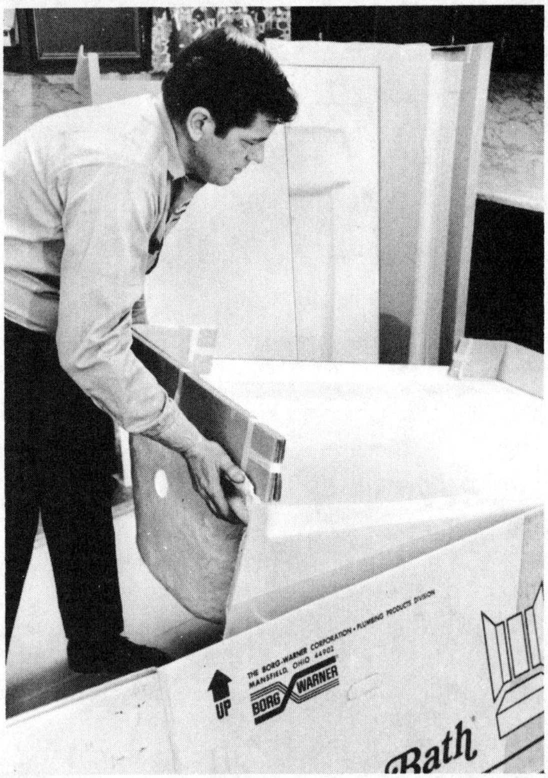

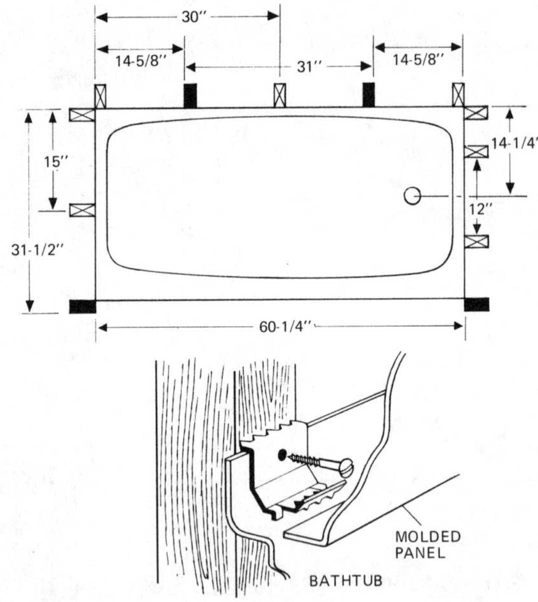

EXISTING FRAMING requires four additional studs (diagram) for attaching three panels in Versa-Bath system. Barbed fasteners lock the panel.

lightweight but strong fiberglass, the tub and wall sections are easy for one man to carry upstairs, through doorways and into place. They can be installed in any standard 5-ft. alcove in a matter of hours with little more than an electric drill, screwdriver and level.

The pictures here show how easily Borg-Warner's Versa-Bath goes into place. Once the alcove is stripped of the old plasterboard and additional studs are added as required, installation is accomplished in four steps.

First step: The tub is set in place and leveled. A leveling runner on the bottom of the tub permits shimming if necessary. The tub is held with

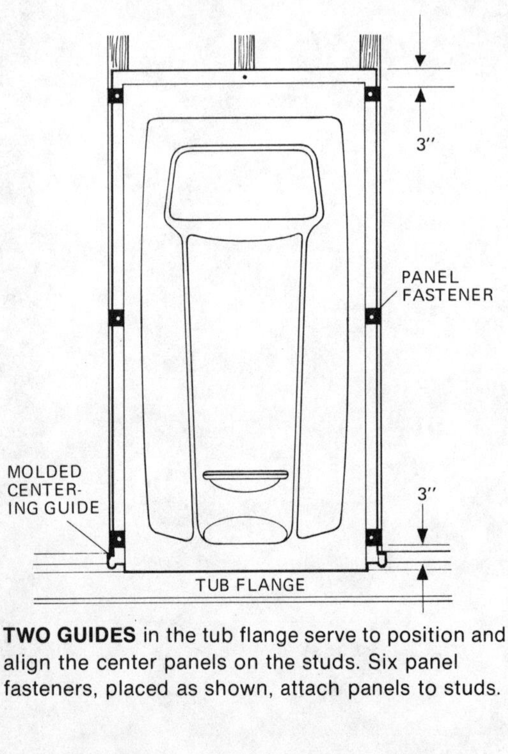

TWO GUIDES in the tub flange serve to position and align the center panels on the studs. Six panel fasteners, placed as shown, attach panels to studs.

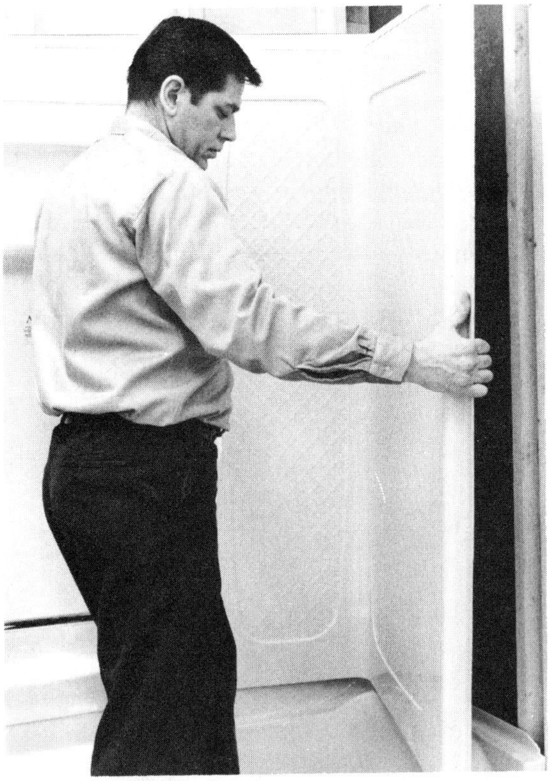

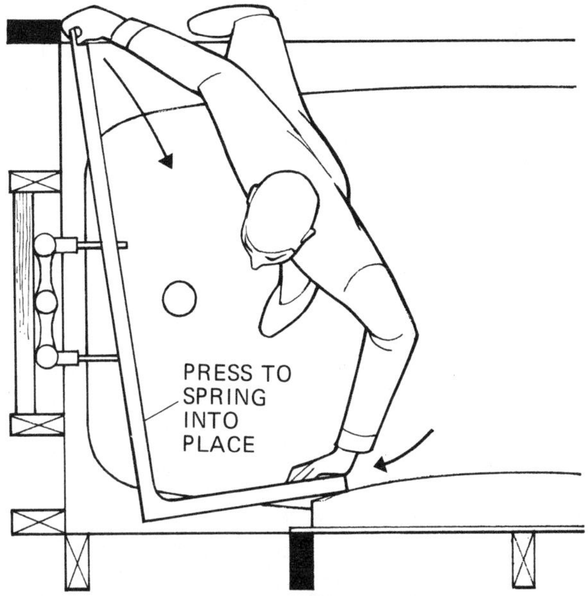

TO INSTALL the L-shaped corner panel, place it in position as shown, spring it slightly to clear the edge of the center panel and let it snap back.

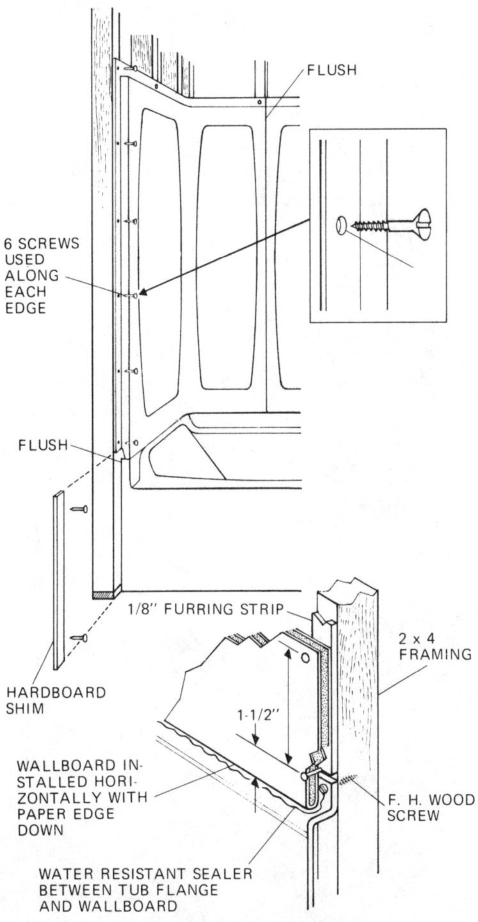

four special fasteners attached to studs with screws. Overflow and drain connections are made and tested.

Second step: The center wall panel is attached to the studs with fasteners and screws. Guides molded in the flange of the tub center the panel.

Third step: Holes for the faucets, spout and shower head are located and drilled through the corner panel with a hole saw.

Fourth step: Finally, the two L-shaped corner panels are inserted into fasteners along the center panel and pressed into place. Top and front edges of the panels are secured to the studs.

WATERTIGHT JOINTS are assured by caulking vertical and horizontal seams with mildew-resistant sealant. Surplus sealant can be removed with turpentine.

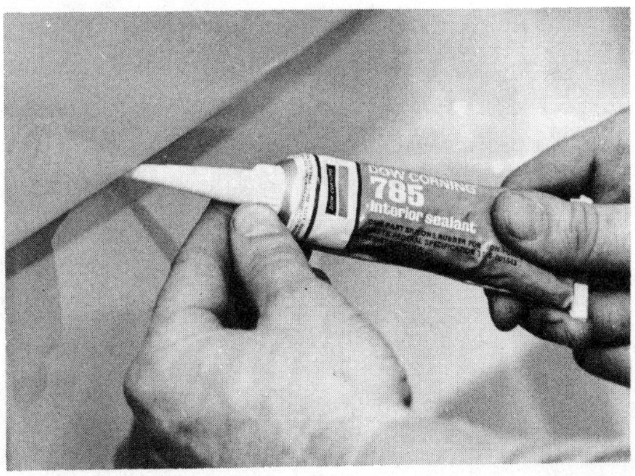

Remodel your bath for easy care

A LOT OF BATHROOMS are designed to look nice, but few are built for easy maintenance. In our remodeling project shown here, easy care is built into the design. It was obvious that the shiny new installation would look great in the beginning, but we wanted it to stay that way over the years with minimum cleaning. Here's how we went about eliminating those

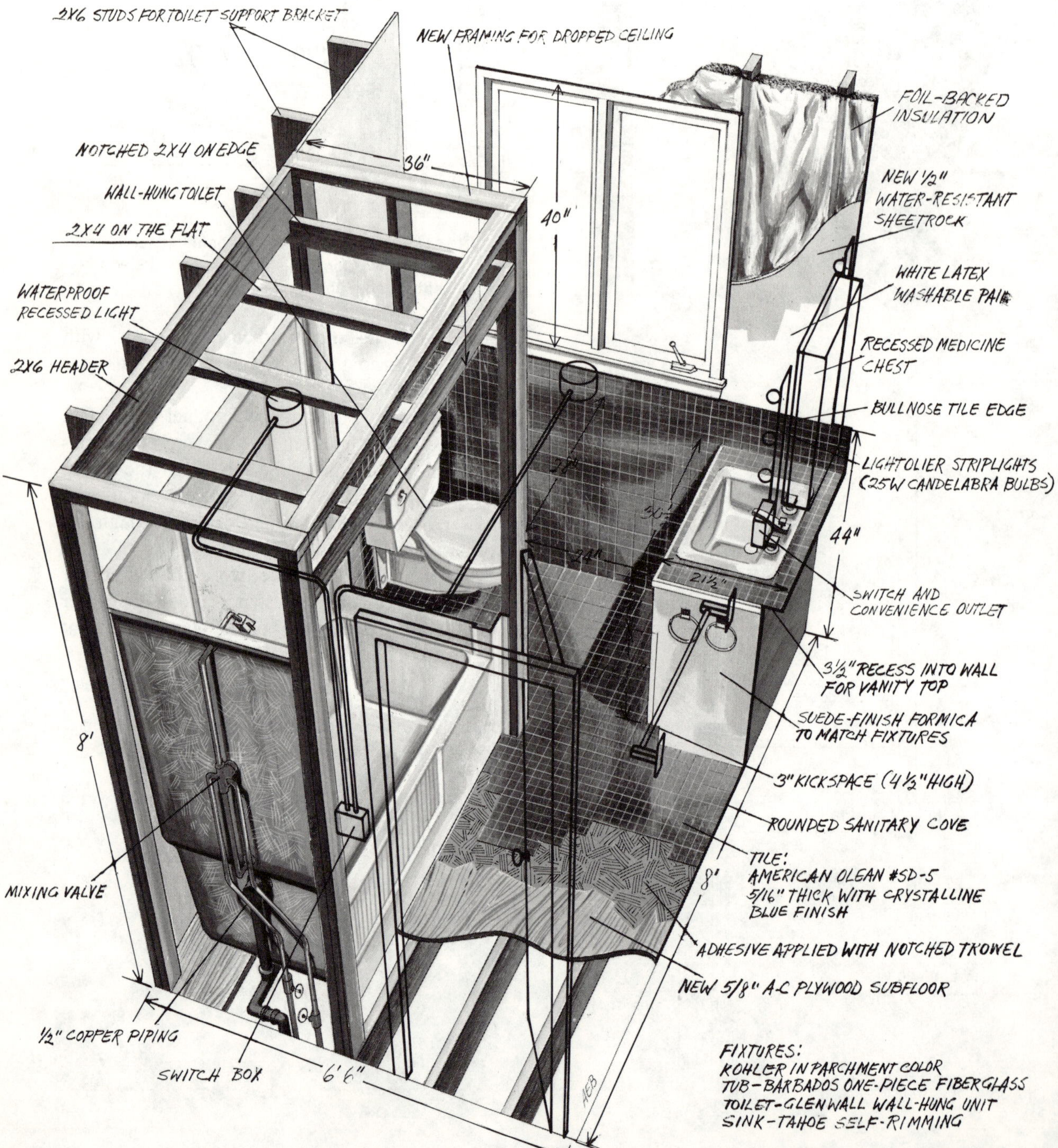

nooks and crannies that can trap dampness, germs and dirt that make a bathroom look old before its time.

The first job was a real pleasure—getting rid of the old fixtures, cracked vinyl tile and wallpaper.

Underneath this old skin were mildew, stains and soft spots from years of typical bathroom spills and splashes—not a good foundation for

Easy-cleaning tiles on the vanity are recessed in the wall. In a small bathroom you need all the floor space you can get. The white, dry-cure grout is sealed with liquid silicone. Combined with a crystalline finish on tiles, it forms a waterproof barrier

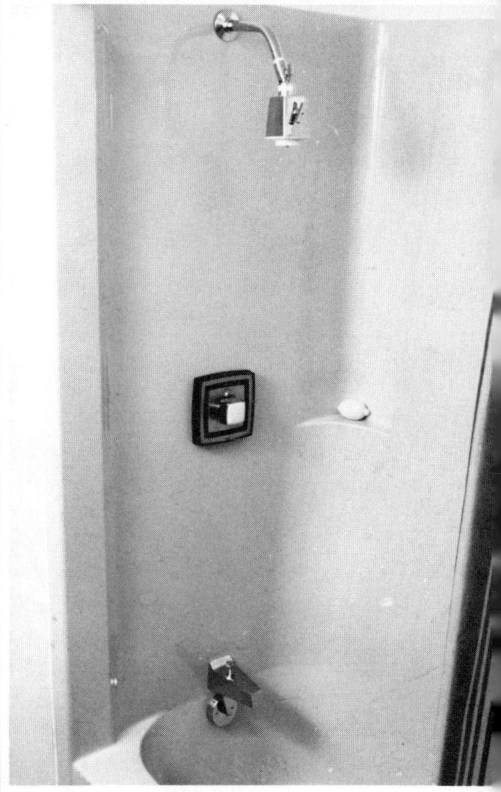

The one-piece tub and shower enclosure is made of fiberglass by Kohler. The smooth surface has many advantages; no hard corners, no seams or joints to crack, and the whole installation is a one-step operation. The off-white color is parchment

CARPENTRY AND AN EASY-CLEANING TUB

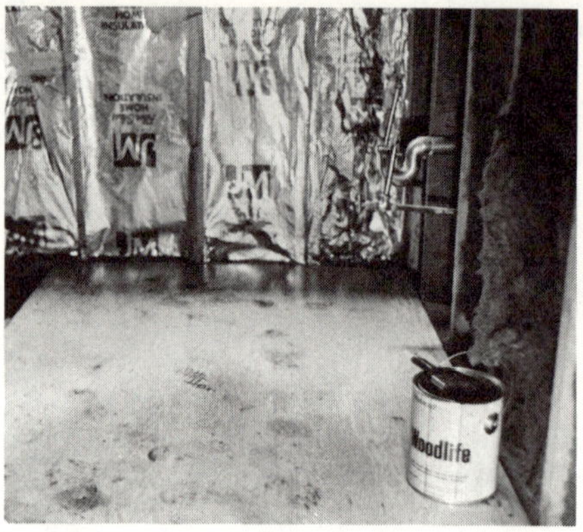

A new ⅝-in. A-C exterior-grade plywood subfloor provides a durable and solid surface for the ceramic tile

The wall-hung toilet is supported by a steel hanger that must be bolted through two new 2x6 studs

A new dropped ceiling joins the partition separating the tub and the toilet. The one-piece unit fits inside

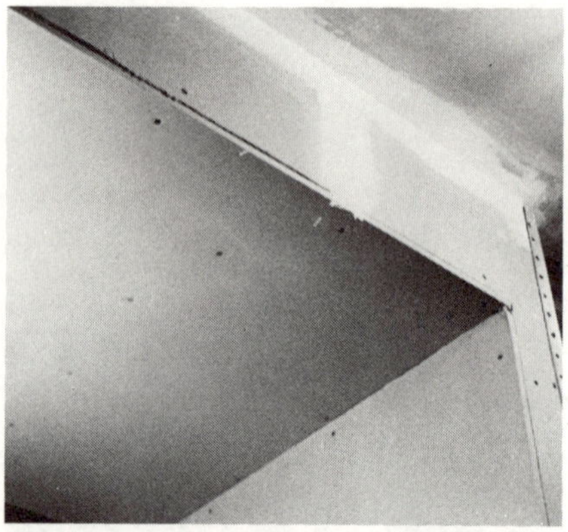

Moisture-resistant Sheetrock ½-in. thick is a durable wall surface that's ideal for ceramic-tile applications

the new fixtures and tile. So we went farther. Old, moisture-ridden wallboard was easy to pull off the studs and the water-logged plywood subfloor came up in pieces. We replaced insulation batts that had settled in the outside wall with new 3½-in. foil-backed fiberglass insulation.

With the walls totally open, it was a simple matter to run a new BX cable for the built-in light over the new tub enclosure. Good access also made it possible to solder a copper cap onto the toilet waste drain below the floor and extend the line to meet the in-the-wall drain of the new wall-hung toilet. (This is a good time to snake through your drains to avoid septic blockages later.)

After we coated beams and sills with Woodlife (a moisture-resistant sealer), we laid ⅝-in. A-C exterior-grade plywood down to make a new subfloor. Rough carpentry included adding two 2x6 studs at the corner of the room to give extra support for the steel hanger that carries the weight of the wall-hung toilet. We measured the rough opening for the new tub and shower enclosure and framed a 3-ft.-wide 2x4 partition to separate tub from toilet. Using 2x4s on the flat, we framed a dropped ceiling over the enclosure.

For the new skin for the bath we re-covered all walls with ½-in. moisture-resistant Sheetrock. You can identify this special board at the lumberyard by its light green color. Its surface is ideal for ceramic-tile installations. A three-coat taping job completed the new surfaces.

We wanted a one-piece, fiberglass tub and shower unit. The only problem was how to get it into the room. The existing door was 32 in. wide; the tub, 34 in. wide. Although it meant removing

The built-in "highhat" fixture has a rubber washer between glass bowl and the bulb to lock out moisture

Install the tub drain first. You can work the copper supply pipes around it to the single mixing valve (inset)

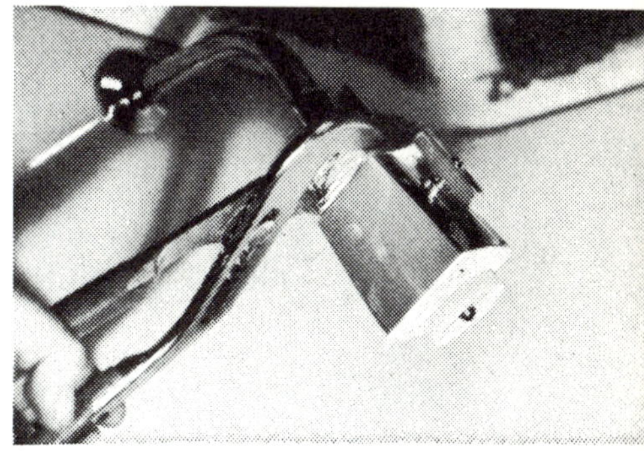

Kohler's showerhead has a water-saving lever to cut down the flow. A rag will protect the finish from the wrench

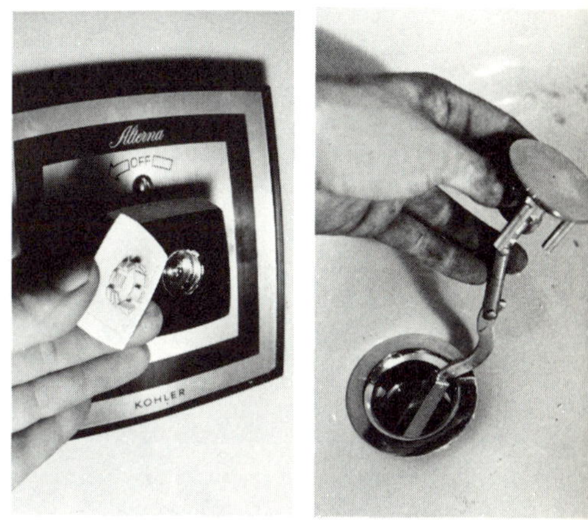

Four optional cover plates are provided for each faucet. The drain flange was sealed with silicone.

the door and jamb, getting the maintenance-free unit into the bathroom was definitely worthwhile. There are no hard corners on the smooth, glossy-surfaced enclosure; no seams to caulk, no tiles to fall off the walls and no nooks and crannies to collect dirt.

Our unit is made by Kohler in a new off-white color called parchment. We opted for this more subdued tone and added color with the tile, shower curtain and towels. It's easy to change if you tire of the color, but fixtures are there to stay.

The only other fixture to install was the vanity. We saved space here by recessing the vanity in the stud wall 3½ in. Front and side were covered with a suede-finish Formica colored like the fixtures. We used the paper template supplied to make the vanity-top cutout.

We chose a crystalline-finish, deep blue tile made by American Olean. Although you can find less expensive imported tiles, in general they are not as uniform in finish and size as American-made tiles. Even seams from one end of the bath to the other are essential for appearance.

First we established the tile height on the walls. For convenience, adjust height to accommodate the nearest full tile. We used a bullnose-edged tile to form the top border and a rounded cove tile at the base. We started work on the walls by spreading 3 or 4 square feet of adhesive with a notched trowel and placing the tiles next to each other with a firm press of the hand.

A durable finish is achieved with a two-step process. First, force the dry-cure grout into the seams with a rubber-coated trowel. Several

A GOOD-LOOKING VANITY

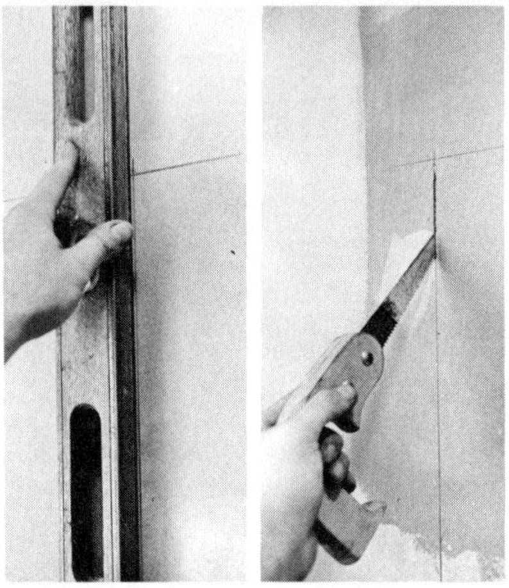

Pencil in the cut lines for the medicine chest with the aid of a level. Cut with a keyhole saw

Light strips flanking the chest are wired to a junction box above the opening. Use wire nuts on all splices

EASY-CARE TILE

Establish the wall height and lay out dry tiles to check it. We recessed the vanity 3½-in. into the wall

Spread three square feet of adhesive at a time with a trowel and press each tile into place firmly

Most local tile suppliers can rent you a cutter and chippers. After you score the surface, the tile snaps

A coved base eliminates one more hard-to-clean crack. Make sure no nailheads protrude from the plywood floor

Apply the grout liberally, forcing it into the seams by making continuous passes with a rubber-coated trowel

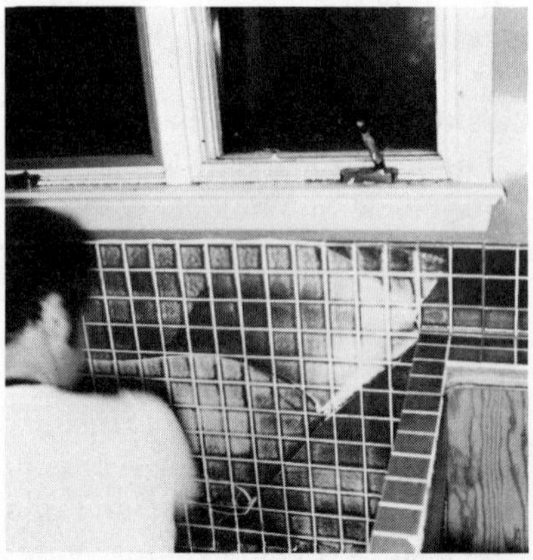

A window washer's squeegee is ideal for removing the excess grout. A rag removes the final film

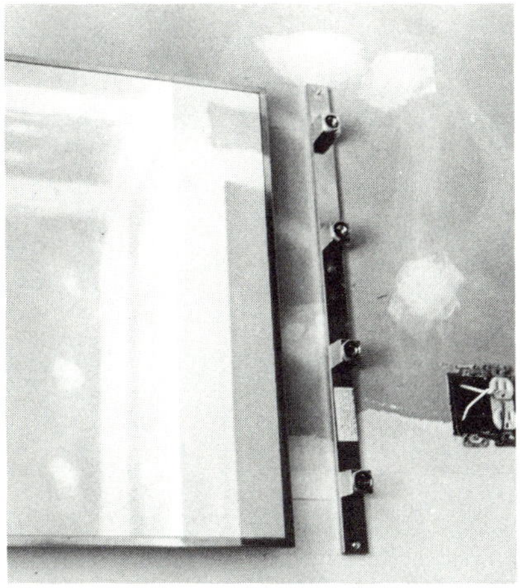

Soft light, 25-watt bulbs throw an even light on the vanity. Install a grounded receptacle next to the switch

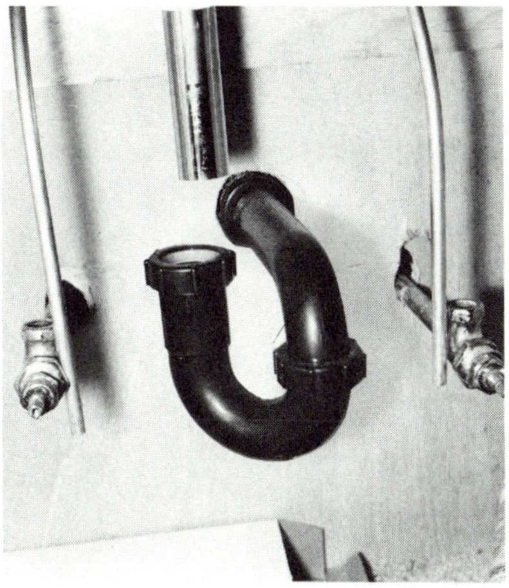

We used a noncorroding PVC trap and copper tubing to connect the old pipes and new sink as shown above

AN EASY-MAINTENANCE, WALL-HUNG TOILET

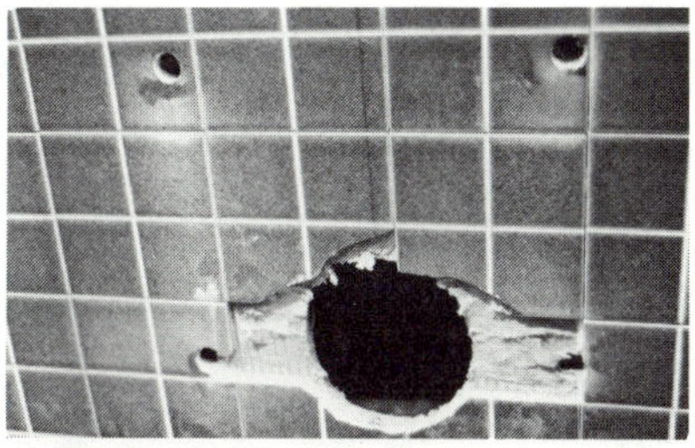

The wall-hung toilet is supported by a steel hanger. Drill holes for the bolts and remove enough tile for the waste drain connection. A plastic sleeve will protect the fixture as the threaded bolts pass through the wall.

Careful layout is essential for proper alignment of the bolts and the openings in the hanger. If your measurements aren't exactly right, you can loosen the bolts to the 2x6s and insert shims

passes over the same area will compact the grout. Don't worry about the excess. A window washer's squeegee will remove it. Follow this with a damp sponge; it will remove all but a fine film which can be "polished" away with a dry rag.

The following day we finished the tile job by brushing a liberal coating of liquid silicone on the grouted joints. This is tedious, but it will save you hours of maintenance.

Two coats of washable latex paint completed the resurfacing of our modern, efficient bath. The thorough installation will keep it looking good with a minimum of effort.

BOARD SHELVES rest on rungs of ladder-like uprights, and bridge toilet to provide extra storage space.

Ladder shelves put waste space to work

IF YOU HAVE NEED for more storage and shelf space in your bathroom but can't see how to manage it, American-Standard shows how it can be done in most bathrooms, large or small. Make use of the wall space over the toilet. Supported by ladder-like, floor-to-ceiling uprights placed on each side of the toilet, several roomy shelves can be installed without interfering with the use of the toilet.

Even if you can't duplicate the arrangement above, in which one ladder upright supports one end of the lavatory counter and an overhead valance, a pair of uprights alone, plus two or three shelves, will provide a lot of the handy shelf space most small bathrooms sorely need. The ladder uprights are 1 x 2s, the rungs 1-in. dowels glued in equally spaced holes. The shelves are no deeper than the toilet tank.

SEE ALSO

**Bathtubs . . . Drains . . . Etageres . . . Fasteners . . .
Home improvement . . . Plumbing . . .
Shaving cabinets . . . Shelves . . . Storage walls . . .
Towel racks . . . Wall tile**

How to caulk a bathtub

■ EVENTUALLY, an annoying crack may develop where the top of your bathtub meets the wall tile. It's usually the result of slight sagging due to weight changes after repeated filling and emptying of the tub. This unsightly crack permits water to seep in, deteriorating the wall and loosening the tiles.

The solution is to fill the crack with a flexible, waterproof caulking compound. Be sure to use the type made for sealing the joint around tubs—not the kind sold for exterior house caulking. Such tub caulking comes in squeeze tubes or disposable cartridges for use in a caulking gun. It's white in color, dries quickly.

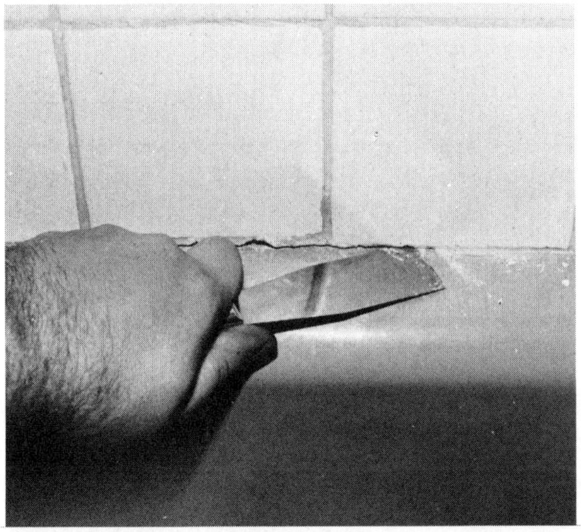

OLD CAULKING must be removed completely or it will deteriorate and affect the life span of the new caulk. Using a stiff-bladed putty knife, gouge out the caulking along the seam between the tile and the tub. This work must be done very carefully to avoid damage to both the tile and the enamel on the tub.

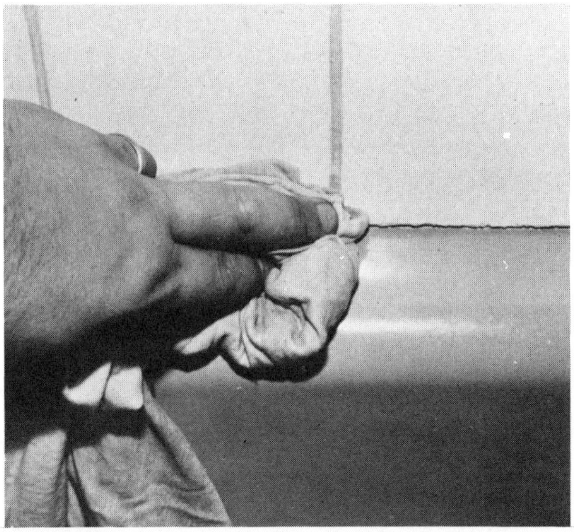

THOROUGHLY CLEAN the seam and adjacent areas to remove all dust, grime and soap film. Even a trace of residue will hinder adhesion of the caulking compound. Cleaning should be done with alcohol or another cleaning solvent. The caulk line should then be rinsed clean with water and allowed to dry thoroughly.

APPLY THE NEW CAULKING in a long, unbroken bead. The bead should be slightly wider than the open joint. The plastic applicator tip on the tubes of some caulking compounds such as the one shown in the photo above have gradations to provide a cutoff guide to obtain the correct bead thickness for the job.

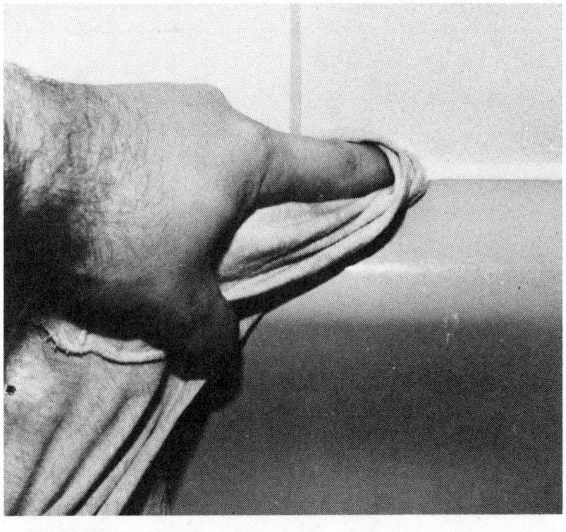

THE BEAD OF CAULK can now be worked or forced into the opening. Moisten your finger with water or wrap a cloth tightly around a finger and push the caulk firmly into the joint. With the type of caulking shown, the excess caulk can be wiped off the tile and tub with a wet cloth. Allow the caulk to dry thoroughly before painting.

IF YOUR CHUCK KEY IS MISSING, insert a drill bit in the keyhole. Use it as a fulcrum while prying sideways with a screwdriver that's engaged in the ring gear of the chuck.

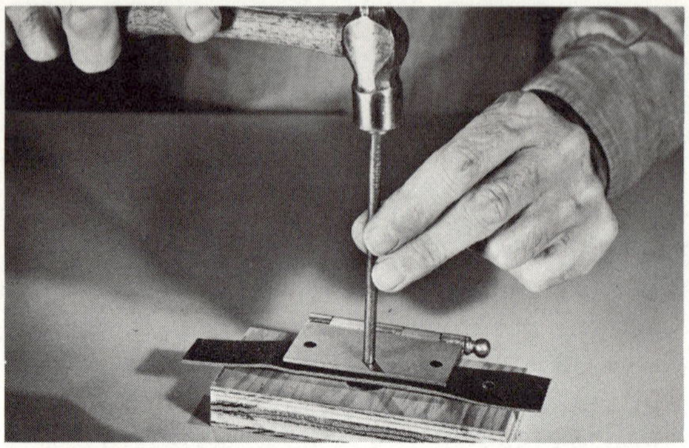

A LEATHER PUNCH can be improvised with a butt hinge and a nail. The nail must fit the hole snugly and have its point cut off square. The hinge is placed over the hole in the block.

A TAUT CLOTHESLINE will stay so if you secure it to a spring-mounted eyebolt. Drill a hole in the post crossarm for a 6-in. eyebolt and fit it with a 2-in. coil spring and two washers.

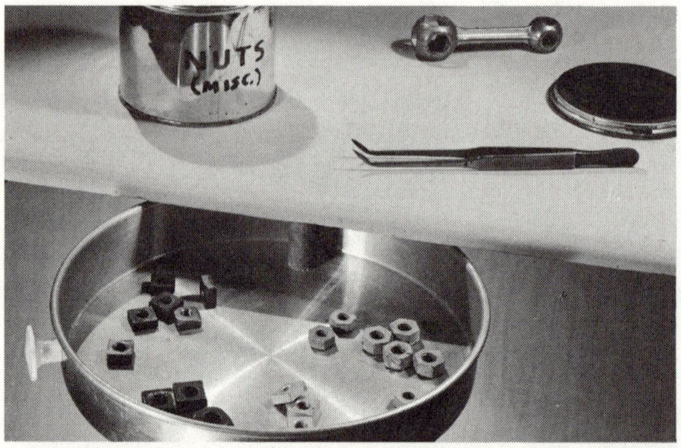

WASTE SPACE UNDER SHELVES can be put to work holding swing-out trays. A bolt passing through a hole in the shelf and a hole in a wood spacing block can pivot a round cake pan.

FOR A FREE MARKING GAUGE, drill a row of holes in a wooden clothespin and cut off one leg. Drill the holes big enough for a pencil point and space them to suit the work. A gauge is useful for marking duplicate pieces.

SAVE THE PLASTIC FORKS you get with take-out lunches—they make fine spreaders for glue. The tines hold a surprising amount of glue, they distribute it evenly, and the forks are cheap enough to throw away at cleanup time.

A DULL PENCIL SHARPENER can quickly be revived. You can touch up the roller cutters without removal by looping an emery-cloth strip around them and cranking the handle backward.

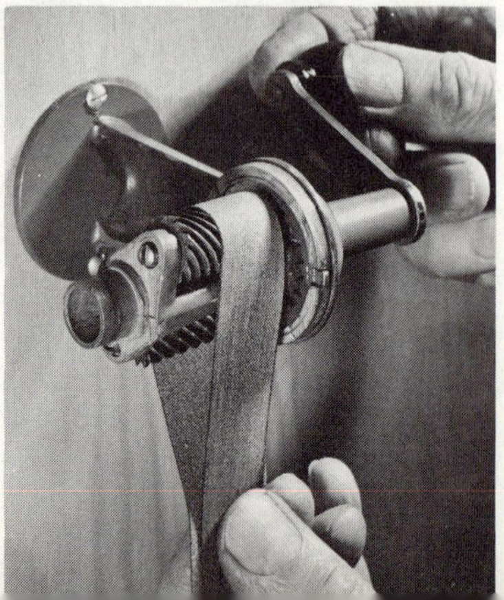

Everything you need to know about small batteries

More and more of today's electronic gadgets depend on batteries for power. There are literally hundreds of battery types. How do you choose the right one? Check our handy guide

By JEFF SANDLER

THINK BACK. Not long ago you had no electronic games, LCD watches, cassette recorders, television games or portable fluorescent lights. Now you do. And they all gobble batteries, which are no longer cheap.

Luckily, 85 percent of batteries sold are 9-volt radio flat cells or AA, C and D round cells. It makes selection much easier; there are more than 400 different batteries available.

carbon-zinc batteries

The common carbon-zinc dry cell has been sold for more than 90 years. Today, it is still the most widely used battery. Because of its low cost, in low-drain applications such as in radios, it can outperform the next best battery (the alkaline) by two to one in cost-per-hour use.

But—because of its internal chemistry—heavy, continuous current drain drives its efficiency way down. The faster you have to draw out power, the less you get. Other batteries have this problem, too, but not to the degree of the carbon-zinc.

Therefore, if Junior has a super-strong, walking, talking, motorized space robot that he wants to show off to his friends, avoid using carbon-zincs. The huge current appetite of this type of device will exhaust the batteries rapidly.

Despite this, there are some heavy-drain situations where it is smart to use a carbon-zinc. A flashlight or toy that draws heavy current may be used so infrequently that even a carbon-zinc won't run down. There is little point in buying a more expensive battery when its capacity will never be used.

Current drain isn't the only consideration. For example, carbon-zincs are essentially useless below 20° F. So forget using them for auto-winding your camera on a ski trip. However, their performance improves steadily with increased temperatures, reaching a peak at about 100° F.

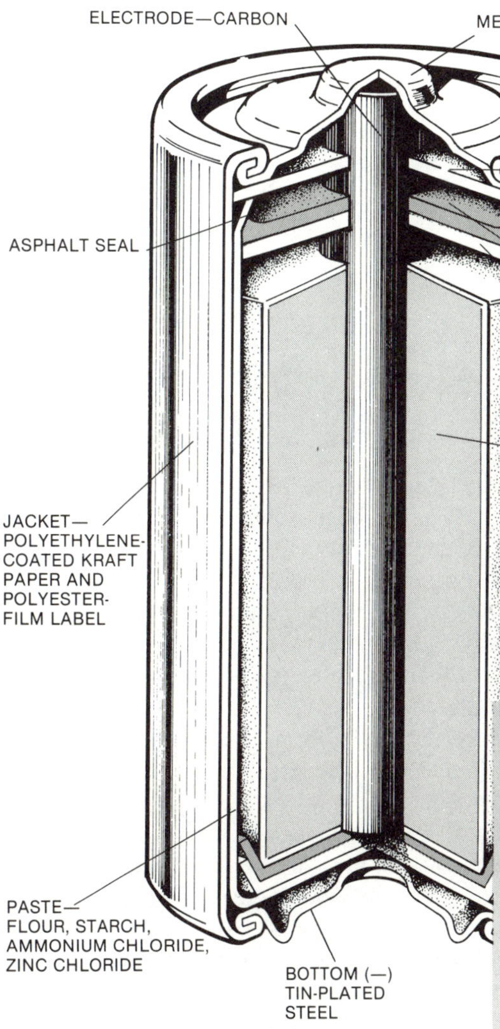

CARBON-ZINC battery is the workhorse of batteries, and the lowest priced.

SEE ALSO

Battery testers . . . Checkers, outlet . . . Doorbells . . . Testers, continuity

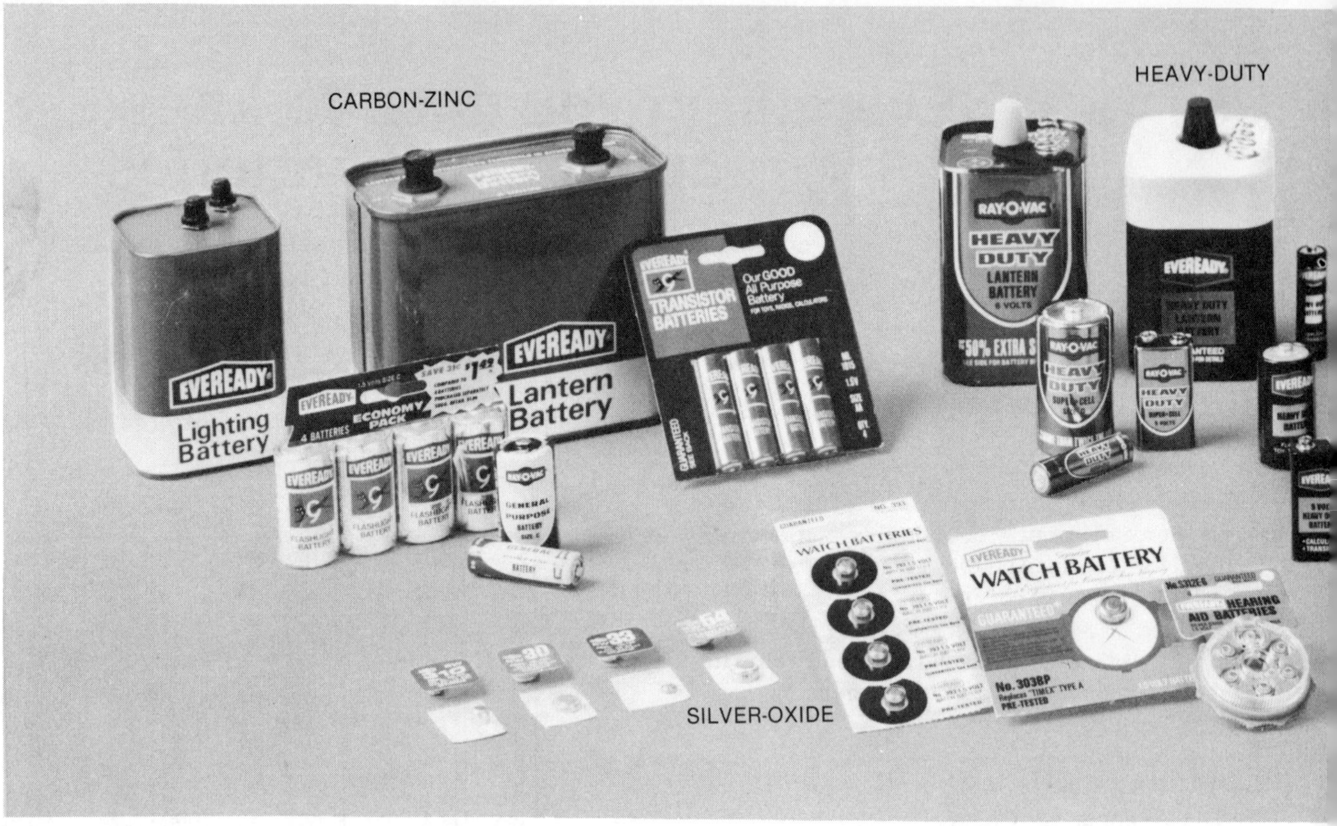

Important: Just because carbon-zinc batteries perform well in the heat, don't expect that they will store better that way.

High temperatures will greatly accelerate self-discharge, causing rapid battery deterioration and destroying their otherwise good shelf life.

You've probably seen batteries marked "heavy duty." But, are they really?

Generally, they are a form of carbon-zinc that uses a different construction and an electrolyte (zinc chloride).

You get 50 percent more capacity and somewhat better cold-temperature performance, along with—you guessed it—a 50 percent higher price tag.

You get what you pay for. Alkalines outperform all except the expensive, special types. They are good at high currents, work well in the cold, and have an excellent shelf life. In sum, they perform well in precisely the areas in which the carbin-zinc fails.

When the carbon-zincs are suffering under heavy currents, losing 90 percent of their capacity, it's the alkalines' turn to shine. Now they have the advantage, by a whopping 5 to 1 margin. What they say in the ads about alkalines is true. In toys, photoflash and other heavy-current devices, don't even consider another battery.

Of course, there has to be a break-even point. Generally, it falls at medium currents. However, since rest periods help carbon-zincs, the break-even point rises to somewhat higher currents with intermittent use. Also, the edge goes to the alkalines if you need very long (over five years) shelf life.

Alkalines and carbon-zincs share what is called a sloping voltage discharge. This means that their voltage falls gradually as they are discharged. The lower the cutoff your device can tolerate, the more energy you will get from the battery.

The major battery cards are on the table, and you've picked the best hand. So that's it; you're not going to save any more. Wrong! How would you like to take your low costs and cut them in half, or even two-thirds?

Just look for sales! Don't laugh. This one tip may save you more than anything we've said so far. The battery-marketing structure is such that there are often sizable discounts (and cash rebates) of 50 percent or more off list price.

Silver-oxide, the type of battery that powered the lunar buggy, would make a fantastic battery for your flashlight. It would power it three times as long as an alkaline, and your light wouldn't dim at all until the battery was totally exhausted.

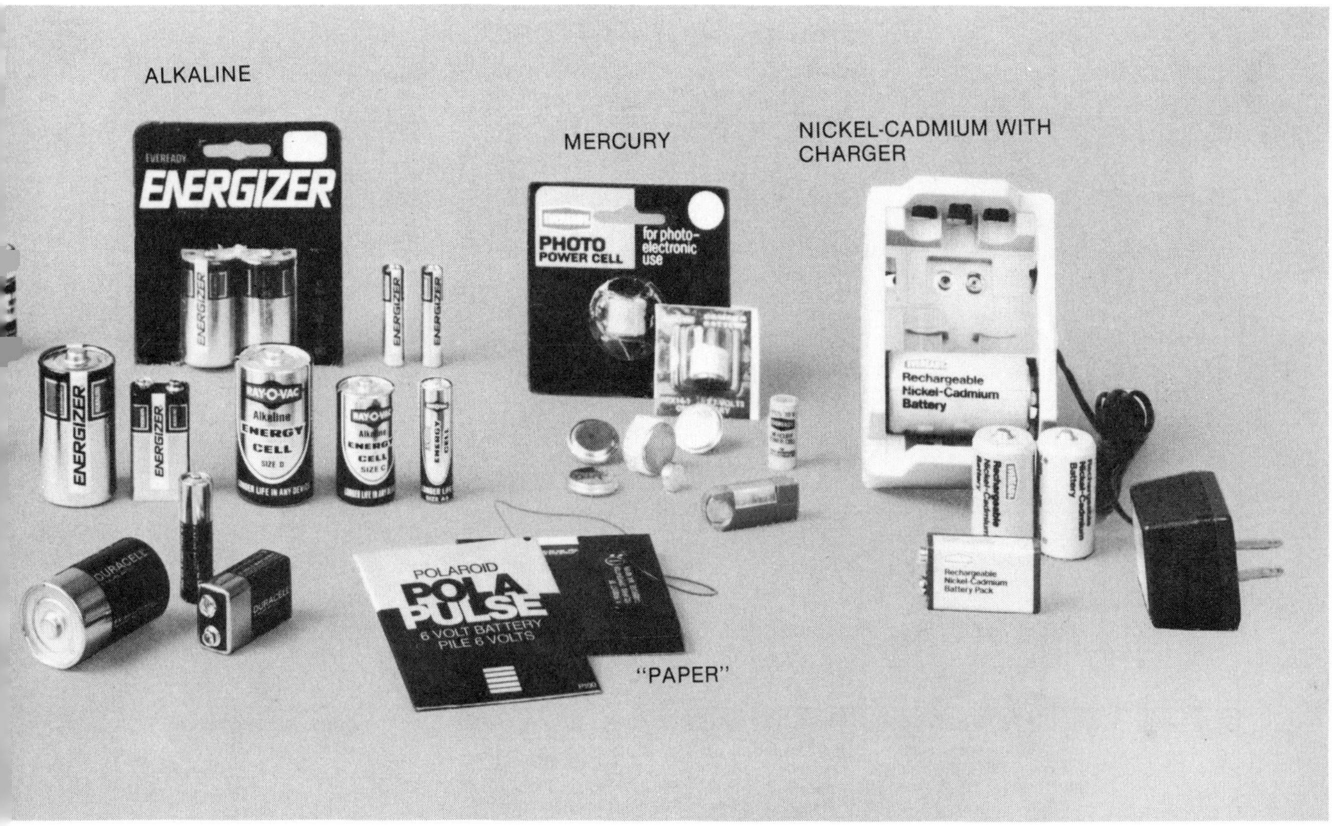

There's just one tiny catch —it would cost $9.10 per hour!

Here on earth, you'll find silver-oxide batteries in watches, calculators, hearing aids and cameras as "button" cells. They are ideally suited to these applications because they have very high energy content for their size. Unlike carbon-zincs and alkalines, the voltage doesn't fall gradually during discharge, and this is important for the accuracy of watch circuits. Yet, despite their tiny size, they cost about $3 each.

Like the silver-oxide, mercury batteries find wide use in button-cell applications, but they cost half as much. However, *you can't indiscriminately replace a silver cell with a mercury.* This is because mercury has a lower operating voltage (1.35 or 1.4 volts). Many circuits, especially timekeeping ones like watches, can't take the one-fifth of a volt difference between the silver-oxide and mercury.

Luckily, hearing aids, which use up a lot of batteries, will not be damaged by a change from silver to mercury. Often, the only ill effect, if any, is slightly lower volume. In the future, we probably will see more devices designed around the cheaper mercury system.

Recently, alkaline button cells have appeared on the market as inexpensive replacements for the silver-oxide and mercury, which have a flat voltage discharge. The alkaline doesn't, and this can cause a problem in some devices, particularly watches.

If you find that your battery costs are high, then you need rechargeable nickel-cadmium (nicad) batteries. Once you get past the initial high cost, you have virtually free batteries for life, because they can be recharged over 1000 times. Often, the cost per discharge cycle is under a penny.

Usually, they come in the AA, C, D and 9-volt radio sizes. Unlike the button cells, you don't have to worry about the fact that the nicad has a 1.25 voltage rating. The devices that are designed to run on these batteries take into account that the voltage of carbon-zincs and alkalines falls in use. So the nicad's lower voltage is okay.

These batteries can crank out current levels that would put the powerful alkaline to shame. That's why you see them in extra-heavy-current applications, like hedge trimmers and soldering irons.

Recently, lead-acid lantern batteries appeared on the market. These are rechargeable, have a "gelled" electrolyte, and don't need added water. If you use over two lantern batteries a year, these batteries would be a good investment.

COMPARISON OF BATTERY LIFE

Type	Voltage	Composition	Weight (in ounces)	*Low drain	Hours of life	*Medium drain	Hours of life	*High drain	Hours of life	Approx. price
AAA	1.5	Carbon zinc	0.3	2	300	10	43	50	2.3	$ .35
AA	1.5	Carbon zinc	0.52	5	240	30	25	100	2.5	.35
C	1.5	Carbon zinc	1.5	10	220	50	20	250	1.5	.45
D	1.5	Carbon zinc	3.0	20	260	100	45	300	4.3	.45
9V	9.0	Carbon zinc	1.5	5	80	10	38	25	1.0	.99
AA	1.5	Zinc chloride	0.6	5	275	30	38	100	6.0	.50
C	1.5	Zinc chloride	1.6	10	330	50	56	250	7.0	.65
D	1.5	Zinc chloride	3.3	20	375	100	65	300	13.0	.65
9V	9.0	Zinc chloride	1.5	5	94	10	45	25	15.0	1.59
AAA	1.5	Alkaline	0.4	2	375	10	73	50	10.0	.90
AA	1.5	Alkaline	0.75	5	340	30	54	100	13.0	1.90
C	1.5	Alkaline	2.2	10	470	50	90	250	13.0	1.13
D	1.5	Alkaline	4.5	20	470	100	91	300	29.0	1.13
9V	9.0	Alkaline	1.6	10	52	30	17	60	8.0	2.25
A76	1.5	Alkaline	0.09	0.1	950	1	90	10	8.0	.99
AA	1.4	Mercury	1.05	5	480	30	80	100	23.0	1.90
675	1.4	Mercury	0.09	0.1	2200	1	215	5	42.0	3.25
AA	1.25	Nickel Cadmium	1.95	5	100	30	17	100	5.0	3.80
C-D	1.25	Nickel Cadmium	2.2	20	60	100	12	300	4.0	4.40
509	6.0	Carbon zinc	21.5	20	500	150	60	500	10.0	2.50
76	1.5	Silver	0.08	0.1	1900	1	190	5	37.0	2.40
544	6.0	Silver	0.5	0.1	1900	1	190	5	37.0	13.90
303	1.5	Silver	0.09	0.1	1650	1	165	5	32.0	4.15
357	1.5	Silver	0.08	0.1	1650	1	190	5	37.0	4.15

* Measured in milliamperes.
Note: 85 percent of carbon zinc and zinc chloride batteries, 95 percent of silver and mercury, 50 percent of nickel cadmium batteries get one year shelf life.

HOW DIFFERENT TYPES OF BATTERIES WORK

	Performance at:			Performance at:		Shelf life at:		
	Low current drain	**Medium current drain**	**High current drain**	**Low room temp.**	**High room temp.**	**Low room temp.**	**Medium room temp.**	**High room temp.**
Carbon-zinc	E	G	P	P	G	G-E	G	P
Zinc chloride	E	G-E	F-P	F	G	G-E	G	P
Alkaline	E	E	G	G	G	E	E	G-E
Nickel-cadmium	E	E	E	G	G	E	E	G-E
Mercury	E	E	F-E*	F	E	E	E	G
Silver oxide	E	E	F-E*	F	E	E	E	E
Lithium	E	G	P	E	E	E	E	E
Lead-acid	E	E	E	F	G	F	F	F-P

* Depending on type. Legend: E = excellent; G = good; F = fair; P = poor.

THE INFORMATION on this page is valuable. The chart above, "How Different Types of Batteries Work," outlines the relative strengths of each battery-chemical.

Once you decide on the battery chemistry, get specific data from the top chart, "Comparison of Battery Life."

Finally, use the chart at the right and the top chart to calculate battery life.

CURRENT DRAIN IN VARIOUS DEVICES (Measured in milliamperes)

Device	Current Drain (volume)
Radios (with 9-v. battery)	9-12 (low) 10-15 (medium) 15-45 (high)
(with round batteries)	10-20 (low) 20-30 (medium) 30-100 (high) 100+ (blasting)
Cassette Recorders	70-130 (low) 90-150 (medium) 100-200 (high)
Calculators	
LED (9-v. battery)	20-30
LED (AA batteries)	40-100
Fluorescent (green)	20-50
LCD	under 1
Fluorescent Lamp (one 6-w. bulb)	500-1000
Flashlights	500-1000
Toys	
Motorized type	400-2000
Electronic games	20-200
Video games	20-200
Cameras	
Photo flash	1000-2000
Autowind	200-300
Watches	
LCDs	10-25; back-lighted
LEDs	10-40, lighted
TVs (portable)	500-1500, depending on unit

You may see lithium cells taking over a good portion of the watch (button) and calculator market in the next five or 10 years. They have an incredible shelf life that is measured in decades!

In a photo on page 235 is the same type of 6-volt, carbon-zinc battery that was an integral part of the Polaroid film packs. It is now available to the consumer as a separate battery for special applications where space is at a premium or there are momentary, large surges of current. Other than the fact that it's able to put out a 25-amp. pulse, it's similar in basic characteristics to the ordinary carbon-zinc battery of comparable size.

BATTERY BRAIN clips are connected to the battery to be tested. If it needs charging, you plug in the battery eliminator or another power source at jack J1.

Build a 'brain' to test and recharge most batteries

Here's the answer to your battery blues. This tester sorts batteries into the good and the bad, and rejuvenates those that aren't too far gone

By JEFF SANDLER

■ EVERYBODY KNOWS that batteries "give up" just when you need them most. You can prevent this frustrating annoyance with our Battery Brain. It has features not normally available on chargers, such as an adjustable charge rate. But particularly valuable are an automatic current cutoff that prevents a damaging overcharge and a light that lets you know your batteries are "ready."

Testing is a snap. All you do is flip a switch that corresponds to your battery voltage, touch the clips to the battery terminals, then watch the meter. If the meter needle moves, your battery has life. How much depends on how far the needle moves toward the 1.5 mark (0.9 means dead and 1.5 indicates a full charge).

If the needle doesn't move at all, throw out the battery.

how it works

Consider a single carbon-zinc or alkaline flashlight battery. Fresh from the store, it's rated at 1.5 v., but this falls steadily as the battery is used. The 1.5 and 0.9 on the Battery Brain meter scale represent the working voltage range of a single-cell, 1½-v. battery.

But say you want to test a more powerful 9-v. radio battery (composed of six 1½-v. cells in series). The Battery Brain simply divides all the voltages by six.

RECHARGE YOUR BATTERIES

Percent of energy remaining in carbon-zincs and alkalines for various voltages:	Recommended charge currents for different-size battery cells:	
1.5 = 100%	AAA	20 ma.
1.4 = 85%	AA	40 ma.
1.3 = 65%	C	60 ma.
1.2 = 35%	D	100 ma.
1.1 = 20%	9-v.	10 ma.
1.0 = 10%	Lantern	140 ma.
0.9 = 0%		

PARTS LIST—BATTERY BRAIN

All resistors are ¼-w. carbon unless otherwise specified.

R1—1-ohm resistor
R2—100-ohm resistor
R3—200-ohm resistor
R4—300-ohm resistor
R5—390-ohm resistor
R6—510-ohm resistor
R7—680-ohm resistor
R8—4.7K (4700-ohm) resistor
R9—110-ohm resistor
R10—3.3K (3300-ohm) resistor
R11—10K (10,000-ohm) resistor
R12—10K (10,000-ohm) resistor
R13—100-ohm resistor
R14—10K (10,000-ohm) resistor
R15—1K adjustable trimmer control
R16—1K adjustable trimmer control
Q1—2N4403 PNP transistor (TO5 case)
Q2—2N4403 PNP transistor (TO5 case)
Q3—2N4403 PNP transistor (92 case)
Q4—2N4403 PNP transistor (92 case)
Q5—2N4401 NPN transistor (92 case)
D1, D2, D3—1N4148
M1—0-200uA edge meter
S1 = S8—8-position DIP switch
L1, L2—6-v., 70-ma. lamp
J1—Jack, open-circuit type
Misc.: Wire, clips for batteries, solder.

Note: A complete kit of parts for the Battery Brain is available from Circuit Craft Inc., 10 Idell Rd., Valley Stream, NY 11580 (includes everything listed above). A completely assembled Battery Brain is available. A plug-in-the-wall, 15-v., modular power source is also available separately.

charge! (and save)

Nobody has to tell you that you are spending plenty on batteries nowadays—probably $20 or more over a year's time.

Charging is as simple as testing with the Battery Brain. Once it is set up to test a battery, plugging a 9- to 15-v. source into the Battery Brain's jack automatically converts it into a charger.

measures rising voltage

The meter still works, except that it now measures the rising voltage of the battery as it is charged. A light shows that you're charging and goes out when your battery is fully charged. If you want to charge a battery of different voltage, just flip the switch on the case to whatever new voltage is desired.

One of the best and most convenient sources for the 9- to 15-volts is one of the little modular, plug-in-the-wall battery eliminators. Since any 9- to 15-v. source will power the Battery Brain, you can also make an adapter that plugs into your car's 12-v. cigaret lighter.

when to recharge

Generally, it's best to recharge a battery when the voltage falls between 1.2 and 1.4. Normally, you can count on more than 10 recharges on such batteries as carbon-zincs, heavy-duties and alkalines. Nicads are even better; they're designed to be recharged repeatedly and can go more than 1000 cycles.

Just as falling voltage indicates the state of discharge, how far the voltage rises toward 1.5 v. indicates how much charge the battery has taken. You adjust the cutoff trimmer control so the charging lights go out *just* at 1.5 v. This way, the cutoff is set properly for all the different battery voltages you will use in charging.

different charge currents

Different-size batteries need different charge currents. The chart shows the recommended rates for various batteries. You set the current level with the charge control and judge by the brightness of the lights: Dim red = 20 milliamperes (ma.); bright red = 30 ma.; orange = 50 ma.; yellow = 60 ma.; white = 70 ma. These values are doubled when you flip the "C" switch. So you get a charge current range of 20 ma. to 140 ma.

construction

Construction is easy if you order our kit. You install and solder all the components on the drilled, etched and labeled printed-circuit (PC) board. If you prefer to make your own PC board, we supply a template herewith.

Resistors R1 through R7 divide the different battery voltages down to 1.5. Which one is in the circuit is selected by one of seven switches. Before the meter gets the voltage, the "unwanted" 0.9 v. is subtracted out by diodes D2 and D3. The circuitry on the left shuts off the charge current (which flows through the lamps) when the voltage per cell of the battery you are charging reaches 1.5 v.

Note: In order for your battery to get a charge, the voltage of your source has to be higher than that of your battery. So if you are charging 9- or 12-v. batteries, you need at least a 12-v. or higher source.

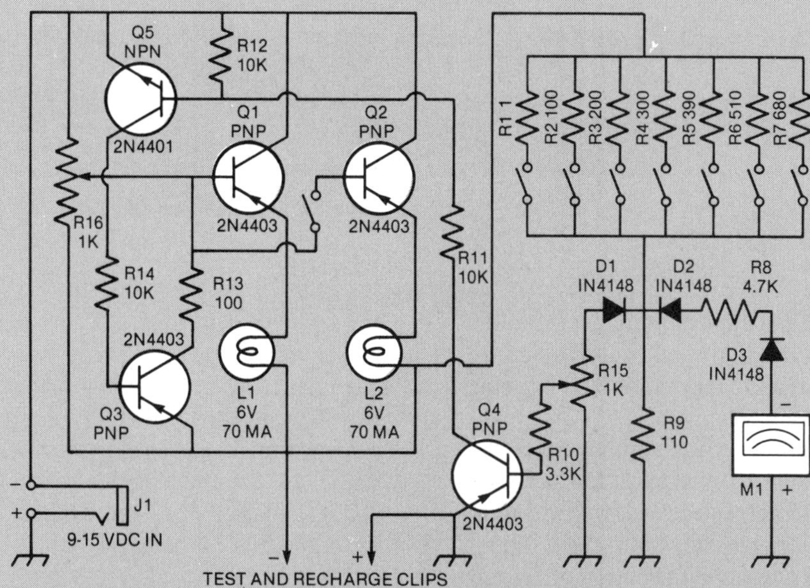

THE SCHEMATIC diagram (above) details how Battery Brain's components are interconnected.

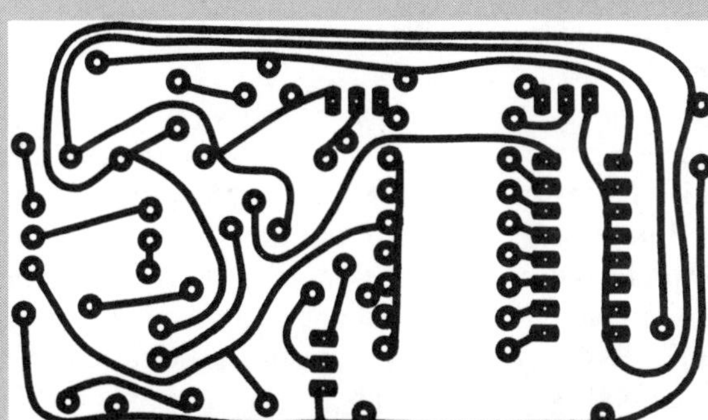

COMPONENT-SIDE view (below) shows how all the parts of the Battery Brain are to be placed on the printed-circuit board. You can easily make the PC board by using the template which is shown above.

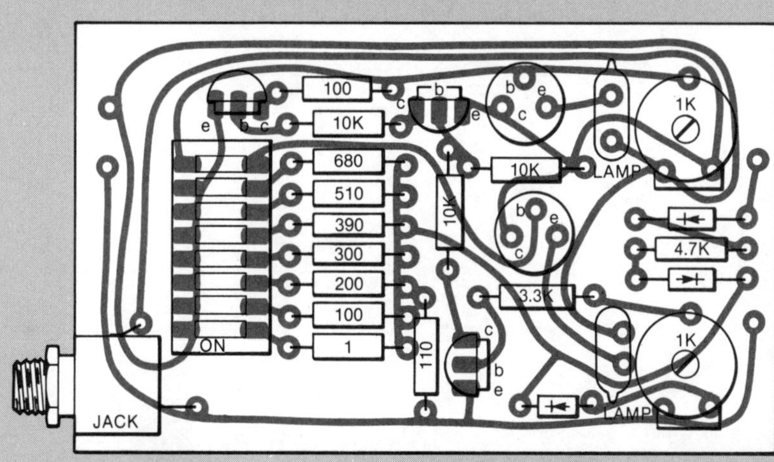

Don't electrocute your car battery

By JEFFREY SANDLER

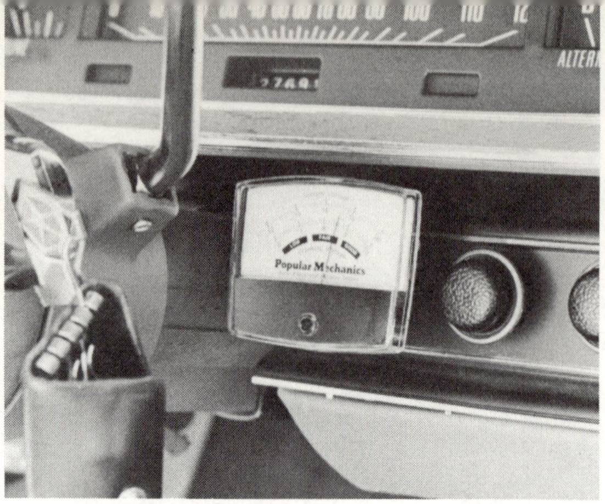

■ THE AMMETER supplies more useful information at a glance than any other instrument in your car. Unfortunately, the ammeter is going the way of the passenger pigeon.

You are driving blind when you rely solely on warning lights. If you really want to know what's going on, build the auto electrical-system tester. This simple meter plugs into your car's cigaret lighter and supplies all the information of an ammeter and some extra.

An auto battery isn't just a black box that puts out exactly 12 volts until it dies. During normal car operation, it may vary from 12 to 15 volts depending on whether it is being charged or discharged. Hidden in small voltage shifts is plenty of information about the electrical system. A single volt can be the difference between a running car or one stuck somewhere with a fried battery.

Let's change the scale on a meter to spread the range of 12 to 15 volts over its face. Use a meter which normally reads 0 to 1 milliamp. (Radio Shack No. 22-052) to display the automobile's voltage.

Our electronic trick is to get the meter to display a voltage range between 12 and 15. To make our magic, we'll use a *zener diode* (Radio Shack No. 276-563) that will not conduct any electric current until there is a certain voltage across its leads. Our expanded meter will not indicate until voltage reaches 12. Then it reads correctly from 12 to 16 volts.

You'll also need a cigaret-lighter plug (Radio Shack No. 274-331) and a 3900-ohm resistor. Wire the diodes so that their polarity bands face this resistor, not the meter.

In a properly working car, before the car is started, with everything turned off, the meter reads about 12.5 volts. Open a car door and the meter will drop a notch due to the current drain of the dome light. The meter falls below 12 when the engine is cranked due to the tremendous current drain of the starter. The battery can fall as low as 9 volts. Remember, our meter scale starts at 12 volts.

WIRING DIAGRAM

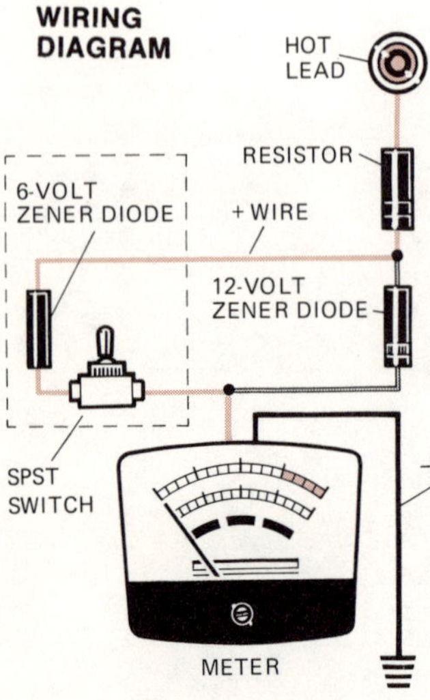

HOW TO HOOK UP THE TESTER

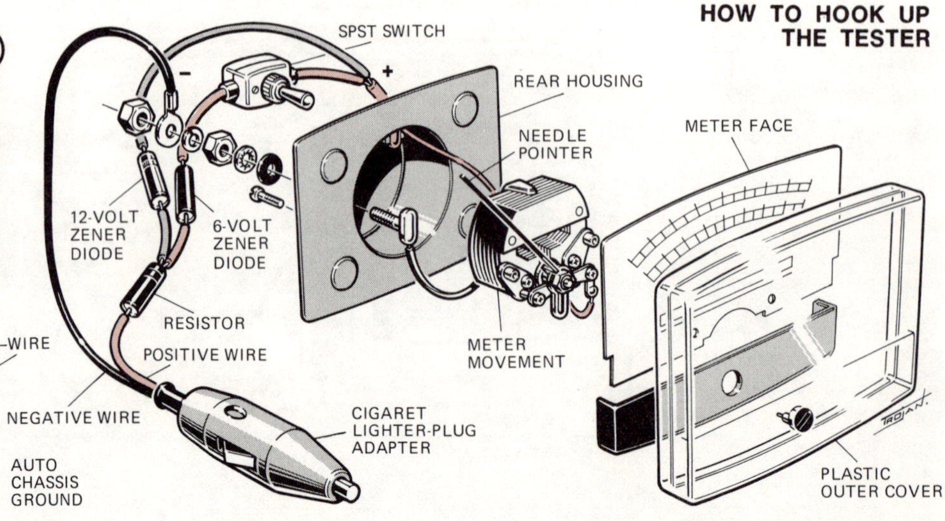

Once the car is started, the generating system supplies its electrical needs. System voltage is brought up to 14 to 15 volts.

dead meter

If the meter is below 12.8 and doesn't move in response to changes in engine speed, don't sit there and watch the needle fall. Get the car off the road immediately. But don't shut off the engine yet. Check to see if your fan belt is broken. If so, stop the engine right away.

If you have an intact fan belt, the charging system is dead and the battery is powering the electrical devices in the car. The coil is the first thing to die as the battery runs down. Don't waste time. Turn off all electrical accessories and head for the nearest service station.

If heavy electrical use makes the meter drop below 14 to 15 when the engine is going faster than idle, watch out. In severe cases, the meter never reaches 14 or 15 volts.

As the generator or alternator is called on to deliver more power, it drags harder on the fan belt. A loose belt slips, reducing output and system voltage. Tighten the fan belt.

If the meter stays near or above 15 during driving, the voltage regulator is set above the proper 14.6 volts. As you drive, the battery is being overcharged. Your dashboard light or original-equipment ammeter will not indicate there is a problem. They respond only to current, not voltage levels. The life of the battery is being shortened. Adjust or replace the regulator.

The meter never moving above 13.8 volts is the opposite of frying your battery. The regulator is set too low. The battery never gets a full charge. Your light or ammeter won't tip you off to this one either. Another symptom is weak cranking.

If, over several months, the meter falls farther when you turn on your lights than it did before, the battery is getting old and weak. Other symptoms include lazy cranking and, on generator cars, a noticeable dimming of the lights when the car engine is idling.

By adding a switch and a 6-volt zener diode, (Radio Shack No. 276-561) you can tell when you are not getting proper cranking voltage to start your car. Switching the 6-volt zener into the circuit lowers the meter scale to read from 6 to 9.5 volts. The scale is expanded, reading 6 volts on the left and 9.5 volts on the right. When you switch in the 6 to 9.5 volt range, the 12-volt zener has no effect in the circuit. Check out your cranking voltage by reading low, fair or good on the replacement meter face we've provided.

CUSTOMIZE your tester. Pop the clear cover from a Radio Shack 0-1 milliamp. No. 22-052 meter. Paste on the exact-size replacement face (above). Don't bend the pointer needle.

TEST READINGS: 12–12.8 (top left) normal vols with no use of battery; 12.8–13.8 (top right) undercharging, fast idle; 15.1–16 (middle left) overcharging, fast idle; 12–12.6 (middle right) engine off but lights on; 12.1–13.9 (bottom left) generator car at idle; 13–15 (bottom right) alternator car at idle.

A ONE-PIECE plug-in version is made by taping or gluing the lighter plug to back of smaller meter.

How to remove a bearing wall

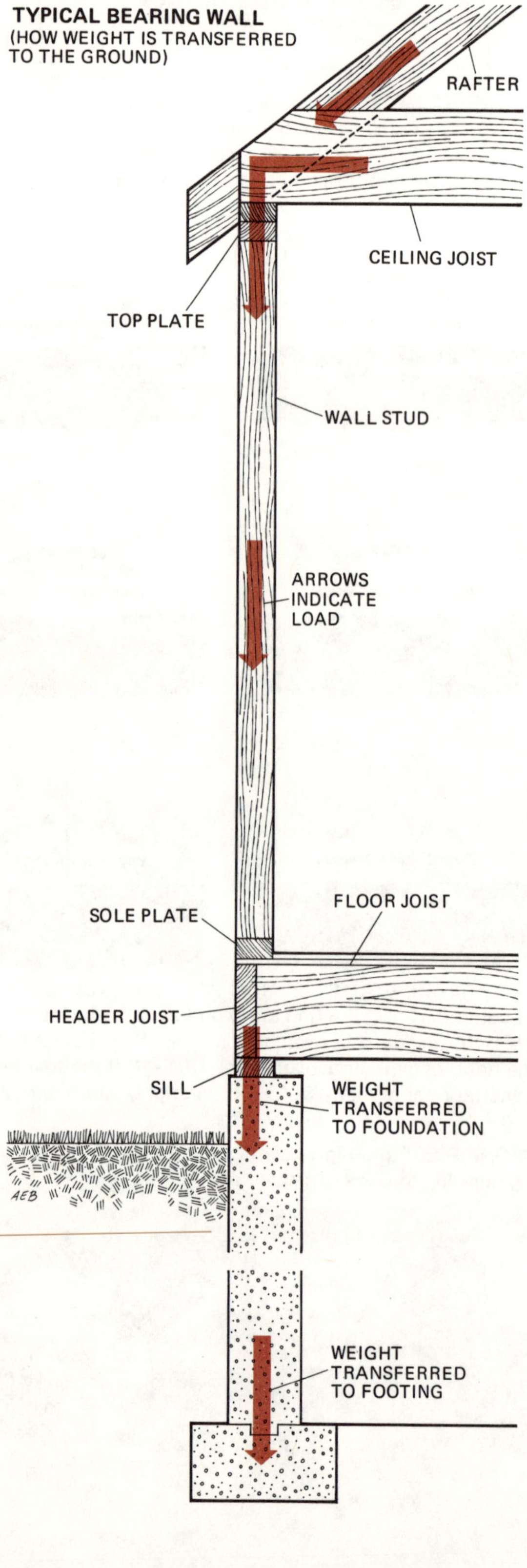

OFTEN A MAJOR home-remodeling project requires the removal of an existing wall. The usual reasons are to create a one-room effect between dining and living rooms and to enlarge a room by knocking out the wall between it and an unused bedroom or garage. Often, however, wall removal is only partial: When redecorating plans call for installation of sliding doors, for instance, or making a wide-arched opening where a single door now exists.

If the wall to be removed is simply a partition wall—that is, nonload-bearing—the task is relatively simple. But if the wall supports weight from above (see drawing, left), it is a bearing wall. In this case, it's important that a proper-size header be installed over the new opening (span) to handle the load adequately from above—and its transfer to the foundation.

Though removing a large section of a bearing wall is a job usually best left to a pro, you will be well advised to have a working knowledge of just what this task involves. Most smaller jobs can be tackled with confidence by a knowledgeable home handyman; the information on these pages will help you do that. As can be seen in the drawings and text, the first big chore is to determine whether the wall is, in fact, a bearing wall. If it is, here's how you can remove it.

Removing the wall finish

Before starting to remove the surface of any wall, determine where all electrical, heating and plumbing lines run. If any are in the wall, do not use power tools near the area. Turn off power to all outlets in the wall and use a hammer to remove plaster or drywall from these sections. Also, protect the floor with a dropcloth. Better yet, use a canvas tarp over the dropcloth. Tape the floor covering along the edges which will be walked over, or debris kicked beneath will scratch the floor. For safety, stop periodically and haul accumulated debris outside. If this is left underfoot, it can cause accidents.

The best way to remove a drywall is with a sabre saw. Simply run its blade alongside studs to make vertical cuts, and make horizontal passes to create the

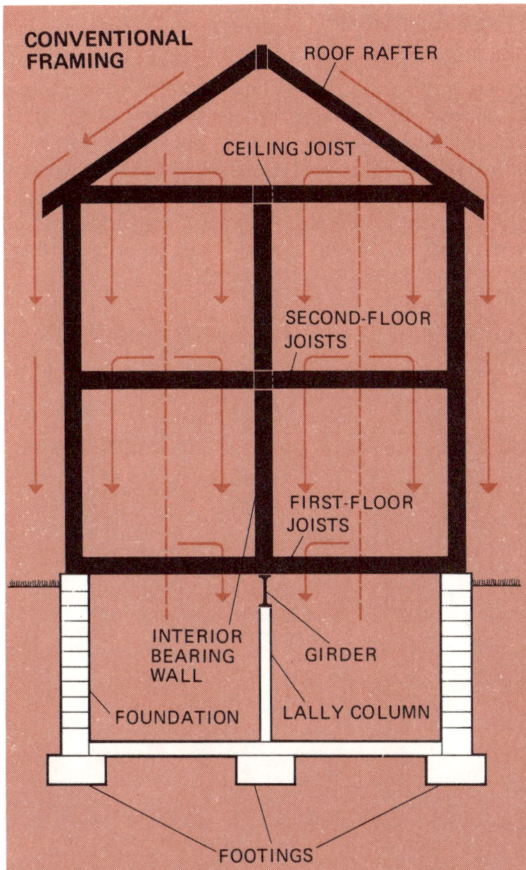

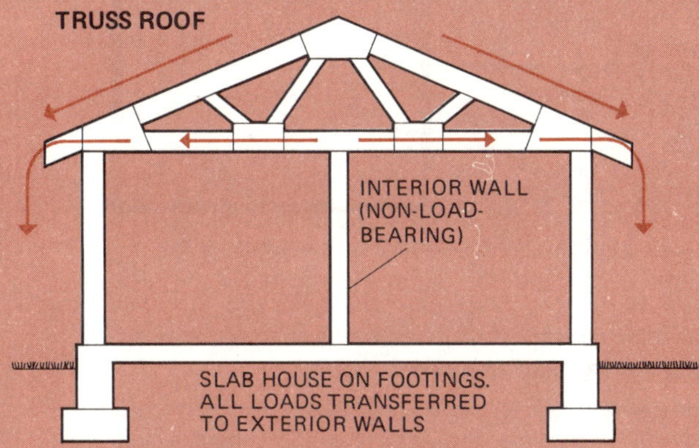

Determining if a wall is a bearing wall

In conventional framing (see sketch at left), two opposite walls of a house are bearing. They partially support floor loads (joists), exterior walls, roof, and ceiling loads (rafters and ceiling joists). The interior wall is also a bearing wall. In a basement or crawl space, you can see the direction in which joists run. Their support points determine which of the walls are bearing. Bearing walls usually continue right on up to the underside of the ceiling joists for the top floor.

In trussed-roof construction (sketched above), there are no interior bearing walls supporting the room. It is supported by the exterior walls upon which the trusses rest. But in a two-story house with a truss roof, this will be true *on the second level only;* interior walls on the first level *may* have ceiling joists resting on them

SEE ALSO

Basement remodeling . . . Concrete blocks . . . Family rooms . . . Fasteners . . . Garage remodeling . . . House additions . . . Insulation . . . Lumber . . . Measurements . . . Moldings . . . Nails . . . Remodeling

desired-size chunks. When all of the plasterboard is removed, clean the nails from all the studs you plan to save and reuse. If the studs are to be thrown out—rather foolish in these days of high lumber prices—drive home all nails before ripping out the studs.

Removing plaster and wood lath is a different—and dirtier—story. Besides protecting the floor, it's a good idea to drape dropcloths over doorways to keep white dust from spreading through the house. Open windows for ventilation and be sure to wear a face mask.

The handiest tool to have when removing a plaster wall is a bayonet-type power saw. A sabre saw does the job, too; it just takes a little longer. Use a plaster-cutting blade in either type of saw; an ordinary blade will soon become dulled and useless.

To start, make a plunge cut in one of the bays between studs and run the saw horizontally until you come to a stud. Then turn the saw in a vertical position, either up or down, and continue cutting. After you've made both horizontal cuts and one vertical cut, you can start the last vertical cut. Here you'll find that as the tool cuts into the wood lath behind the plaster, the lath chatters. Thus, it is best to have a helper hold a board against the wall on the outboard side of the saw to minimize lath chatter.

It's a good idea to give your power tool a thorough cleaning as soon as the job is completed. There will be considerable accumulation of white dust in the tool's air ports, and unless it is completely blown out, excessive heat can build up and burn out the tool.

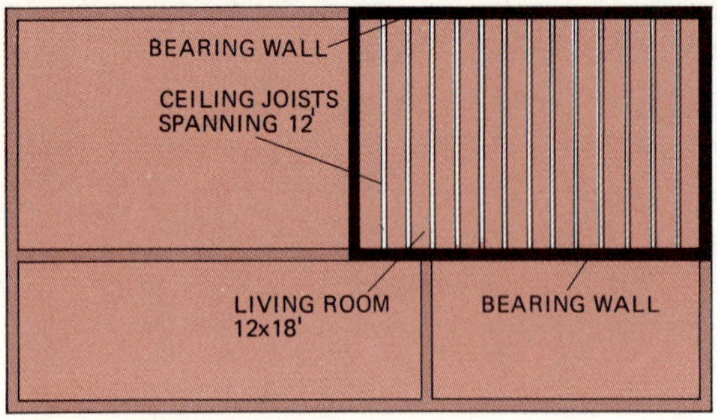

Slab-house bearing walls

In a slab house where visual inspection of the joists above is impossible, the easiest way to check which walls are bearing is by living-room dimension. If, for example, your living room measures 12x18 ft., ceiling joists will normally run the shortest dimension—12 ft. The bearing walls will be the 18-ft.-long walls. Also, it is often easy to spot the plasterboard nails in joists—by the rows of dark spots on the ceiling

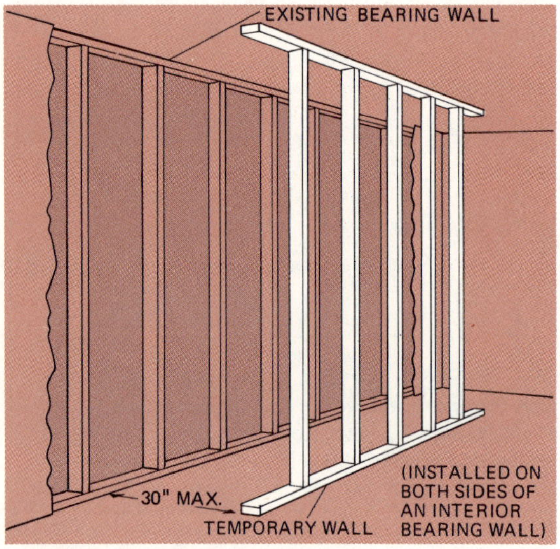

Temporarily supporting the load

Since a bearing wall denotes a wall which is supporting some structure above, it should not be removed until a temporary wall is installed (about 30 in. away from the wall). If you are removing an interior bearing wall, construct a temporary wall on both sides. A temporary supporting wall is constructed in much the same manner as a permanent wall: Studs are positioned 16 in. on centers between top and bottom plates. The main differences are that the plates are *not* nailed to the floor and ceiling, and the stud-holding nails are not toe-nailed all the way home into the plates (so they can be easily removed later).

It is important that all temporary wall studs be cut so they are a tight fit. If either ceiling or floor are uneven, use shims (undercourse shingles) between these surfaces and the plates

Installing a header

When wall studs and plates are removed, the header can be wedged up tightly under the ends of joists it will support. If required, use shims for a tight fit. If a lower header is desired, use cripple studs as shown below. The header must bear (rest) on solid wood—i.e., supporting studs, not plaster or dry wall. To make up your header, check the finished wall thickness. If the existing stud width is 3⅝ in., you'll need a ⅜-in. filler (plywood or lath) in the header

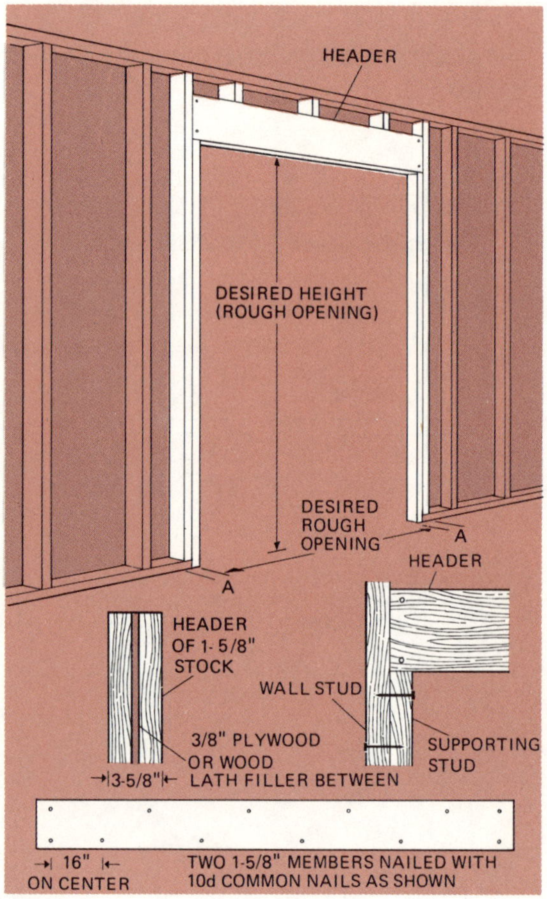

Installing new rough opening

With wall finish removed and the exact location of the desired opening determined, intermediate studs (A) may have to be installed to provide a nailer for the supporting stud or studs. With these up, the appropriate-sized header is installed, supported by a stud at each end. For openings over 6 ft., double supporting studs are required at each end of the header. For openings over 8 ft., a contractor should be employed for the job.

The chart at the bottom of the facing page is a guide for maximum loading conditions. If your room is narrower, which means less floor load, or your opening is less than that shown, your header size may be reduced. For exact sizes, consult an engineer

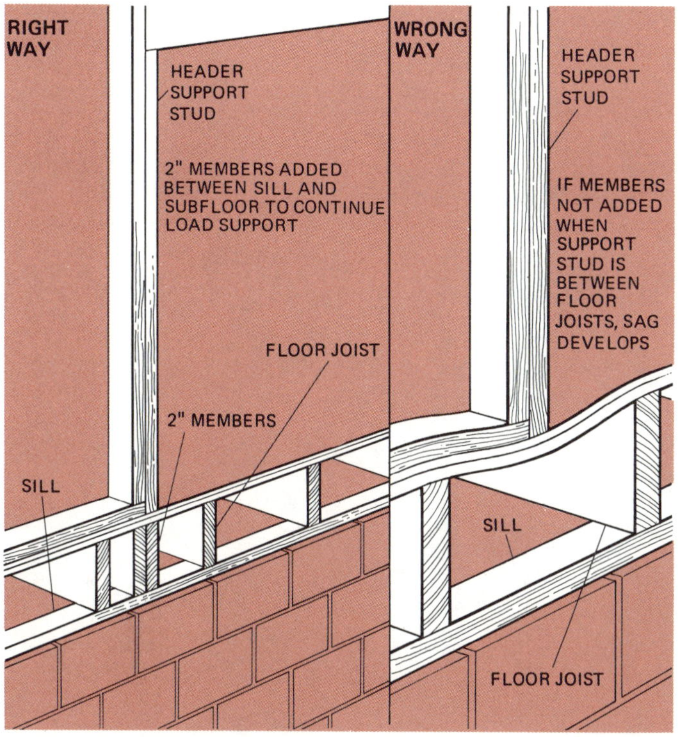

Supporting new load from below

Studs supporting the newly installed header must also bear on solid structure; they must not simply rest on flooring and subflooring or a serious sag will develop. In this event, the easiest solution is to cut short lengths of 2-in. members (1-5/8-in. actual dimension) equal in *length* to the *width* of the floor joists.

These "jacks" are then wedged—with grain running vertically—between the subflooring and the sill supporting the floor joists. If under an interior bearing wall, they're wedged between beam, or girder, and sub-flooring. Use at least two jack studs under each supporting stud and, when satisfied the fit is tight, secure jacks with 10d common nails.

In this way, the structure load is transferred from header to supporting studs through jack studs to the main support below. Once header and supports are installed and nailed, the temporary wall may be removed. The opening can now be finished on both sides to match the existing coverings

Finishing the job

Use plasterboard to re-cover the exposed studs in walls. If matching up to plaster thickness, add shims of wood to stud faces so that the drywall surface will be flush with the plaster wall. Spackle joints and nailheads to finish. If your floor is of wood, it will be necessary to custom-fit a piece in the hole (where the old soleplate was). Fit the piece and install it with glue and nails through predrilled holes. Sand and finish

What size header do you need?

Header size is determined by span over the opening and weight it must support. In sketch of house at right, interior wall is a bearing wall. The chart lists header sizes needed for various widths in such a wall—with 12 ft. of floor on both sides. 2-in. stock now comes in 1½-in. actual dimension (old 1-5/8-in. size is still in stock at some yards)

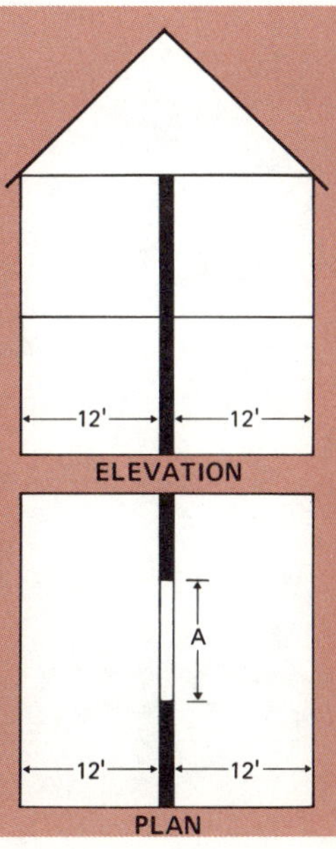

IF THE FLOOR ABOVE THE BEARING WALL IS 12' WIDE ON EITHER SIDE, AND OPENING A IS:

A (OPENING)	HEADER SIZE
3'	2-2x6
4'	2-2x6
5'	2-2x8
6'	2-2x10
7'	2-2x12
8'	2-2x12

Build a buffet-bed table

By WAYNE C. LECKEY

Covered with wood-grain plastic laminate, this multipurpose table earns its keep in many ways. With leaves extended it's a buffet counter. Straddling a twin bed it makes a handy bed table

■ STANDING BY TO SERVE a dual role, this double-duty buffet-bed table will prove to be one of the handiest pieces of furniture in your home. As a buffet table with its drop leaves extended, it becomes a 7-ft. long counter.

When used during sickness or just for breakfast in bed, the table can straddle a twin-size bed and let you eat, read, or write in comfort. Rolled to the foot of the bed, the table affords a perfect viewing place for a portable TV set.

From its handsome wood-grain finish you'd never know it was made from common fir plywood and pine lumber. All exposed surfaces are faced with Formica's English Oak laminate to provide a durable finish. The table's height must be determined by the particular bed, since some beds are higher than others. Likewise, the table should be wide enough to clear the sides of the bed by a couple of inches.

Basically, the table consists of four separate parts: two built-up legs, a top assembly and a countertop. The latter (including its drop leaves) goes on last after you've covered it with laminate and hinged the leaves. As you will note in studying the drawing, the top assembly has two same-size (top and bottom) frames of doweled 1x2s (¾ x 1½ in.) which are glued and nailed flush to 3¼-in. side rails (B, C and D) and a center divider (A).

The top frame differs in that it has cross mem-

SEE ALSO
Bars . . . Butler's tables . . . Hutch tables . . . Joinery . . . Legs, furniture . . . Mobile furniture . . . Occasional tables . . . Sofa-beds

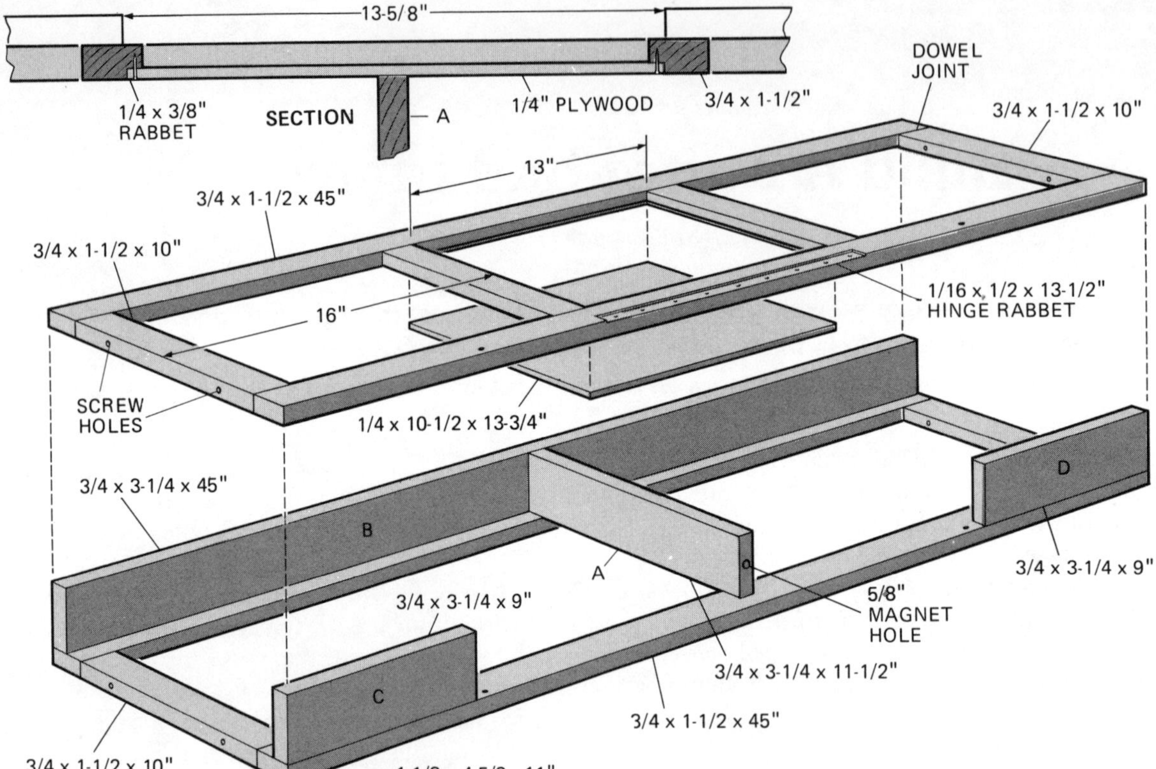

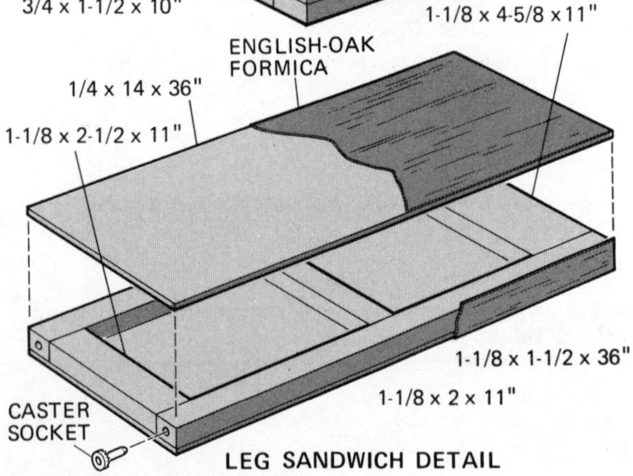

bers 13 in. apart to support the hinged center section, a ¼-in. dust cover which fits flush in rabbets cut on the underside, and a hinge rabbet for the book rack (see section view). Each end member is drilled before assembly for two ¼ x 3-in. screws which are used to attach the legs, and a ⅝-in.-diameter hole is made in the end of center divider (A) for a button magnet. Screw holes are also made in the two frames for the drawer pivots although these holes can be made after assembly.

AN 8½-IN. wrought-iron hinge screwed to the underside of the bookrack is used as a prop.

SOCKETS DRIVEN in the ends of the table legs accept the stems of 2-in. Shepherd casters.

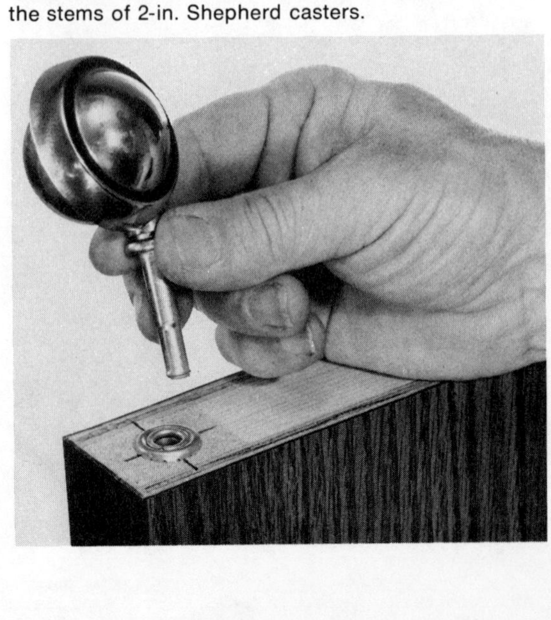

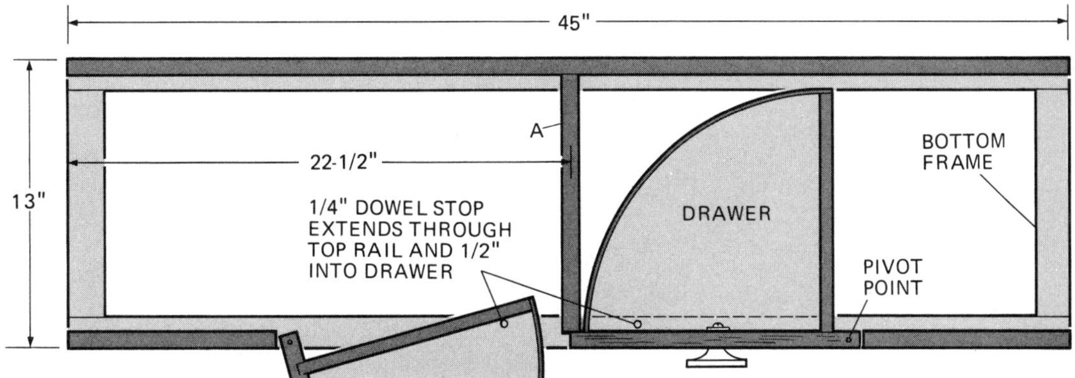
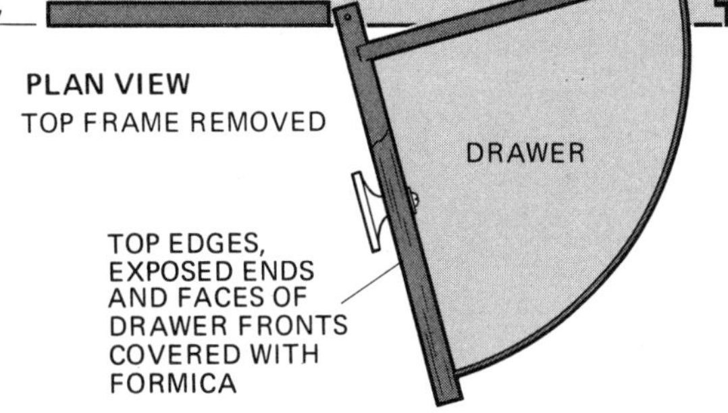

The two built-up legs are identical, each consisting of an inner frame of 1⅛-in. pine and faced on each side with ¼-in. plywood. Note that the inner top member of each leg is wider than the others, and that holes for the caster sockets are made in the lower ends of the side members.

To apply the Formica, cut the $\frac{1}{16}$-in.-thick laminate a bit larger than the wood surface to be covered and "glue" it in place with contact cement. The latter is applied with a brush to both wood and laminate, allowed to dry until tacky to the touch, then the surfaces are joined. Bond is instant; once the two coated surfaces touch, they can't be shifted. Therefore, it's necessary that the laminate be positioned carefully the first time.

When in place, the laminate is tapped all over with a hammer and wood block to assure good contact and bond. When an edge is to be covered with laminate, such as the table legs and countertop, it is covered first, then trimmed flush with the surface. Faces are covered last; let the laminate overhang the edge previously covered ap-

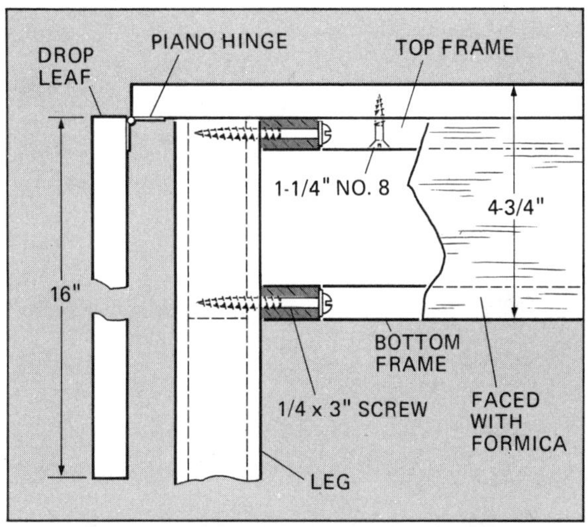

THE CUTAWAY DRAWING above shows how long wood screws through holes in the end rails are used to attach the top section rigidly to the hollow table legs. The screws enter wide blocking inside the legs at the top. The legs are attached before the countertop and drop leaves have been added to the table.

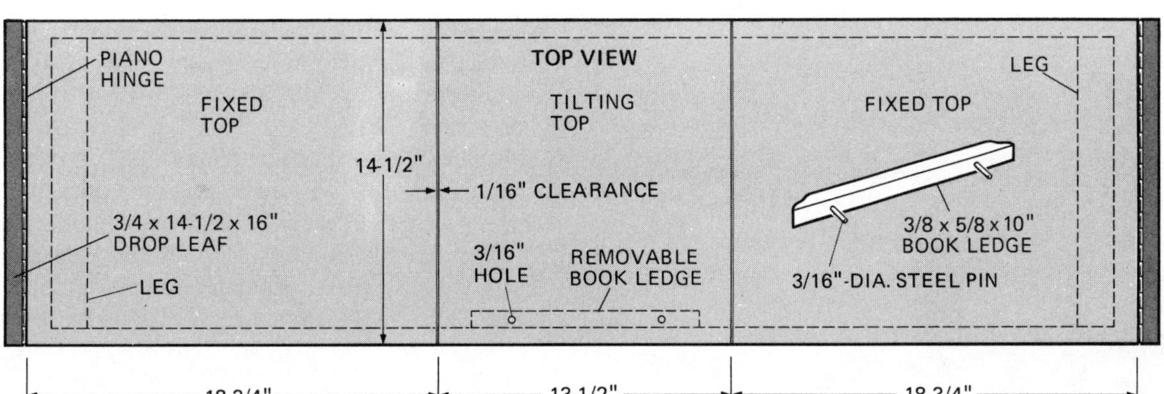

QUARTER-CIRCLE drawers swing open on screw pivots driven through the rails from above and below. The ledge strip at the bottom of the slanting bookrack is removable when the table is used for buffet serving. Short sections of 20d nail in the ledge strip fit mating holes in the bookrack.

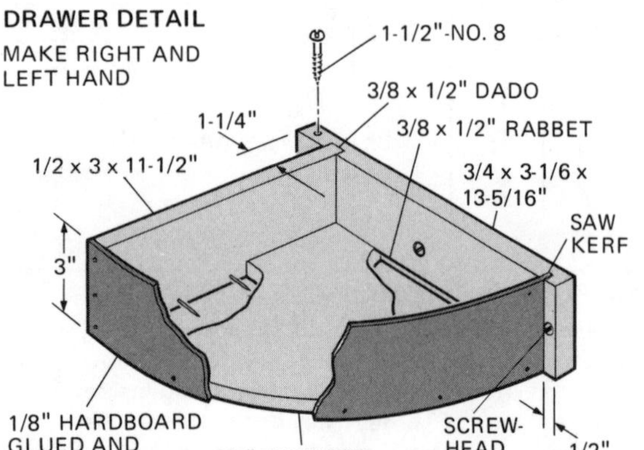

THE DROP LEAVES are supported by standard leaf supports made by Stanley, New Britain, Conn.

with laminate, it is applied, then trimmed flush with the surface. Faces are covered last; let the laminate overhang the edge previously covered approximately ⅛ in., then trim as before. Trimming is done quickly and professionally with a portable router and special cutter, but it can be done by hand with a flat mill file. Be careful not to scratch the finished surface of the laminate.

The front and back surfaces of the top assembly are faced with 4¾-in.-wide pieces of laminate. Like the back, the front is covered with a single piece, then cut out over the drawer opening and filed even with the frame edges and ends of pieces C and D.

The right and left-hand drawer fronts are fitted to their openings so there is a $1/16$-in. clearance top and bottom after they are faced with laminate. A thin washer placed over the pivot screw maintains this clearance at the bottom. The two drawers meet in the center of divider (A). They are held shut by flathead screws which contact the magnet. The latter, which is available from J. C. Armor Co., Inc., Box 290, Deer Park, N. Y. 11729, is set flush and glued in its hole.

Lengths of brass-plated piano hinge (cut 14½ in. long) are used to hinge the drop leaves to the 18¾-in. counter sections. Here all four edges of the five-piece counter are banded with laminate before the top surfaces are covered. Finally, 1¼-in. No. 8 wood screws are driven from below through the top frame to attach the counter.

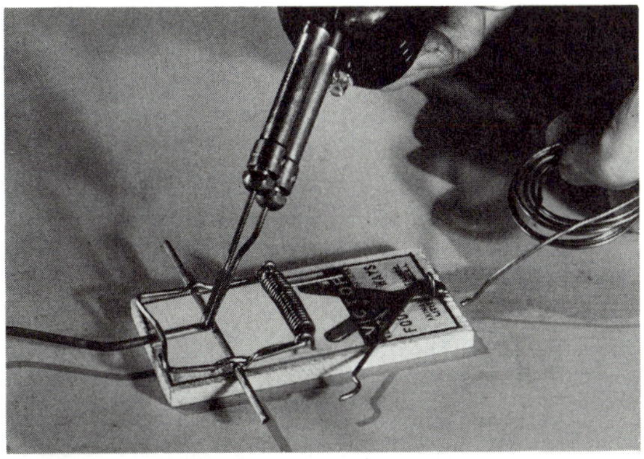

WHEN SOLDERING LIGHT PARTS, a common mousetrap can be as good as a third hand. Parts are arranged as required and held in place by the spring jaw. Kink the wire jaw if necessary.

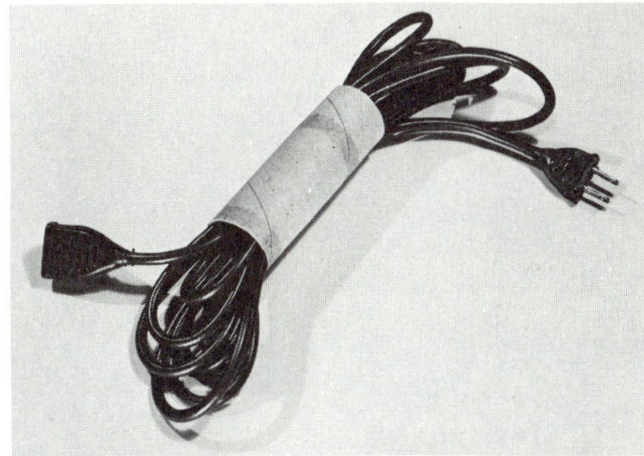

LEFTOVER TUBE from a roll of toilet paper is just the right size to keep an appliance cord neatly stored in a drawer. Coil the cord in a hank and slip the cardboard tube over it.

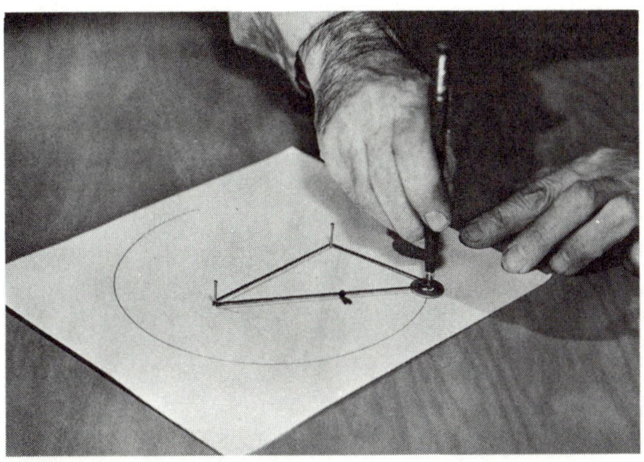

KEEPING THE STRING from slipping under the pencil point when drawing an ellipse by the string-pins-and-pencil method is no problem if you first place a small washer under the string.

SMALL TWIST DRILLS will remain rust-free if you store them in a capped glass jar fitted with a roll of corrugated cardboard. A little oil poured over the cardboard does the trick.

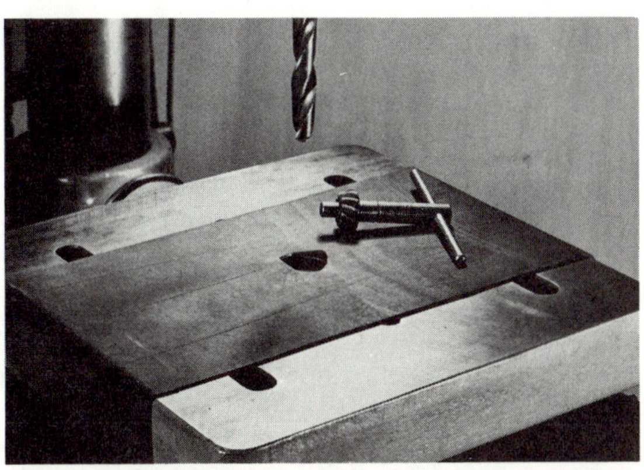

DRILL-PRESS WORK will be less difficult to keep from spinning when the table has a rubber surface. A 6-in.-wide sleeve cut from an old inner tube and stretched over the table will do the job.

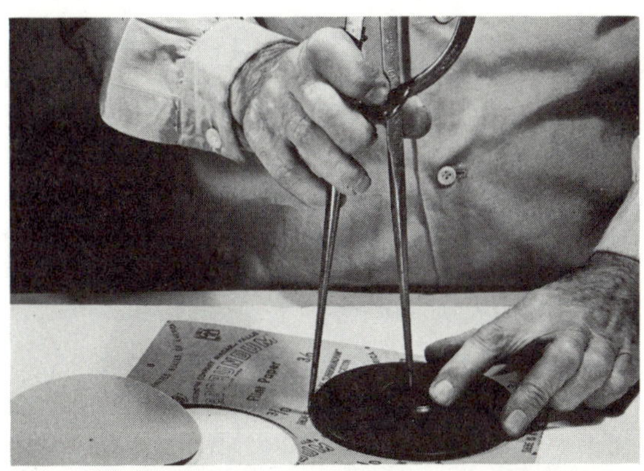

THE QUICKEST WAY to cut your own sanding discs is with dividers. Set them to the radius, place the abrasive paper face down on cardboard and score it. The disc is then simply pressed out.

Three handsome platform beds

Platform beds are the living end for any bedroom. Put one in a prime location and decorate the rest of the room around it. Here we present three different styles. Choose the one that best fits your needs, and start building dreams

■ PLATFORM BEDS seem to sit comfortably in just about any bedroom. They can be decorative with a wooden add-on shelf for creature comforts or seating, they can provide extra storage space or they can just seem to "float" in air. Included here are plans for building three platform beds. They are all different, but all are built around sturdy, handsome wooden platforms.

building the bed surround

The framework for the surround is constructed of 1 x 3 material assembled as shown. The cantilevered platform gets its sturdiness from the 10 x 10-in. corner irons that secure it to the vertical wall framing members spaced 16 in. on centers. When the wall and seat are skinned with the diagonal 1 x 6 tongue-and-groove boards, the structure achieves full rigidity.

Since the structure must be built to suit the bed it will contain, start by taking careful measurements of the bed. Make a sketch on graph paper and note all measurements thereon. Refer to your drawing when you lay out the framework. *Make certain you allow some space* (i.e. if bed is 36 in. wide, the inside measurements of the U-shaped frame should be a minimum of 36½ in. wide). Allow similar spacing for the length dimension.

Your drawing should show locations of the various framing members. On the prototype, vertical members (studs) are located 16 in. on center to provide adequate nailing for the tongue-and-

SEE ALSO
**Bed tables . . . Chairs . . . Chests . . .
Children's furniture . . . Desks . . . Lowboys . . .
Sofa-beds . . . Upholstery**

groove boards used on the surface.

You can use pine or other softwoods, such as spruce or fir, but make certain you bore lead holes for any fastening with nails. Since, for the most part, the structure is built of ¾-in.-thick stock, the prebored holes are a must to prevent splits and weak, poorly fastened joints.

Cut all parts for the walls and temporarily tack them together so the unit can be checked for fit with the bed. If you've built too close for comfort, now is the time to sneak in a filler strip or two, if needed, because they will be hidden when the framework is skinned with the tongue-and-groove boards.

When satisfied with the fit, disassemble the walls and haul the parts back to your workshop. Reassemble the three wall units using finishing nails and carpenter's glue. All assembly of the ladder-like wall frames should be with 6d or 8d finishing nails; the rule of thumb is to use the largest size that won't cause splitting.

When dry, stand the units in position and check the corners for square; hold them that way with diagonal braces tacked at the corners. You will need one long straightedge tacked to the sides near the head of the bed structure. Install the filler strips at the corners with screws, and then join the corners with screws *only.* The idea here is to build a unit that will be relatively easy to move should the need arise.

Construct the cantilevered shelves using the technique shown above. The corner irons provide the fastening and the strength for the shelves. These may not be readily available, even in an otherwise well-stocked hardware store. But the dealer can get them on special order.

Since the diagonal lumber goes on over the brackets, it is necessary to plow out grooves in back to receive the hardware. You can make the groove with a router, straight cutter and clamped-on guides, or handsaw and chisel. Grooves do require careful layout and cutting.

You can eliminate this task by using 8 x 8-in. (or larger) shelf brackets. If you make the switch, keep in mind that the shelf brackets will be mounted on the face of the diagonal boards; thus, they will be somewhat in view on the finished project.

Install the shelf framework on the walls using glue, screws and nails. If you want to retain the

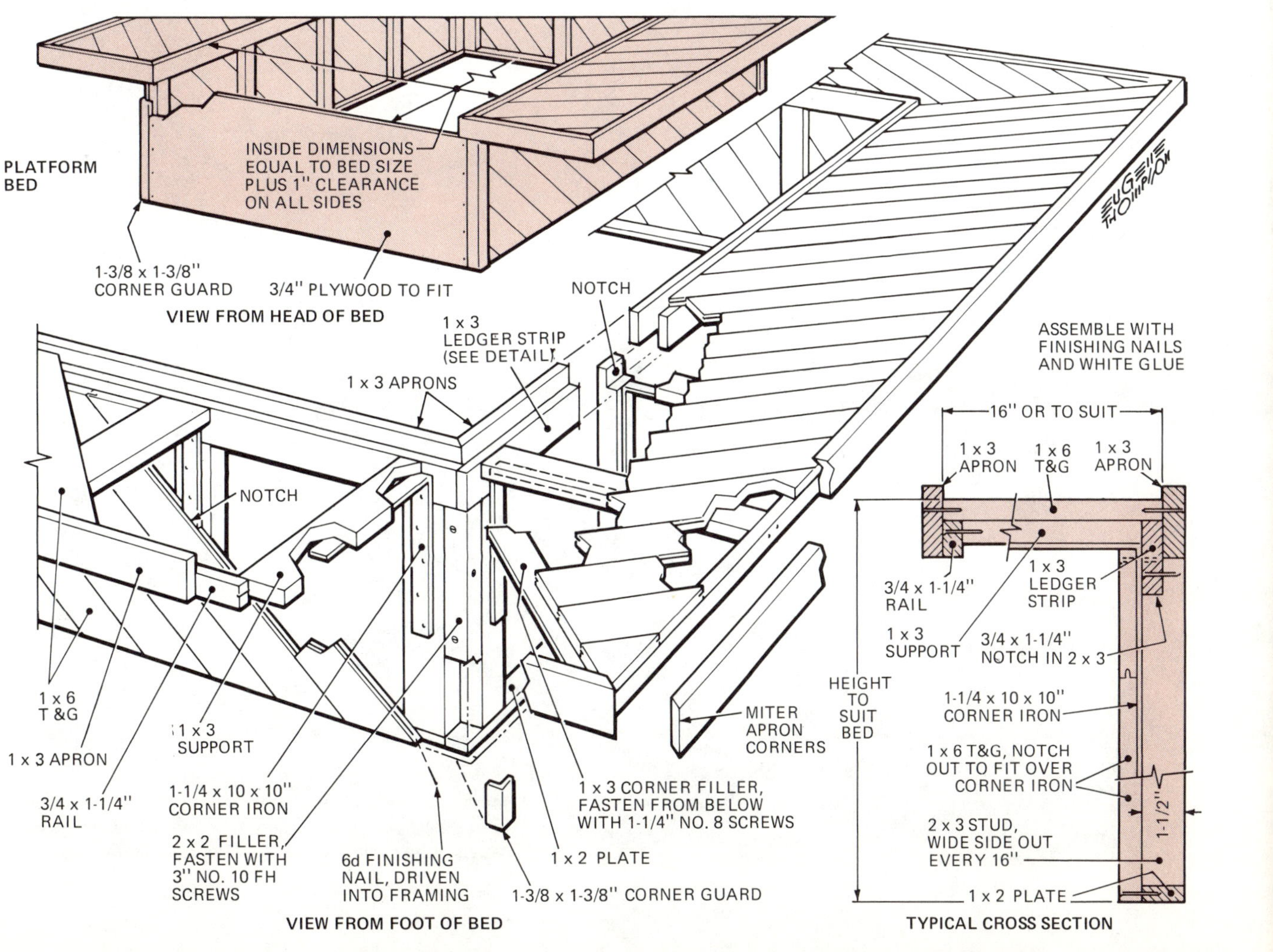

THE SWEEPING elegance of this luxurious platform is matched by its versatility. Full-length storage drawers slide out easily on casters, and convenient end tables can be placed at any point along the 1-in. aluminum rails

take-apart advantage, the U-shaped platform can be built as a unit and completely screw-fastened to the walls.

Make certain that you predrill lead holes in the tongue-and-groove boards for the shelf. If you do too much banging with a hammer, you are apt to do more destroying than building. In fact, it is recommended that you do a minimum of nailing from above and complete the shelf fastening task by using screws in predrilled holes from below.

king-size bed

One of the best features of the king-sized platform bed is that hidden beneath the elegant styling and generous proportions is more easy-access storage than you are likely to find in most closets. When you first look at this bed it may seem to be too luxurious for your bedroom. But when you begin to study the plans you will see that every decorative detail is built to serve an important purpose. Notice that the platform part of the bed has a significant overhang. It is designed this way to create a floating effect that makes a large piece of furniture seem less imposing in your bedroom. But the design also puts to use one of the biggest dust collectors of all time—the dead space under a conventional bed. Here are the full-size drawers, bigger than you will find in any dresser. They

KING-SIZE BED

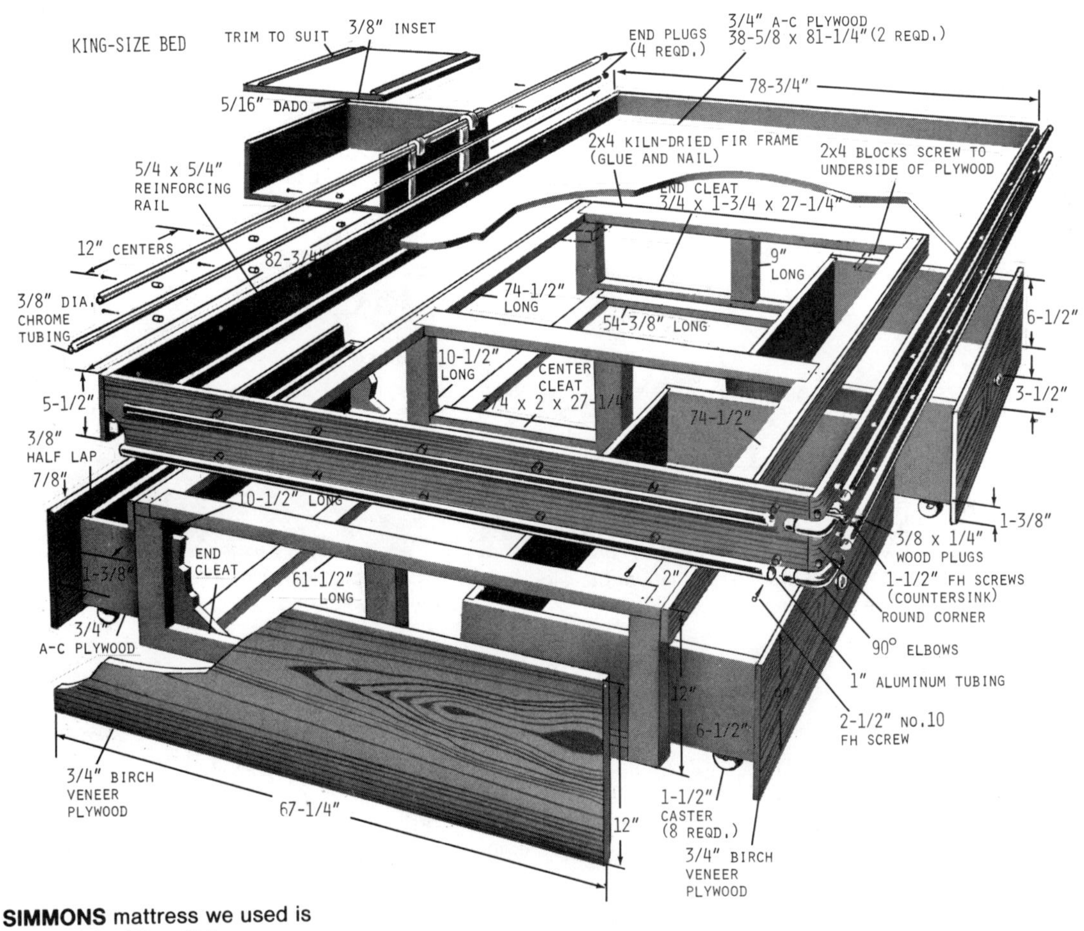

THE SIMMONS mattress we used is about 6-in thick. Allow ½ in. between the mattress and the side rail to accommodate bedcovers

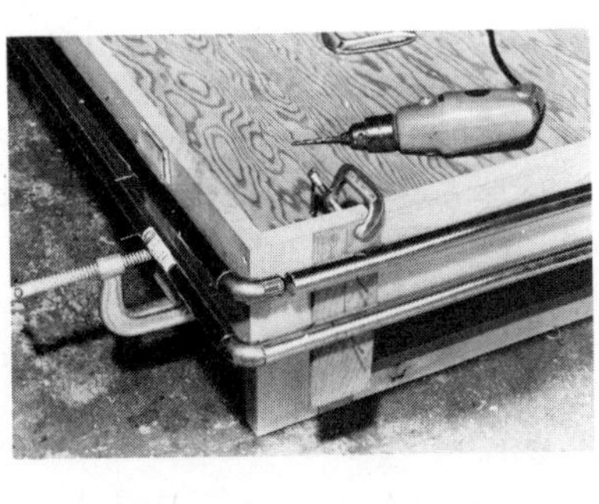

A PLYWOOD jig with nails supports the aluminum tubing for marking the screw holes. Sliding drawers (far right) have casters on the front and Teflon glides at the rear

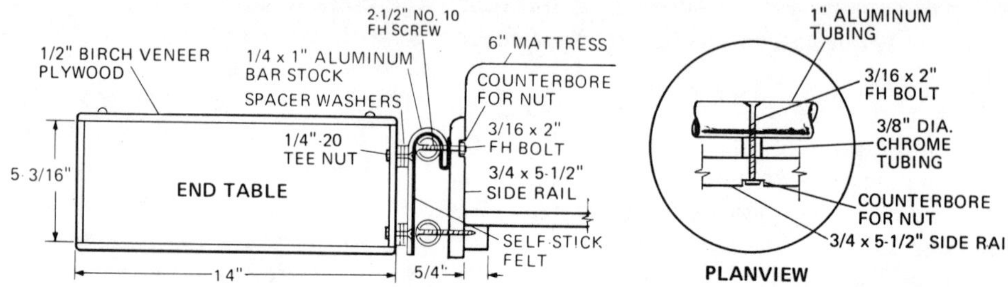

END TABLE DETAILS

A GROOVED 2 x 2 will support the 1-in. aluminum tubing during drilling

A BLOCK with a 1½-in. hole and a simple pipe tee guide the rail bending

WITH THIS JIG, the aluminum bar stock can be bent by stages in the vise

SELF-STICK FELT lines the inside of the bar stock where it rests against the rails

are made with casters on the bottom to roll out easily on a hard floor or even on a rug.

The interesting and attractive rails on the sides of the bed are made from 1-in. aluminum tubing with compression-socket elbows connecting the straight lengths. The rails are attached to the side with screws and spacers every 12 in. as is shown in the details above.

The end tables are designed in keeping with the free-floating design of the total bed by hooking onto the side rails. Aluminum bar stock is used and bent like an upside down "J" to hook over the top rail and bear against the bottom one. The straps securely hold the end tables at convenient right angles to the bed. But the design of the straps lets you freely move the tables to any point along the rails. Since the tables are supported without any permanently fastened hardware, you can move them aside for better access to the drawers or for a more convenient position. Since the siderails run around the foot of the bed as well, you may even want to move one of the tables around to the end of the bed to support a TV set.

construction tips

We strongly suggest that you use kiln-dried 2 x 4s for the frame of the bed. This dimensionally stable wood won't shrink and tighten up the drawers. To keep the drawers sliding and operating smoothly, install Teflon guides at the back corners of each to reduce friction against the support cleats. Much of the construction of the bed is in the supporting members and won't be seen. Devote the most attention and time to critical areas like the side rail corners. If you cut carefully with a good sharp saw blade, a simple butt joint is all that's needed.

You should first clamp the joint in place and then counterbore for the screws and plugs. Then carefully drill pilot holes through the joint so the screws will seat firmly without splitting the ¾-in. end grain. Take the joint apart to apply some glue, then tighten up the screws in the predrilled holes. If you cut plugs (the same size as your counterbore) from your railing material, they'll be unnoticeable when you finally sand them flush.

the single sleeper

You may already have a good double bed for yourself and don't want to attack the king-size bed described above. But how about the kids? Couldn't one of them use a single, smaller version of the platform bed? Our small platform bed is a less challenging project that you can probably build in an afternoon. Study the plans carefully. The simple base is made from plywood panels that are reinforced for strength and stability at each of the corners. Carriage bolts and wingnuts hold the pieces together. This means that the bed can easily be taken apart for moving.

YOU CAN BUILD this simple platform bed for about $50, including the foam mattress. The solid platform is surrounded by pine rails, mitered at the corners and reinforced with 5/4-square kiln-dried strips. The support platform is made of plywood and painted to suit. Pull out the eight carriage bolts and bed will store flat

SMALL PLATFORM

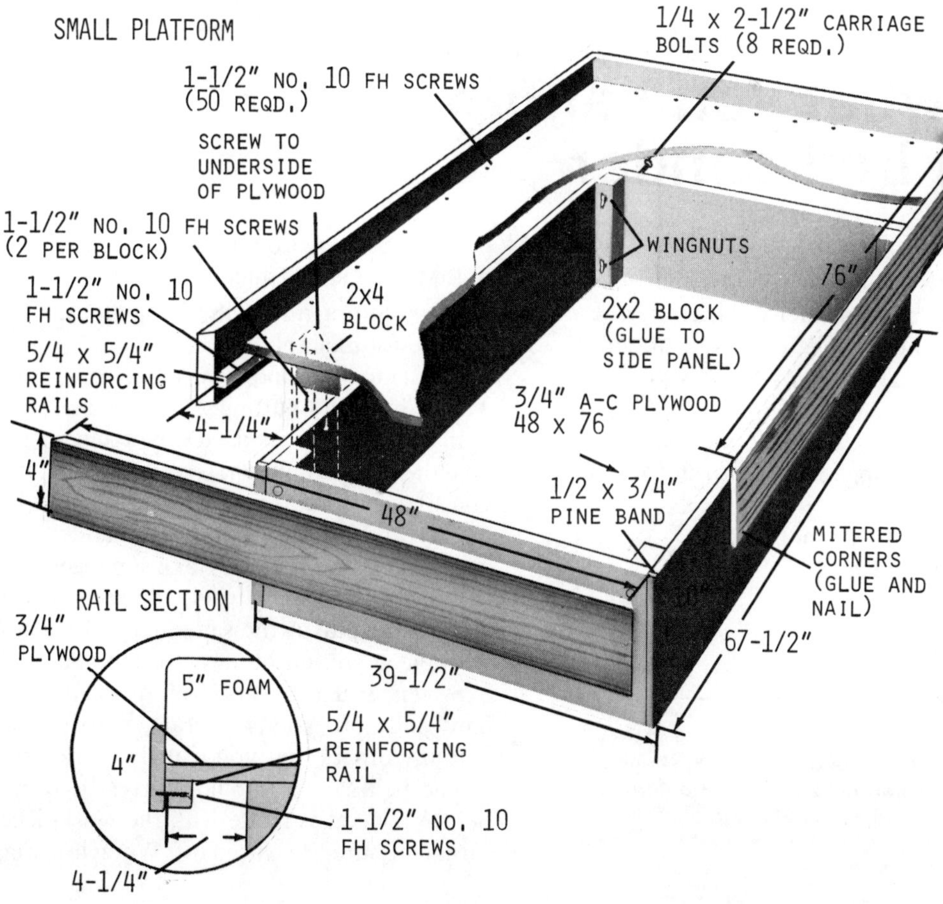

You may be surprised how versatile a belt sander can be. Whether your work is in wood, metal or even concrete, the belt sander may be the rugged tool you need for the job

By BURT MURPHY

Look what you can do with a belt sander

THE BELT SANDER is a workhorse of a tool. Faced with a job that would be dirty and tedious by hand, a belt sander will literally chew its way through the chore effortlessly. Actually, once you own one, you'll wonder how you ever got along without it.

Using a belt sander, you will find that with a little practice you'll spend a lot less time on such tasks as:

- Sanding rough stock smooth.
- Removing old finish.
- Putting a bevel on a door.
- Reducing stock thickness.
- Back-cutting miter cuts for neater joints (casings, for example).
- Dressing up a poor saw cut.
- Polishing and buffing.

If you have never used a belt sander before, take the time to familiarize yourself with it when you first get one. Since a belt sander is larger, livelier and heavier than a pad sander or drill-disc combination, it does take some getting used to. Hefting, changing belts, adjusting belt tracking and the pull as the sanding belt digs into the workpiece will all be new to you. To gain this experience, use the tool on various materials: hard and soft woods, metals, plastic laminate and any others that you usually work with.

The belt sander should always be turned on before contact is made with the workpiece and turned off after it is lifted off. When lowering the

SEE ALSO
Abrasives . . . Finishes, wood . . . Motors, shop . . . Pad sanders . . . Power-tool stands . . . Routers . . . Sanders, disc . . . Sanding . . . Shapers

LATEST DESIGN TREND by most makers lets you use power for flush sanding next to a vertical surface.

COARSE-GRIT BELT sands rough stock smooth in a few minutes. Finer-grit belts are used to finish the job.

TO WORK small pieces, sander can be clamped upside down on the workbench to free both of your hands.

EVENLY POLISHED FINISHES on metal are possible in the workshop using special belts and lubricant.

TO STRIP PAINT, use a coarse, open paper to start, then complete the job with a finer, closed-coat belt.

NYLON WEB BELT and small amount of cutting oil clean dirty-plywood surface and produce even tones.

sander to the material, you should keep the flat platen parallel to the work. Once it contacts the workpiece, keep the sander moving to prevent "dishing out." The weight of the sander itself provides adequate pressure; all you need do is guide the machine. Bearing down on the sander can, in fact, cause damage. When working with wood, move the sander with the grain of the wood, never across. Work the entire surface, overlapping each succeeding pass. If you attempt to complete a 3-in. strip and then move over for successive strips, you will end up with a wavy surface.

The sanders shown on these pages are all basically the same, with slight design variations. Most manufacturers offer at least one model equipped with a dust collector. It's a good feature and it adds little to the total cost. If you do a lot of sanding, or if your wife hasn't been too happy with the dust settling in the laundry room,

CONCRETE FLOOR STAINS can be cleaned with a belt sander. The tool's not limited to wood and metal.

LUMPY CONCRETE on basement window sill is removed using coarse grit. Here a dust collector pays off.

DUST COLLECTOR on Skil's sander is a tube and bag connected to the unit with a threaded, knurled ring.

A SPRING-TENSIONED slip-in nozzle is connected to the bag on the Black & Decker model.

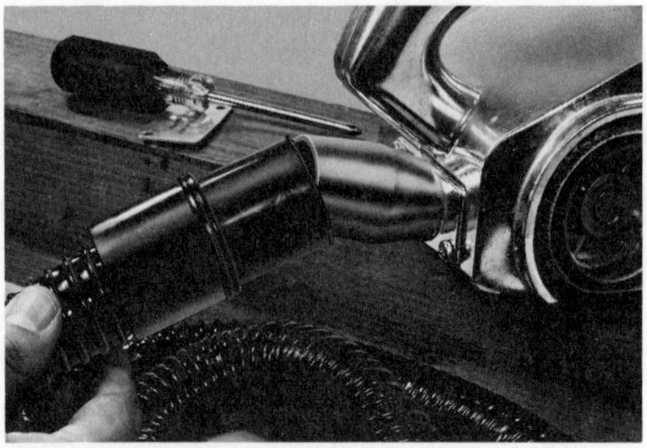

HOSE AND NOZZLE serve as dust collector on the Stanley sander—they're attached to vacuum cleaner.

CLAMPED ON ITS SIDE, the belt sander can be used for "planing" jobs. Vertical board serves as a fence.

the extra couple of dollars that a collector costs will be money well spent.

In addition to on-the-job uses, a sander can also be rigged with clamps for use as a bench-type power sander. Small-size workpieces can then be brought to the sander and, since you are saved the task of hefting the tool, both hands are free to guide the work against the belt.

Both general and special-purpose abrasive papers are manufactured for use with belt sanders. Aluminum oxide, manufactured in a wide variety of grits, is the type you will use most often. Or, you can use special-purpose belts to convert the belt sander for use as a cleaner, buffer and polisher for metals, woods, plastics and laminates.

Belt sanding facts you should know:

- *Wood finishing*. For final finishing of furniture

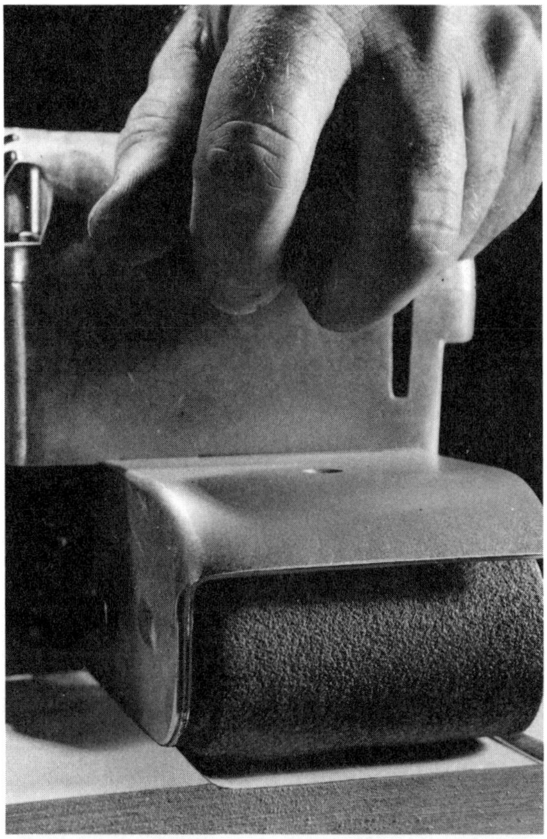

HELD IN ONE SPOT too long, a belt sander will plow a deep groove (shown across the grain here).

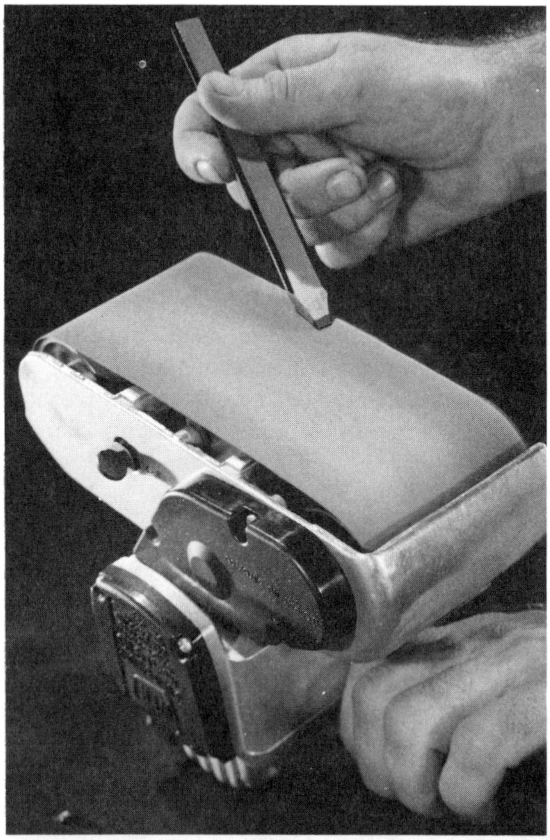

CARPENTERS on construction jobs find that a sander offers a fast way to sharpen a pencil to a keen point.

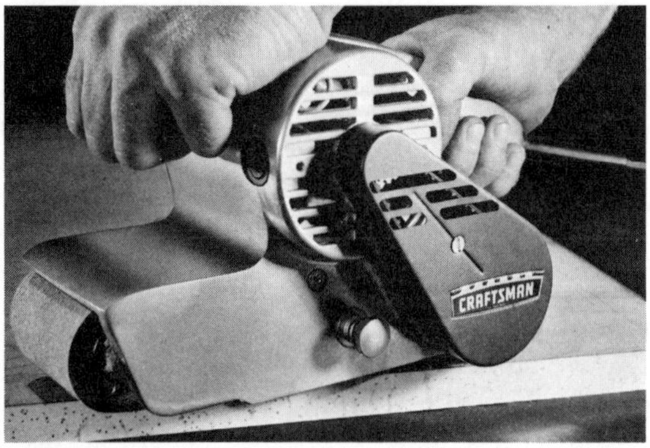

USING AN 80-GRIT BELT, plastic laminate self-edge is quickly and easily smoothed flush with plywood.

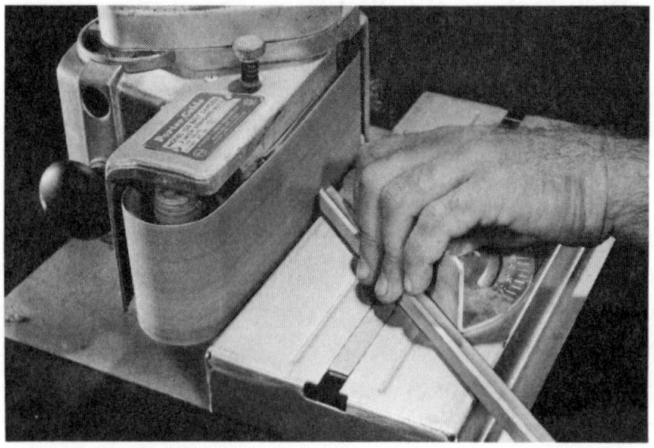

WORKBENCH STAND comes with accurate miter gauge, secures the sander. The one shown is by Rockwell.

or cabinetry, use as many progressively finer grits as possible. The object here is to remove any marks left by the coarser belt that preceded the one being used.

• *Metal finishing*. Beeswax or tallow are recommended for use as lubricants for metal sanding, polishing or stain finishing. Several manufacturers market commercial lubricants for metal sanding. Black & Decker, for example, offers Luster-lube belt lubricant and the Stanley Works markets two products, Tripoli and Greas-tick, for use with its Stanbrite belts.

• *Refinishing*. When removing paint, varnish or lacquer, use a coarse grade, open-coat belt for the initial stripping. Then change to closed-coat belts as the material shows through the coating. Use short, light strokes to avoid burning the coating and for longer belt life.

Check your car's drive belts

Belt maintenance is a lot more than a thumb on the belt to check tension or a spray of dressing when the belt squeals. Here's how to do it right

By PAUL WEISSLER

■ DON'T IGNORE drive belts until they snap—it makes a lot more sense to give them some reasonable maintenance. A belt failure on the road can mean loss of engine cooling, charging, power steering, air-conditioning and loss of your temper if you don't have spares.

thorough inspection

Whenever you do underhood service, take a few minutes to inspect each drive belt. Twist each belt over and look for all of the following; any one is cause for replacement:

■ **Cracks in the underside** (the surface that rides flat against the surface between the pulley rims). Cracks create hinge points that allow excessive flexing. The belt can split apart at any crack.

■ **Peeling from the underside.** This results in a rough surface, and the belt will transfer power unevenly. Belt failure will be sudden.

■ **Split in the sidewall.** A drive belt is something like a tire in that there is a supporting layer of cord between the rubberized surfaces. If there is a separation in the sidewall, often at the cord layer, the belt will not ride the pulleys properly and may fail at any instant.

■ **Glaze on the sides or underside of the belt.** A slick, hard glazing on the sides or underside of the belt is caused by belt slippage. The accessories are not driven properly, resulting in a low battery, engine overheating, poor airconditioning performance and erratic power steering. The slipping belt itself overheats and will fail.

■ **Oil-soaked belt.** A belt that is oil-soaked has been softened and will come apart. Because all belt dressings contain some oil-base penetrant that ultimately softens the belt, they are no solution to belt squeal, even if they temporarily eliminate this noise, which is normally caused by looseness.

Thumb pressure on a belt, midway between pulleys, has been the traditional way to check belt tension. On older cars, up to a half-inch deflection under the pressure has been standard "rule of thumb" for an adequately tightened belt. On today's cars, however, this is not acceptable for these reasons: 1. There is a substantial variation in the deflections under the thumbs of any two people. 2. Accessibility is such that you could never measure the deflection accurately even if you have a calibrated thumb. 3. Deflection is not a positive indicator of tension.

The belt-tension gauge is the simplest way to test tension accurately. It hooks over the belt and when released provides a number—pounds of tension—to compare with specifications developed by the carmaker. The belt can be adjusted to specs in a single operation on most cars. Price of the gauge ranges from under $10 for some basic models to more than $20 for elaborate ones.

adjusting tension

Most drive belts are adjusted by loosening mounting bolts for the accessory or loosening an idler pulley (belt guide), then applying tension on the component with a pry bar, and tightening the adjusting bolt.

There are some exceptions. The simplest is an access hole in the adjusting bracket, so that the pry bar is positioned precisely, and not against something delicate, such as the air-cooling fins of an alternator.

A square hole in the accessory, or idler pulley that accepts a ½-inch drive breaker bar is another popular design. Again, the object is to make sure you don't pry against a part that can't take the strain.

A cam-type adjuster on an idler pulley is used on the Dodge Colt. You slacken the retaining nut, put a wrench on a partial hex section of the pulley and turn (one way to loosen the belt, the other way to tighten). When tension is correct, you tighten the retaining nut.

A stud-nut adjuster used on Ford power steer-

SEE ALSO

**Airconditioners, auto . . . Alternators, auto . . .
Cooling systems, auto . . . Engines, auto . . .
Gaskets, auto . . . Ignition systems, auto . . .
Ramps, auto repair . . .
Steering and suspension, auto . . . Tune-up, auto**

HOW TO TAKE CARE OF YOUR CAR'S DRIVE BELTS

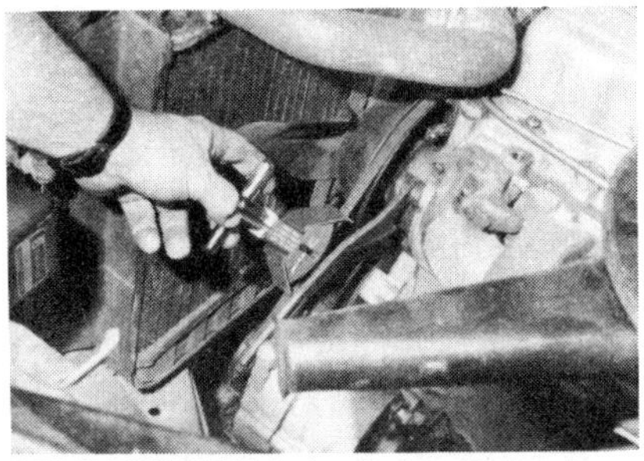

BELT TENSION is best checked using the type of gauge shown here.

STUDNUT ADJUSTER on power steering pump is tensioning device on Fords.

BRACKET with slot is most common means of belt-tension adjustment.

PULLEY NUT is loosened on VW while screwdriver is wedged to hold pulley.

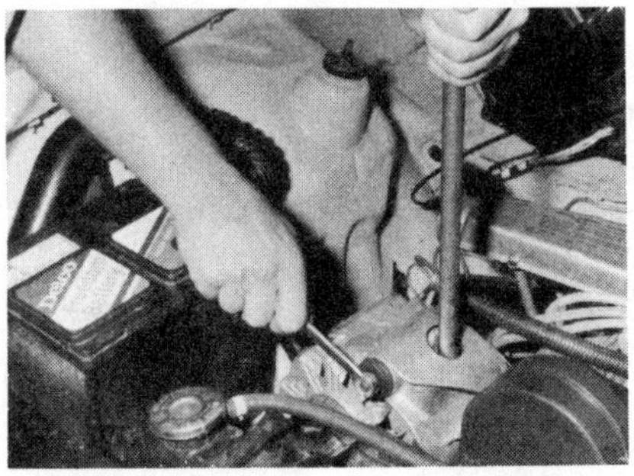

PILOT HOLE for pry bar, as used on Chevette, is accurate and convenient.

ADJUSTER is turned to tension idler pulley on the Dodge Colt.

PULLEY HALVES are separated to remove belt on ageless Beetle.

ing pumps eliminates the need to apply tension with any kind of bar. The pump is mounted on a bracket with studs through elongated bracket holes and retaining nuts. You slacken the retaining nuts, then turn a separate stud-nut adjuster. This moves the stud in or out, repositioning the pump along the elongated holes in the mounting bracket. When tension is correct, tighten the retaining nuts and you're done.

The Volkswagen Beetle, a car that seems to live forever, is an exception to just about all rules regarding drive belts. On the VW, you can check tension with your thumb, and the belt is so wide open, you can even get a ruler into position to measure the deflection (10 mm or ⅜ inch is the spec).

The adjustment is with shims on a generator/fan pulley that comes apart. You wedge a screwdriver through a slot in the inner pulley half and against the engine to hold the pulley, then remove the nut holding the halves together. To increase tension, you remove some shims from between the pulley halves so the halves will come closer together when tightened, forcing the belt to ride higher between rims of the pulley halves. To reduce tension, add shims, which are stored between the outer pulley half and nut. It's a pure cut-and-dried operation.

When a new belt is called for, double-check others for possible replacement, particularly if you're changing an outer belt.

Push the idler pulley or accessory all the way in (in the case of the stud-nut adjuster, back it all the way out), and the new belt should just fit onto the pulleys. You may have to pry a new belt over a pulley rim with a screwdriver, but a new belt should never fit so easily that you are near the outer limits of proper tension adjustment.

Benches to build for your deck

■ THE GANG'S ALL HERE for the cookout, but where do they sit?

From spring through fall, outdoor entertaining is a real part of the American scene. But when there's a big party group in your back yard, you may have a problem finding seats for everybody.

If you are a bit short in back-yard seating, you may want to build one of the beauties shown on these three pages. These benches are very good-looking, sturdy and, best of all, they will last for years. The movable bench (on this page) is constructed of eight standard-size pieces of fir. Thus, it is simply a hammer-and-saw project. You just cut the pieces to length and assemble them. It is

MOVABLE BENCH

A practical approach to extra seating on the patio is this simply designed, but handsome, movable bench. It was created by Western Wood Products Assn., and is extremely sturdy

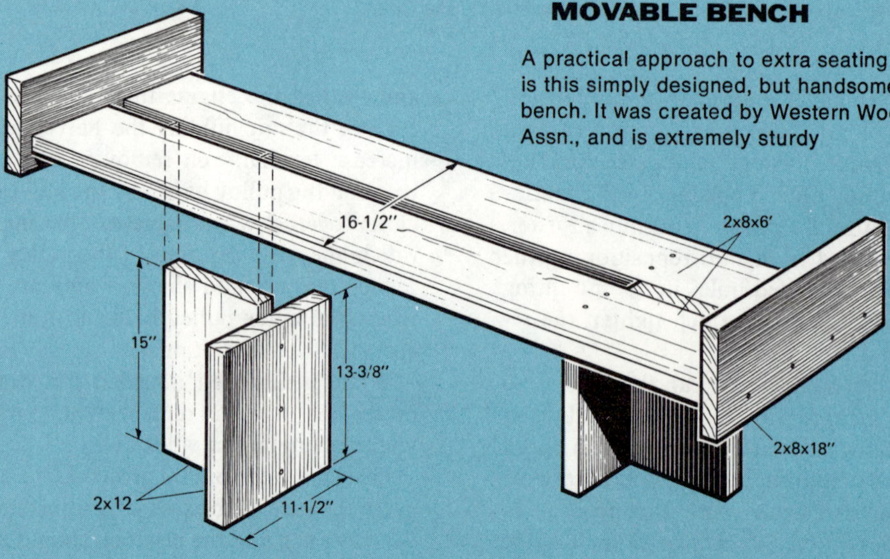

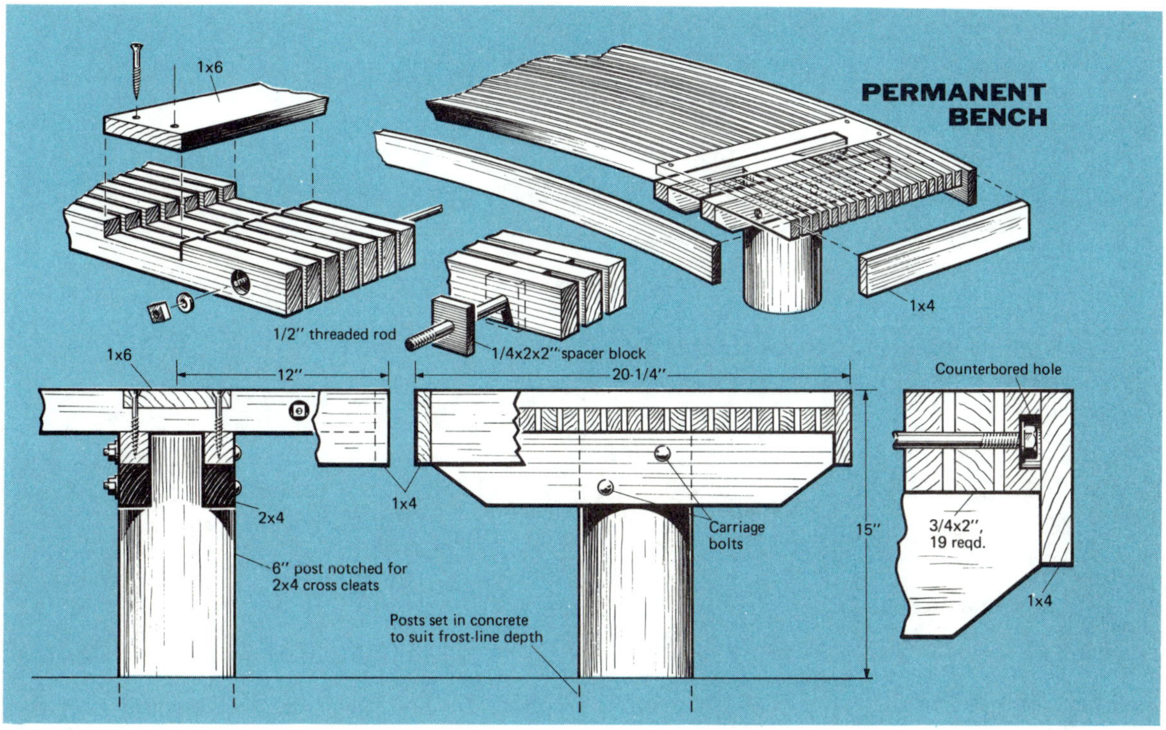

as simple as that.

The curved bench is a little more involved to build and is generously dimensioned, but, if your patio is modestly scaled, simply adjust the bench's length to suit. This bench is permanently installed and is fastened to posts which in turn are embedded in concrete. Designed for the California Redwood Assn., by landscape architect John Staley, the bench, like the privacy screen, is of redwood. Notice how gaps between slats are assured by use of spacers where the threaded rod goes through. These gaps are necessary—they permit water to drain.

The shelves atop the legs of the contemporary

bench can be used to display potted green or blooming plants. Douglas fir was used throughout in this bench design from Western Wood Products Assn. Or you may choose to use a western pine.

Assemble the bench with galvanized finishing nails and waterproof glue. Face-nail all parts, countersink nails and fill depressions with wood putty.

Begin by cutting the leg and shelf pieces **(A, H, J, K)**; cut notches in legs for the crosspieces **(I)**. Clamp and glue the leg verticals **(H)**. Then nail the leg finishing pieces and glue the crosspieces in place. Do not attach the shelves until after the bench seat is in position.

Cut the lower rail **(G)** and end parts **(F)**. Space the legs as needed then glue and nail the lower rails in place.

The bench seat rests on the leg crosspieces. Cut and assemble the seat parts **(B)** and end edging **(D, E)** on the ground. Test fit the bench before you drive nails home. After you have positioned the seat you can cut and nail the rest of the edging **(C)**. Nail the shelves in place. Finish with an oil-base preserving stain.

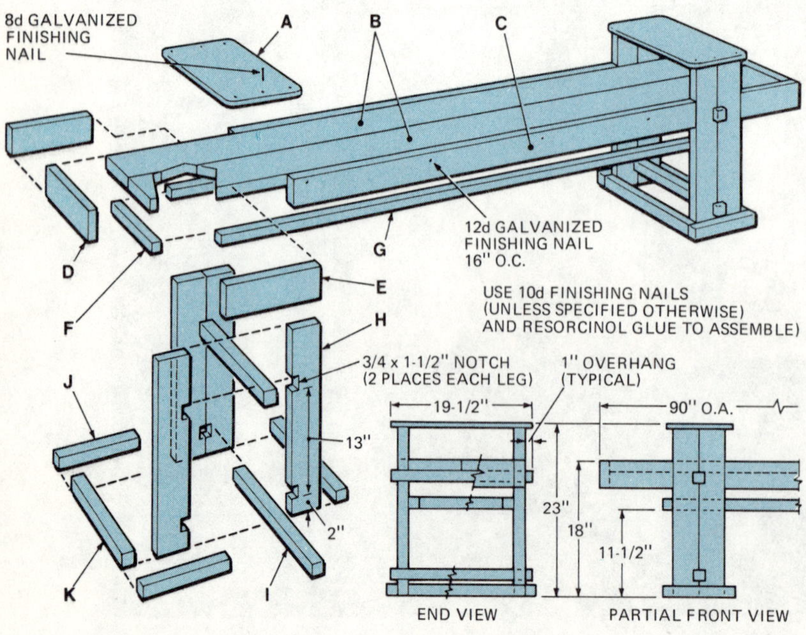

MATERIALS LIST—PATIO BENCH

Key	Pcs.	Size (use)
A	2	¾ x 9 x 19½" (shelf)
B	2	1½ x 7¼ x 87" (seat)
C	2	1½ x 3½ x 56" (edging)
D	2	1½ x 3½ x 14½" (edging)
E	4	1½ x 3½ x 10" (edging)
F	2	1½ x 1½ x 13" (rail)
G	2	1½ x 1½ x 73" (rail)
H	8	1½ x 3½ x 22¼" (leg, vertical)
I	4	1½ x 1½ x 19½" (crosspiece)
J	4	1½ x 1½ x 10" (leg piece)
K	4	1½ x 1½ x 17½" (leg piece)

Misc: 8d, 10d and 12d galvanized finishing nails; resorcinol glue; wood putty.

TOOLS ARE hung on pegs; shelves for pots are installed between studs.

Build a convenient potting bench

■ REPOTTING HOUSE PLANTS and transplanting vegetable seedlings from flats to pots can be messy and time-consuming if you're not fitted out for the task. However, not many of us have the space or time to build a full-fledged potting bench.

Charles and Judith Morgan of Ruxton, MD, solved the problem by designing this compact bench. They constructed it in the storage enclosure which supports the outboard end of their carport.

The bench consists of a tray with pot-holding and soil-disposal holes—and a drawer below to store unused soil. Perforated hardboard surrounds the work surface and organizes tools. A fluorescent fixture with two 40-watt tubes is mounted on the ceiling to provide good lighting. Two 250-watt, infrared bulbs, installed above and in back of the operating position, provide heat.

For easy cleaning, prime and coat all surfaces that contact the soil with a durable, exterior enamel. Line the inside of the soil storage drawer with a plastic sheet. Use the floor space beneath the bench as storage. If there is any floor dampness, construct a removable duckboard-style floor rack.

SEE ALSO
Cold frames . . . Garden shelters . . .
House plants . . . Transplanting

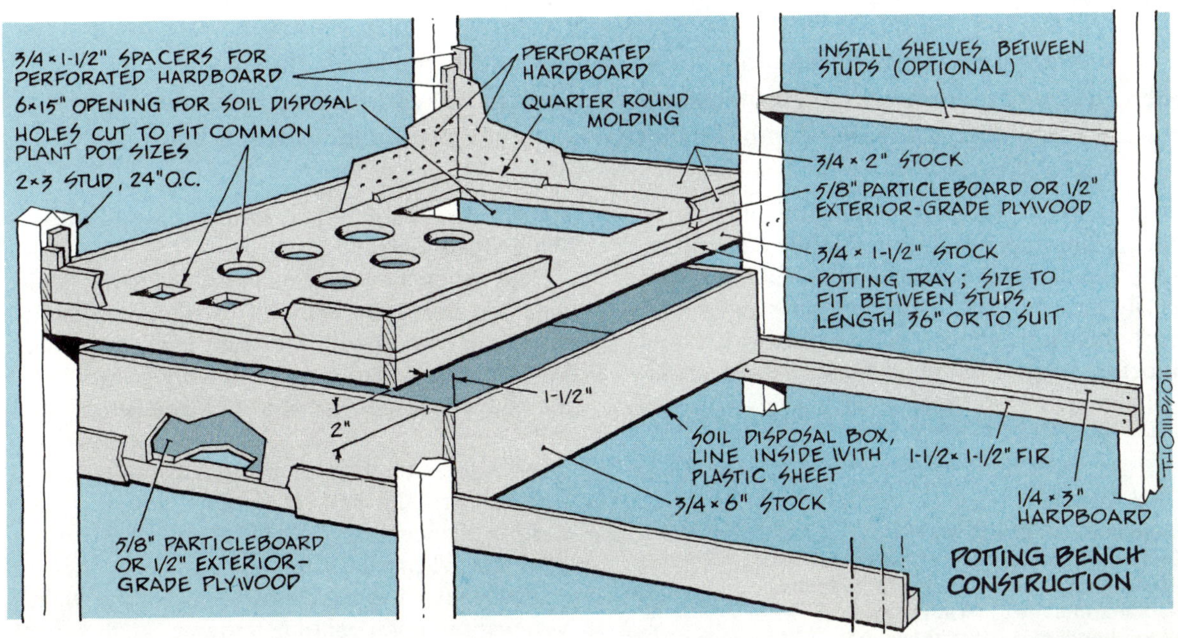

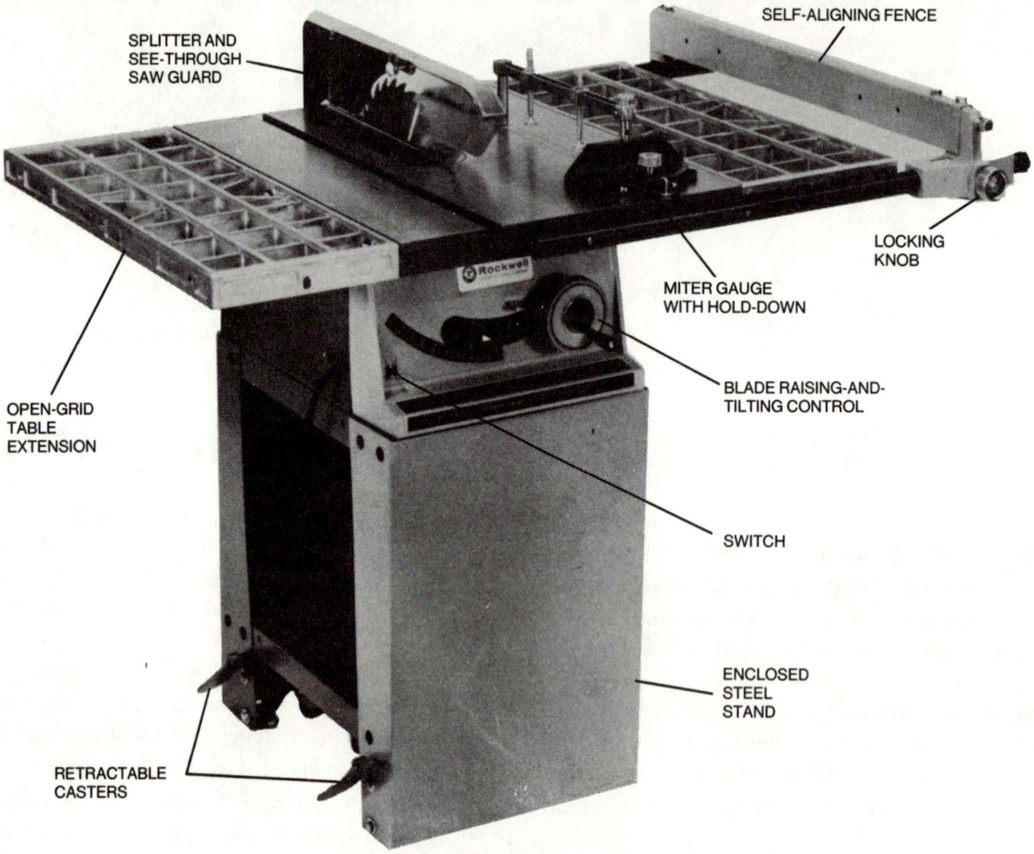

All about using a bench saw

By WAYNE C. LECKEY

A bench saw is one of the most versatile tools in a home shop. Here are the basic techniques and more advanced professional methods to put your saw to best use. Included are some demonstration projects you can build while learning

■ A BENCH SAW is not a difficult tool to run—plain ripping and crosscutting come naturally to most beginners, and other techniques are easily learned. But, as in operating any power tool, there is a right way and a wrong way. Using it before you are fully familiar with its mechanical features is as unwise as dashing off in a strange car without first learning what and where the controls are.

SEE ALSO

Bandsaws . . . Discs, wood . . .
Drill press techniques . . . Motors, shop . . .
Power hacksaws . . . Power-tool stands . . .
Radial-arm saws . . . Table saws . . .
Wood bending . . . Workbenches . . . Workshops

The bench saw (which is also called a "table saw") is not to be feared, but since you can't always operate it with the guard over the blade, you have to regard it as potentially dangerous. You have to respect its whirling blade, keep your mind on what you're doing and not become overconfident. If you always remain a bit "afraid" of the saw each time you flip the switch, chances are you'll never get cut. My best advice is to learn the safety rules and obey them.

All bench saws have a rip fence for use when you want to cut a board lengthwise, and a miter gauge when you want to cut it crosswise. How

Make these initial checks before you saw a board

CHECK THE MITER GAUGE with a square to see if it is at a 90° angle to the blade, thus assuring a square cut.

MAKE SURE that the rip fence is parallel with the saw-table slots so work will not bind against the blade.

THE TABLE must be square with the blade. If it isn't, follow the manufacturer's instructions for adjustment.

KICKBACK will happen when the fence is out of alignment. Adopt the safe practice of standing to one side so you won't be hit by a flying workpiece.

SAFE WORK HABITS AND PRACTICES

1. **Keep floor clean in front of the saw—sawdust can be slippery.**
2. **Roll up your shirt sleeves to the elbow, and remove tie, rings and wristwatch.**
3. **Pull out plug at electrical outlet when leaving machine at end of a work session.**
4. **Never reach across the blade while the saw is running.**
5. **Always use a push stick when ripping narrow work.**
6. **Keep the blade just high enough to clear stock when ripping.**
7. **Stand to one side of the blade—never directly behind it.**
8. **Never rush or force work into the blade.**
9. **Don't hold both ends of the work when crosscutting.**
10. **Always return the miter gauge to the starting point when crosscutting.**
11. **Keep the blade sharp and properly set at all times.**
12. **Never rip against the fence when edge of the work is irregular.**
13. **Wear goggles or a face shield when you're doing close work.**
14. **Always use a guard and a splitter whenever practical.**
15. **Never saw freehand; always use a fence, miter gauge or jig.**
16. **Never use the fence itself as a stop when you're cutting duplicate work.**
17. **Keep your mind on what you're doing.**

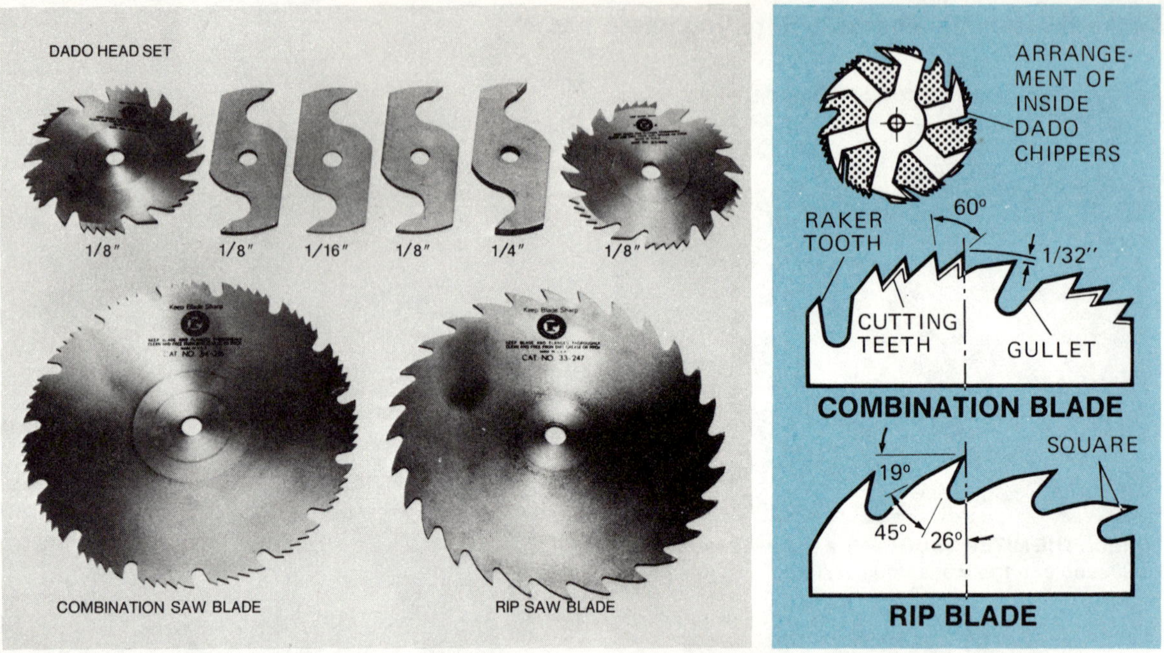

BASIC BLADES: The combination blade, which both rips and crosscuts, is most popular in the home shop. The rip blade is used for ripping only. The dado head consists of two outside cutters and interchangeable inside chippers.

perfect these cuts will be depends on how accurately the fence and miter gauge are set in relation to the blade. So before you cut a board, there are three initial alignment checks to be made: 1. table slots, rip fence, and blade must be parallel; 2. rip fence, miter gauge and blade must be perpendicular to the table; 3. miter gauge must be at a right angle to blade and fence. Each is easily checked with a square. The instruction manual for your particular saw will show what to loosen and adjust to correct any misalignment.

Your saw will probably come equipped with a combination blade, a general all-purpose blade

First projects—a push stick and a wood facing

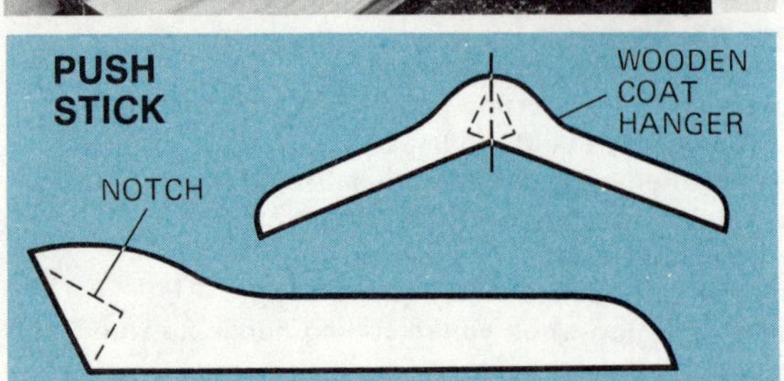

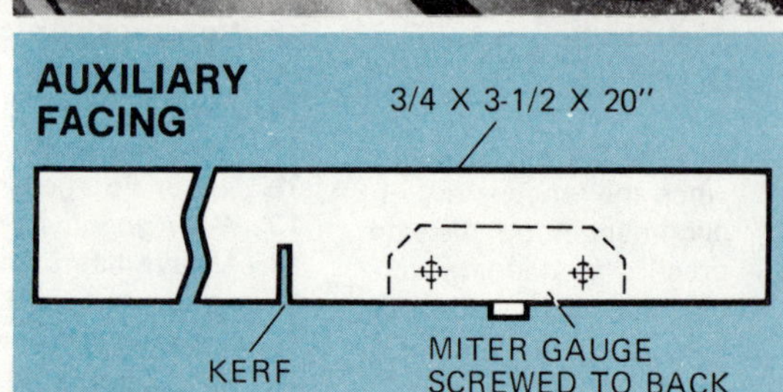

Safe and unsafe bench-saw practices

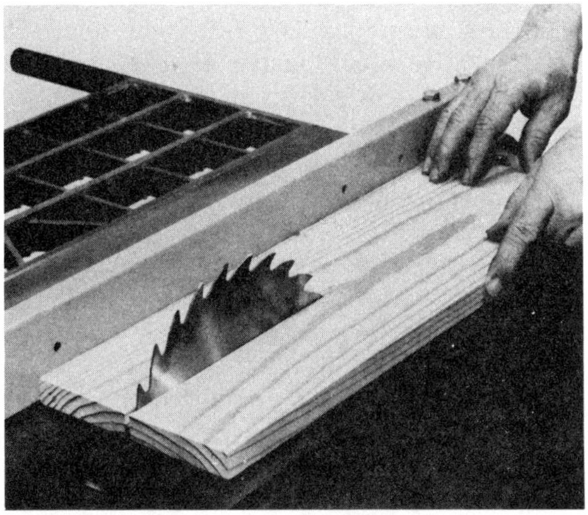

DON'T SAW with the blade this high when it's not practical to use the guard. There's too much chance of injury.

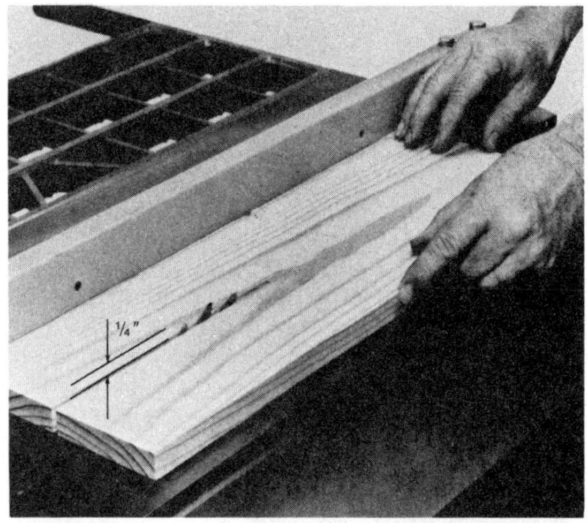

THE LESS the blade is exposed the better. The blade should project no more than ¼ in. when ripping.

A GOOD RIPPING HABIT is to hook your little finger over the fence to keep the hand away from the blade.

WHEN CROSSCUTTING a wide board on a small saw, place the miter gauge backward in the saw-table slot.

NEVER USE the fence as a stop when mass-cutting duplicate work. The work will wedge between fence and blade.

PLAY IT SAFE and first clamp a block to the fence so there will be ample clearance between blade and fence.

Ways to prevent creeping

SANDPAPER GLUED to the face of the miter gauge will provide a noncreep work surface when making miter cuts.

A HOLD-DOWN ATTACHMENT fitted to the miter gauge will keep the workpiece from creeping during miter cuts.

ANOTHER WAY to prevent creeping when cutting miters: Hold the work to the miter gauge with a bar clamp.

that rips, crosscuts and miters, and handles most common cutting jobs. You can add other special-purpose blades, such as a rip blade, a coarse-tooth saw for faster ripping; a hollow-ground planer blade that makes smoother crosscuts, and a fine-tooth plywood blade that's best for cutting laminated woods with minimum splintering.

Another special-purpose cutter, called a dado head, has various combinations of saws and chippers for cutting grooves 1/8 to 13/16 in. wide. It is usually made up of two outside blades and four swaged chippers so arranged on the arbor that the swaged ends fall in the gullets of the two outside blades.

Two of the first things you should make for your saw are a push stick and a wood facing

SHORT TENONS are made with one pass, each side, by switching from the regular saw blade to a dado head.

Two setups for mass-cutting duplicate lengths

A SPECIAL STOP ROD, designed to fit the miter gauge, will assure identical cutoffs up to 27½ in. long.

A BLOCK OF WOOD clamped to the saw table will serve as a stop for mass-cutting short lengths of stock.

Simple jigs and fixtures to use with your saw

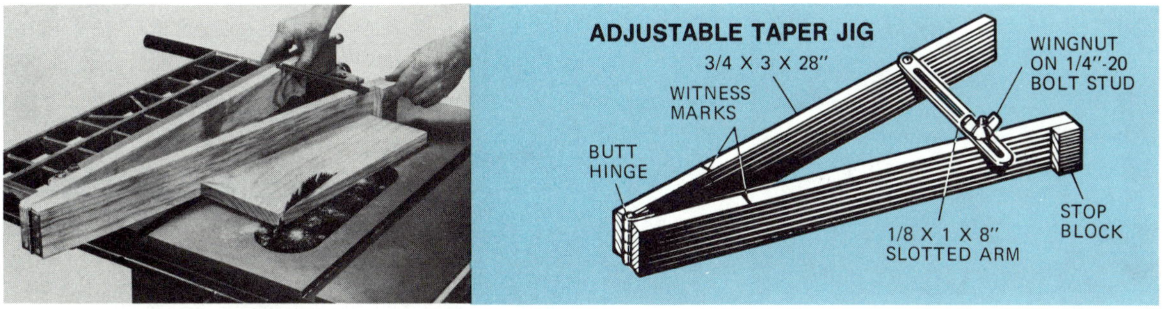

TAPER JIG lets you rip at an angle. Work is hooked on stop block and jig is guided along fence to make cut.

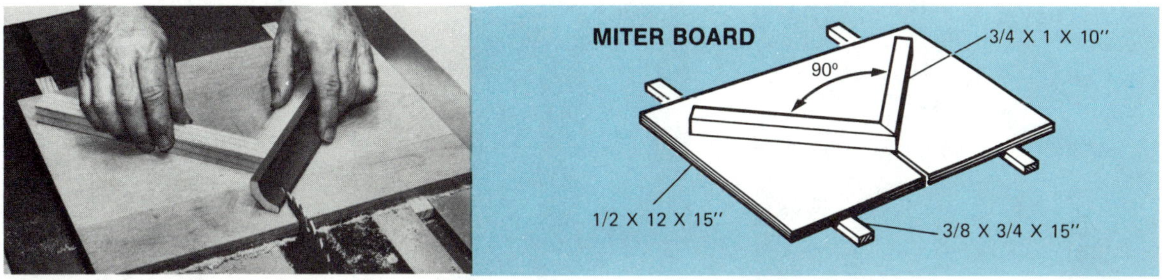

MITER BOARD is better, more accurate, than saw's miter gauge when making right and left-hand miter cuts.

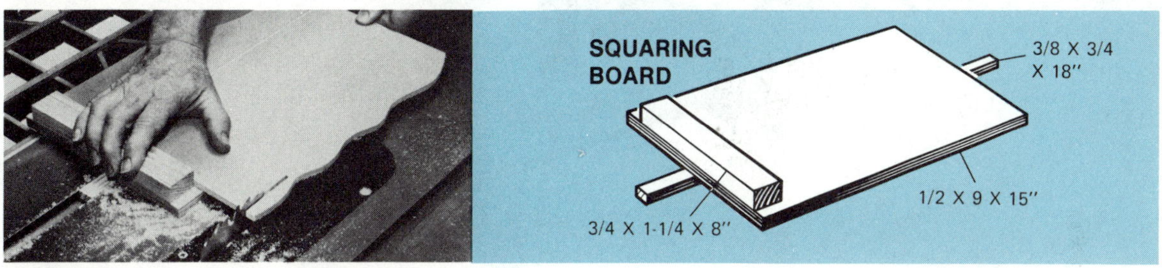

SQUARING BOARD permits straight rip cuts to be made on bandsawed leftovers that have irregular edges.

WEDGE BOARD makes fast work of mass-cutting wedges. Flop work in notch each time to cut next wedge.

STEP BLOCK clamped to saw table sets width of each pass automatically when cutting duplicate dadoes.

THE WORK SUPPORT shown and the special cuts shown in the top photo at the left were made with the tools and shop-built jigs shown at the left.

extension for the miter gauge. A push stick is a must for pushing narrow work safely past the blade. All crosscutting is done more conveniently and with greater safety if the miter gauge has a wood facing. With the kerf in the facing, you can line up the saw mark precisely with the blade.

The photos give graphic examples of the right and wrong ways to perform common rip and crosscut operations. It's always good practice to expose the saw blade as little as possible above the work when it's not practical to operate the saw with the guard in place. A high blade cuts faster, but it's not as safe.

A good habit to follow when ripping is to hook the little finger over the rip fence as you feed the work. This keeps the hand from wandering toward the blade.

When you wish to crosscut a wide board whose size forces the miter gauge off the table, reverse the gauge. Cut about halfway through the board, back up an inch and turn off the saw. Then reverse the gauge—leaving the workpiece untouched—start the saw and complete the cut.

When you want to use the rip fence as a stop in mass-cutting pieces of identical length, don't make the mistake of butting the work against the fence. Clamp a block of wood to the fence; then butt work against it. Then the cutoffs won't jam between fence and blade and be thrown back at you with great force. Too, it's good practice to stand to one side of the blade (normally, left) and not directly behind it when ripping. You'll not be struck by severed work should it be kicked back at you. Usually, this happens when the fence is not parallel to the blade, causing the workpiece to bind.

There are several tricks to follow when sawing a plain or compound miter to prevent the work from creeping as it is cut. Where your miter

LONG WORKPIECE SUPPORT

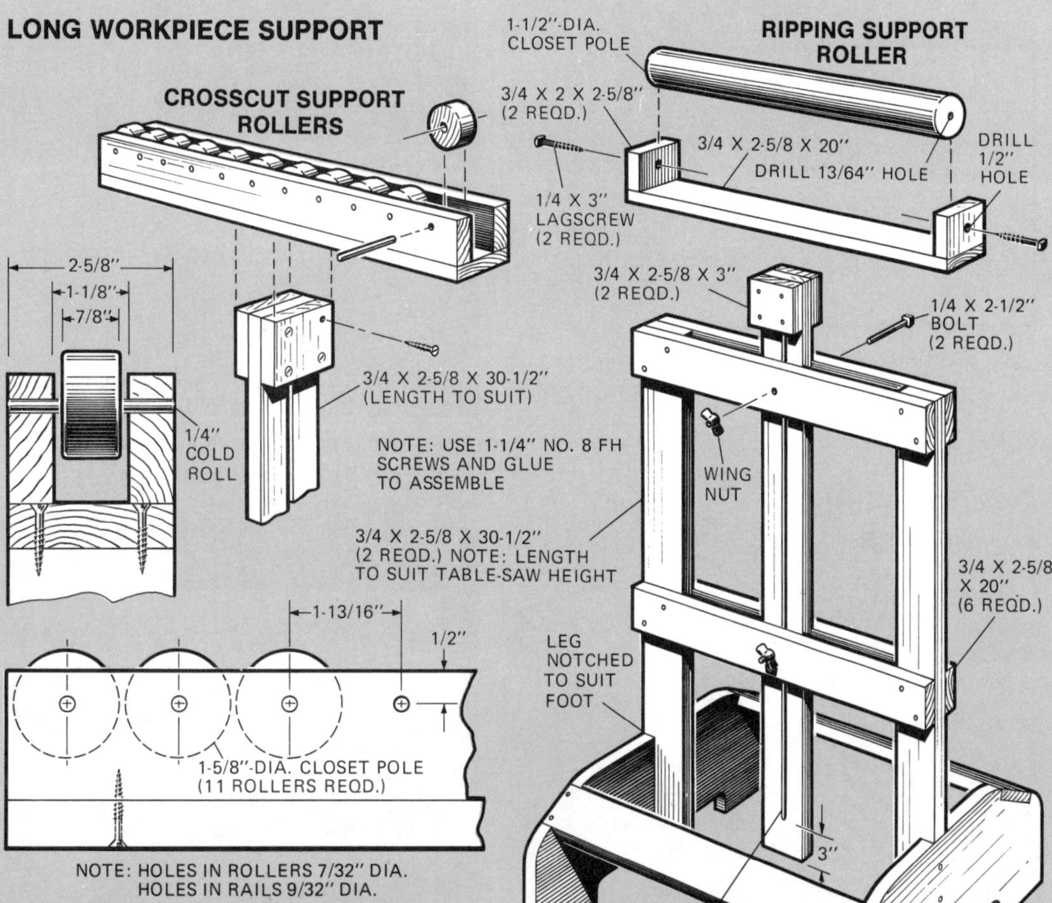

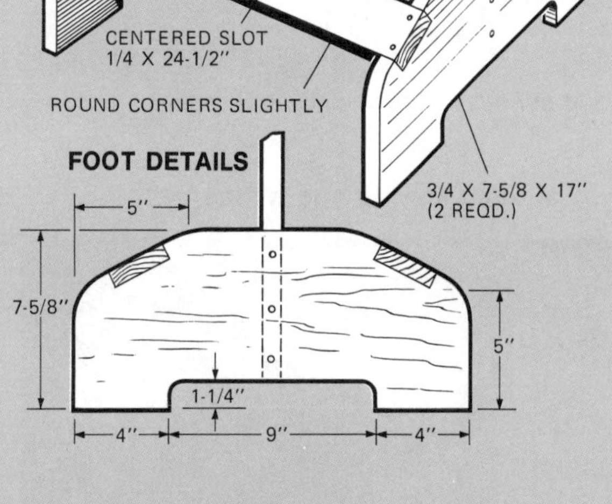

CROSSCUTTING long pieces is simplified because the support has a roller-head for this saw operation.

Bench-saw stunts you should know

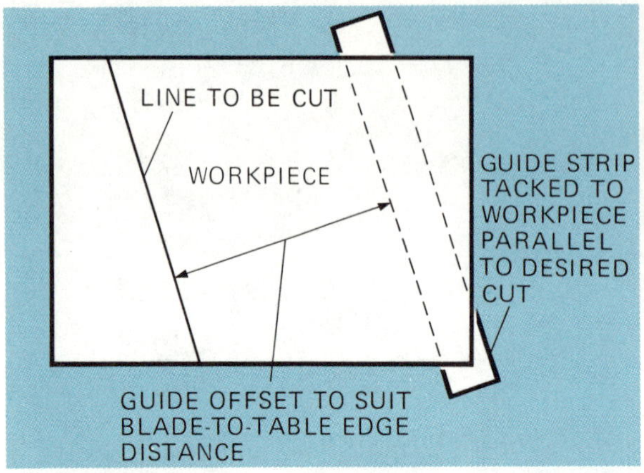

DIAGONALS can be cut on large pieces of plywood by tacking a straightedge to ride along the table edge.

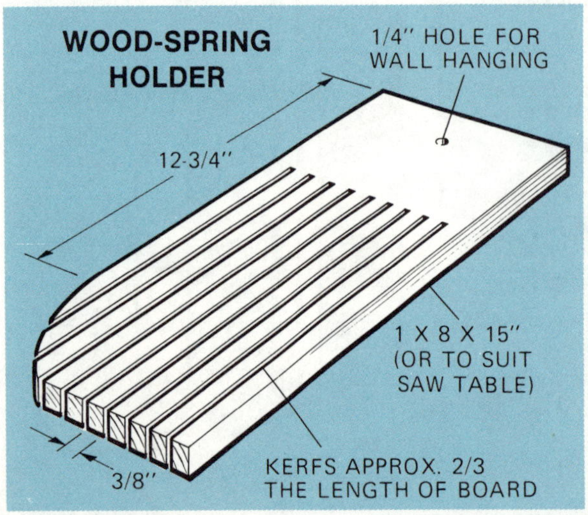

WOOD SPRING HOLDER can be made from scrap. It's always used as a work hold-in when accuracy is required.

Typical dado-sawing operations

DENTIL is simply evenly spaced dadoes. Make the first cut with the end against the pin; loop over for the second.

THE DADOED PIECE is sliced to the desired thickness—usually ¼ to ⅜ in.—for use in trim-molding work.

MAKING A TRIVET is a good exercise in pierce-cutting and dadoing. You can practice both of these techniques at the same time—and wind up with a useful item.

Trivet from a solid block

Here's a project that's fun to tackle once you have become familiar with your dado-head set. Making the trivet is a fine exercise in dado cutting, and your skill in cutting it—as with the "carved" tower—is sure to astound your nonwoodworking friends. Select wood that is knot-free; if you have some hardwood lying about the shop, so much the better. Pine was used for the trivet at left, and it worked well. To make it, the author used the fence and, when work was within 3 in. of blades, a pusher stick. Make the dadoes (across the grain) first, then flop and rotate the workpiece 90° and cut the grooves. For safety, achieve desired depth using multiple passes. To finish the piece, sand thoroughly; sanding is a must—particularly where blades exit the work. Stain the piece and use a tough finish that will withstand heat.

USE 2 X 5-1/2 X 5-1/2" STOCK (ACTUAL)

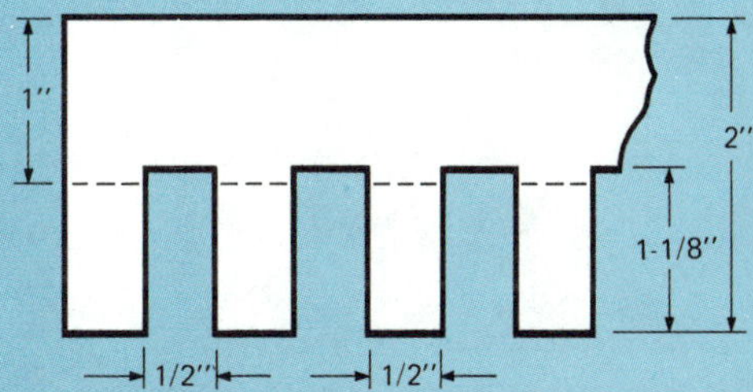

DADO ACROSS GRAIN FIRST, FLOP BLOCK AND USE SAME DIMENS. FOR GROOVING WITH GRAIN

gauge isn't designed to accept a work hold-down, a piece of medium-coarse sandpaper can be glued to the face of the miter gauge to provide a noncreep surface. Or you can simply clamp the workpiece to the miter gauge.

As you become more proficient in the use of your saw, you'll find that it's far from limited to just plain ripping and crosscutting. When teamed up with simple wooden jigs you can make yourself, your saw can take on new jobs in a production-like manner.

Five such jigs are pictured and detailed here. In the case of the adjustable taper jig, two marks made 12 in. from the hinged end permit you to set the jig to any given angle by measuring across the marks. For example, if you open the legs 1 in. at the 12-in. marks, the jig will produce a tapered cut of 1 in. per foot.

Nothing is more accurate and faster than a miter board when it comes to mitering picture-frame molding on a bench saw, and the sliding squaring board makes quick work of squaring up the edges of odd-size scraps with uneven edges. You can produce tapered wedges of any size and amount in jig time with a wedge board. A stepped stopblock takes all the guesswork out of producing perfect fitting half-lap joints with a dado head.

Once you know the basics—and the safety rules—of the bench saw, you're ready for the more sophisticated sawing techniques and accessories.

A basic rule in all power-tool woodworking is to provide the maximum support for the workpiece. A stand for supporting long, overhanging pieces should be one of the first things you build.

Tongue-and groove cutting

A DADO HEAD makes fast work of cutting tongues and grooves. For perfect alignment, test on a scrap first.

TO CUT A TONGUE, the fence is moved and locked. This small amount of stock can be removed in one pass.

Because the stand shown here is of standard, dimensioned pine, it's an inexpensive project. The support has a single-roller head for holding long boards for ripping; a second head has multiple rollers for crosscut sawing.

Dimensions are standard except for overall height, which is determined by the floor-to-tabletop distance of your saw. Build the stand so that when the head is at its lowest position, it is lower than saw-table height. By making the stand's height adjustable, you will be able to use it when working with other tools (jointer, jigsaw or drill press). When laying out parts for cutting, check out the stationary tools you own and try to arrive at a height-variable that gives you maximum use from the stand. If necessary, shorten the four vertical legs of the stand as well as the single vertical on each head.

Rollers must rotate freely. To assure this, drill undersize pilot holes in the closet pole and oversize, loose-fitting holes in the rails. An occasional brushing-off and a blast of silicone spray on the cold-roll and lagscrew "axles" is the only maintenance needed.

To use the stand, set the roller top surface to match the saw-table height and lock the head by tightening the two wingnuts. As the workpiece leaves the table it is supported by the rollers and is easier—and safer—to handle.

While a conventional rip or combination blade can make tongue-and-groove cuts, the job is best done with a dado head because it does a neater job faster. Four passes are required to cut a tongue with a conventional blade, two each for the cheeks and shoulders. The cheek cuts are made first, then the blade is lowered and waste removed by making the shoulder cuts. To make a groove with a conventional blade requires repeat passes until the desired width is attained.

Using a dado head, the groove can be cut in a single pass and the tongue made in two. If you are gluing up narrow stock to make a wide board, do as the pros do and make the tongue slightly less than the groove depth; this trick leaves room for any excess glue to escape.

In wood joinery it is often necessary to cut grooves wider than the typical saw kerf. For this job a serious woodworker owns a dado head. Stated simply, a dado is a U-shaped groove. It is common practice to call this shape a dado when it's across the grain and a groove when it runs with the grain. For a deep dado or groove, it is best to achieve depth by making repeat passes, raising the cutting tool slightly and moving the fence for each pass.

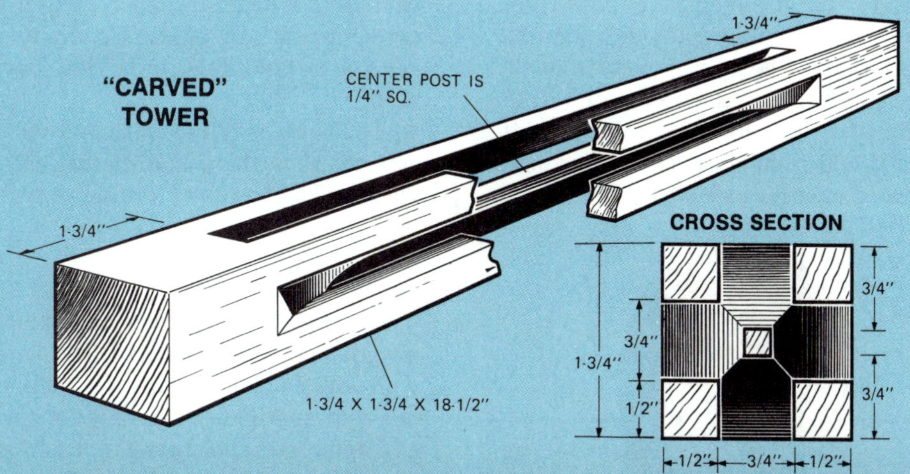

THE BOARD is held against the starter block and fence, then lowered slowly onto the spinning cutting tool.

WHEN THE END of the work aligns with the finish block, back slightly and depress the leading edge to lift off.

Blade projection is always less than the thickness of the stock being cut. A dado (or molding head) table insert with a larger slot must be used, and work is always fed slowly.

The typical dado head comes with two blades (each with a ⅛-in. kerf) and four chippers (three ⅛-inchers and one 1/16-in.). By using these in various combinations, you can obtain 11 different groove widths. Adding paper shims between cutters increases the number of grooves you can cut even more. The blades, mounted outside the chippers, determine the groove width. The chippers clean out the stock between the kerfs.

Almost any cut that can be made with a conventional blade can be made with a dado. You can cut coves faster, for example, but the cut will not be as smooth as the surface of a cove made with a combination blade. And a cove cut with a dado will also be slightly flat at center. As mentioned above, it makes tongue and grooving operations quicker. The same is true of other cutting such as edge-rabbeting, tenoning, saucering, piercing, maximum kerfing and hollowing.

Hollowing, as in fashioning a scoop or trough, is done by making a series of passes. After each pass, the fence is adjusted so that the cutters will overlap the last cut and the work is pushed through. Here, start and stop blocks determine the length of the dado or groove.

Start and stop blocks can be clamped to the rip fence or, simply, magnetic blocks positioned on the saw table. (I prefer the latter method in most instances because it eliminates the need for a fence extension when dadoing long pieces.) Block placement is determined mathematically by raising the blade to ultimate (final) projection and putting pencil marks on the table where the cutting tool will start and stop cutting the workpiece. Blocks are then positioned relative to these marks.

Dado safety rules:

- *Never* use the chippers—or a single chipper—without the mating blades.
- Because dadoing is on the underside it is, in effect, "blind" cutting. *Never* attempt to dado freehand; always use a guide, either a fence or miter gauge.
- *Never* use a dado to cut *through* a workpiece.
- As a rule of thumb, the wider the kerf being

cut with a dado, the more passes—raising the cutting tool for each successive pass—you should make. Keep in mind that a considerable amount of material is being removed from the stock; a too-large bite will place an undue strain on the motor and the cutting tool. And, you. Dadoing hardwood requires even more passes than a softwood such as pine does.

- Because of that large bite, chances of kickback with a dado are much greater than with a conventional saw blade. Generally, it's best to use a work hold-down or hold-in. In many cases, both.
- To insure easy and clean cutting, keep blades and chippers sharp and, periodically, lubricate with a silicone spray during extended cutting operations.

two practice projects

The "tower" and trivet shown on these pages are good practice projects to familiarize yourself with your dado head. Grooves for both should be made in multiple passes. To cut the tower, for example, raise the cutting tool so that it projects about ¼ in. and cut all four sides; then raise the blade ¼ in. each for the second and third passes. The "stop" for starting must be solid enough to press the workpiece against as you lower it. Magnetic types shown are by General Hardware

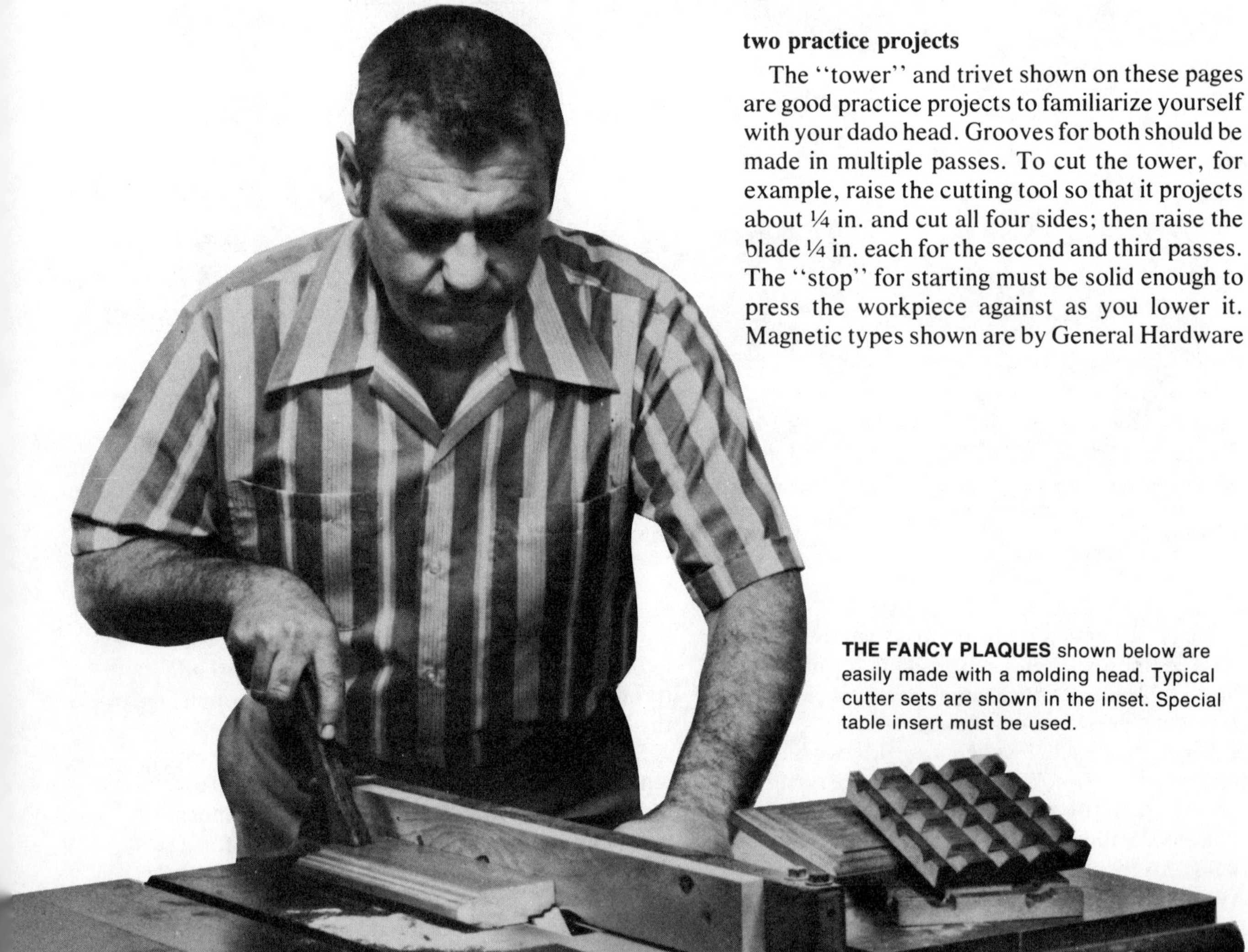

THE FANCY PLAQUES shown below are easily made with a molding head. Typical cutter sets are shown in the inset. Special table insert must be used.

Cutting coves

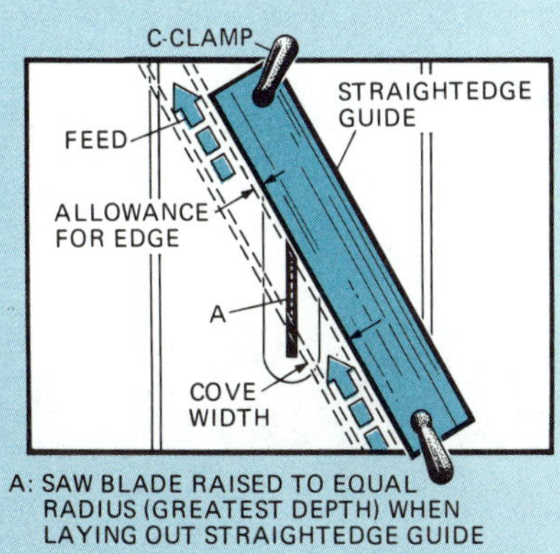

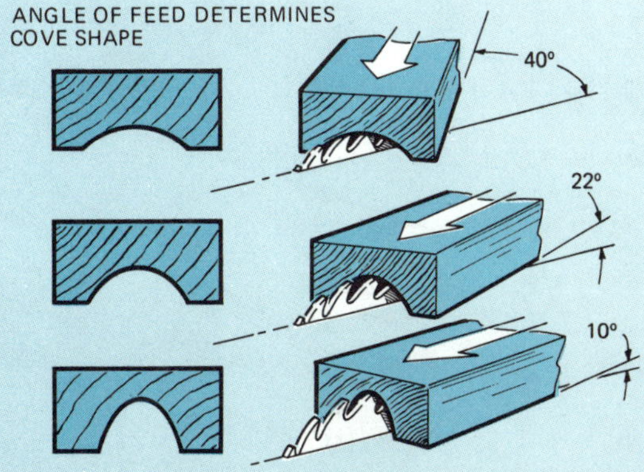

AFTER ANGLE is determined, straightedge is clamped to table. Photo was posed as shown for clarity, but for safety reasons the straightedge should be clamped on *kickback* side of the saw blade.

CORNERS ARE SLICED off the cove molding by using the saw blade set at a 45° angle. This work should be done using the conventional rip fence and a push stick as shown in the photo.

Mfg. Co., 80 White St., New York, N.Y. 10013.

Lower the piece onto the spinning cutters. Push it slowly through until the trailing edge reaches the stop gauge or mark. Back up the piece slightly, put pressure on the leading edge and lift off the piece. Repeat procedure for the remaining three sides. Make the trivet with at least three passes. Cut the dadoes first, then the grooves. Both pieces are examples of pierce-cutting as well as dadoing; that is, cuts from opposite sides intersect, without going through the workpiece, to produce a see-through effect. Both also prove why it is a must to keep dado-cutting tools razor sharp. Dull ones make the job difficult and unsafe.

The tower could be used as an integral part of a leg, or, sprayed with Da-Glo paint, as "pop art." The trivet makes a handsome protective base for hot pots.

In learning the many trick cuts you can make with your bench saw, you'll find it fun to try your hand at oblique sawing—which is the creation of half-round slots (grooves) in a workpiece.

You can use any blade intended for conventional cutting, but experienced shop men prefer a hollow-ground combination, fine-tooth plywood, carbide-tipped, chisel-tooth combination, or dado-head blade. Each leaves a slightly different finished surface, and you are advised to test all blades on scrap to find the one that best suits your purpose.

The important point is to make certain that the depth and angle of cut are such that the front and *not the sides* of the teeth will do the cutting. As can be seen in the drawing, the angle of cut will determine the cove shape. And no matter which blade you use, because coving is done by scraping rather than cutting, you can expect a fair

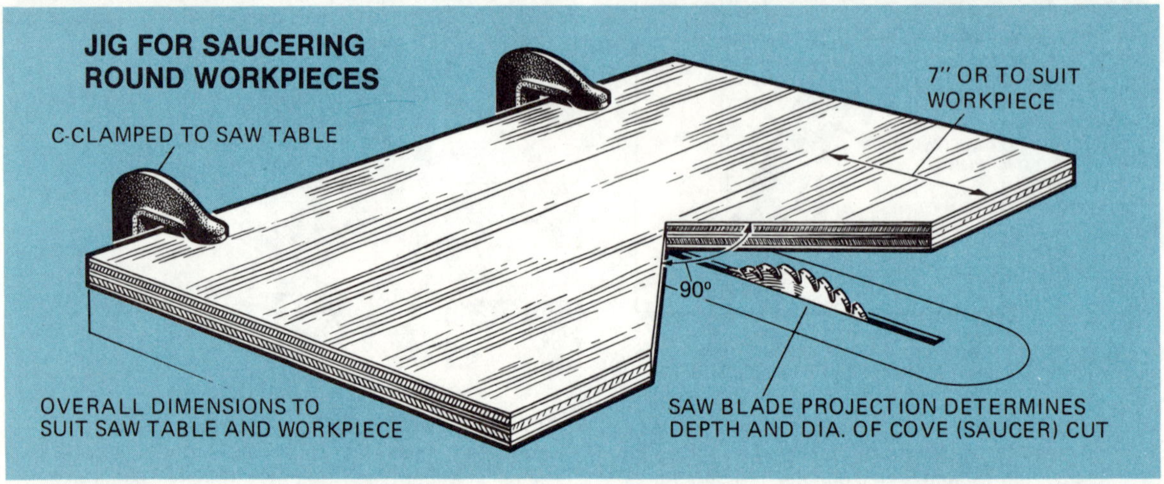

ROUND PIECES CAN BE SAUCERED using a V-jig clamped to the table. The workpiece is centered over a combination blade, and after each rotation the blade is raised 1/16 in. Hold the work securely as you raise the blade.

share of sanding to finish any coved piece.

To design a cove, raise the blade to the height of the finished cove (maximum radius). Place the workpiece on the saw table and angle it relative to the blade so that the cove width you desire will be achieved. Then clamp a straightedge to the table for the work to ride against as it is fed to the spinning blade.

To cut the cove, lower the blade so that there is a 1/16-in. projection. Feed the work slowly and after each pass raise the blade 1/16 in. for the next pass. Continue making such passes until the desired depth is reached.

Bowls can be coved (saucered) too. After cutting the stock to circular shape on a jig or bandsaw, make a V-notched jig out of plywood or particleboard. Clamp it to the table so that the bowl will be centered over the blade and start with the bowl firmly held in position. With your other hand, slowly raise the spinning blade until it projects about 1/16 in. Rotate the bowl—in the direction of the arrow shown in the photo—until you have made a full revolution. Here, matching marks on work and jig will let you know when you have turned the piece 360°. Continue feeding, raising the blade after each revolution, until the desired depth is reached. Make certain that you make a complete revolution at each blade depth before raising the blade for the next revolution.

You should be aware that the final saucer depth is related to the diameter; the deeper the saucer, the larger the bowl diameter.

There are two types of molding head. One uses a single knife; the other employs three. The latter type, as can be seen in the photos, was used here. A molding head can be used instead of the saw blade to create any number of groove pat-

Working with molding head cutters

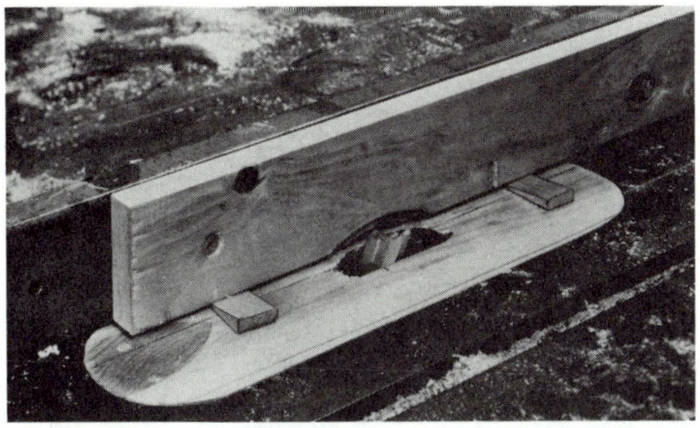

TWO SAFETY MUSTS for working with a molding head are shown at the left: a wood auxiliary fence and the large-slot table insert. If you don't own a metal insert (see photo, page **280**), you can make one of plywood. Cut the outside shape to fit the table opening and, after placing at least two wood shims between the locked fence and the insert, slowly raise the spinning cutter knives. These knives will pierce both the insert and wood fence to provide the necessary clearance for the cutters and for the work to be fed through. *Caution:* You should make certain that the metal rip fence is not directly over the knives. The screw holes in the wood fence should be countersunk on both sides in order that the auxiliary can be used on either side of the rip fence.

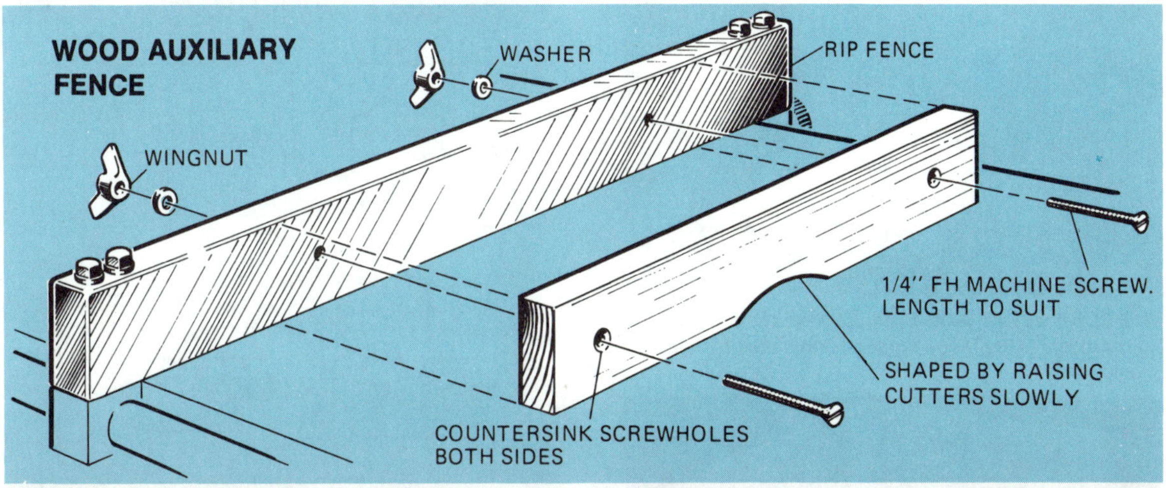

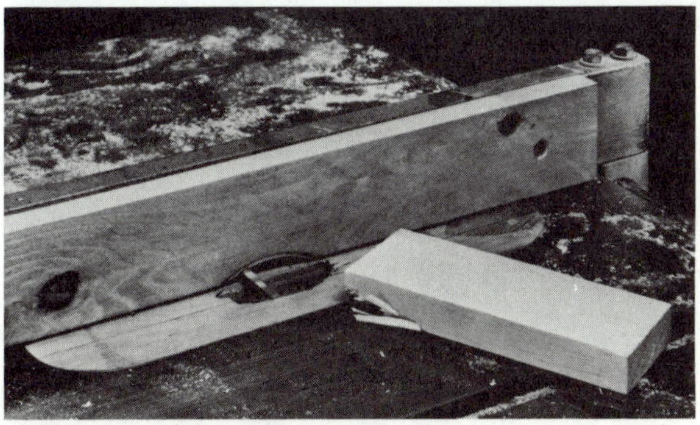

IN SPITE OF A SLOW feed rate, when the cutters leave end grain, the edge inevitably is splintered.

THE RUPTURED EDGE is cleaned by following a pass *with* the grain (see arrows). The knives must be sharp.

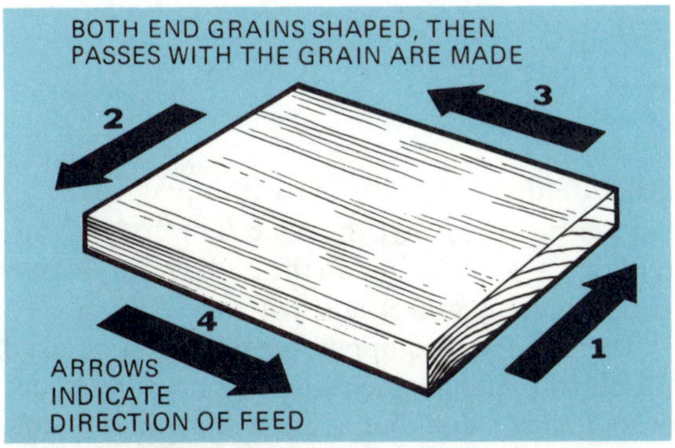

THE CORRECT SEQUENCE for shaping: The first and second passes are across the end grain; next two with grain.

terns. Actually, the method of cutting with a molding head is much the same as with a dado head. The guard and splitter must be removed from the saw and a large-slot molding insert used in place of the standard saw-table insert. These are available commercially or can be shaped of plywood as shown. And, if the fence will be used for end or edge molding, it must be fitted with an auxiliary wood fence. The larger cutout is a must; it provides clearance for partial or full

THE EDGE BEING SHAPED must have maximum support. Here, the fence shifted to the left of the blade provides it.

CRISSCROSS DESIGNS are typical examples of decorative effects that were achieved with a molding head.

CUSTOM EDGES can be made using two or more cutters. By varying the depths, versatility is even greater.

exposure of the cutters. The safest way to make it is with the cutter you plan to use. Just be sure that the fence is tightly wedged so any chance of chatter is eliminated.

A variety of cutter shapes is available. They can be used singly or in combination with other cutters to create custom shapes. To do the latter, simply keep a file of inked tracings of the cutter knife shapes that you own. Then, when you want to plan a pattern, these can be laid one over the other until you're satisfied with the design.

Important: Always make certain that the cutter knives are mounted in the cutterhead following the manufacturer's instructions.

The auxiliary-equipped fence should be used for all straightedge molding. It is possible to cut an outboard edge, but a slip will mean overcutting and a ruined workpiece and, possibly, injury to the operator. It is far safer to support the edge as shown. The work can be either flat on the

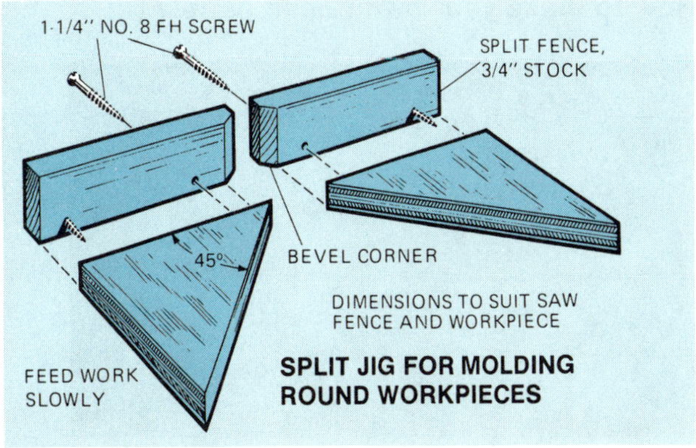

AN ADJUSTABLE V-GUIDE used for molding of round workpieces can be made of plywood or particleboard. The work is positioned over the cutters, then the jig is clamped to the locked rip fence. As with saucering, the work must be securely held while the blade is raised the initial 1/16 in. This is to be followed by repeat passes.

Edge-rabbeting round workpieces

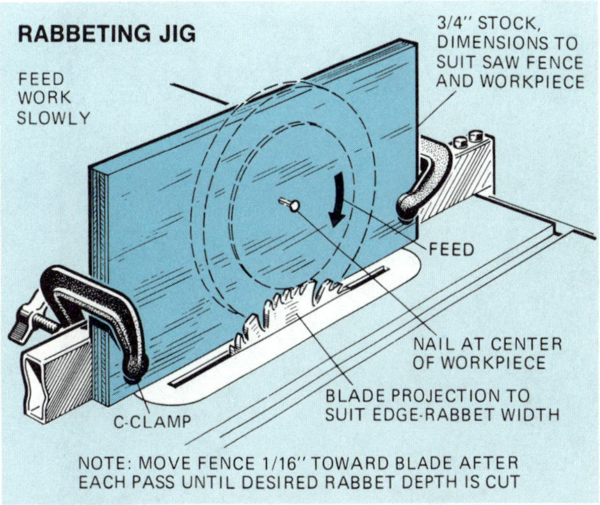

A ROUND PIECE to be edge-rabbeted pivots on a jig clamped to the fence. A nail is positioned directly over the centerline of the blade. After the rabbet width is reached, the fence is moved toward the blade and the procedure is repeated.

table or on edge, depending on the design, but for small or narrow workpieces, use your work hold-down and a push stick.

To mold a circular piece, you will have to first make the two triangular jigs shown in the photo and sketch. As with coving round pieces, you must make repeat passes with the blade raised about 1/16 in. for each pass.

The same split jig can be used to mold the workpiece edge as well. To do it, the V-jig is clamped with the plywood *against the rip fence* instead of on the table. The shaping can then proceed in the same manner.

Though edge-rabbeting of a round workpiece could be done with a dado head, it is safer to use a combination blade and slow feed. The "jig" in this case is simply a rectangular piece of ¾-in. plywood (sized to suit your saw and the workpiece) clamped to the locked fence. The pivot is actually a hefty common nail which passes

How to make your own raised panels

THE PANELS above were cut from the same piece of wood. All work on the finished door was done on a bench saw.

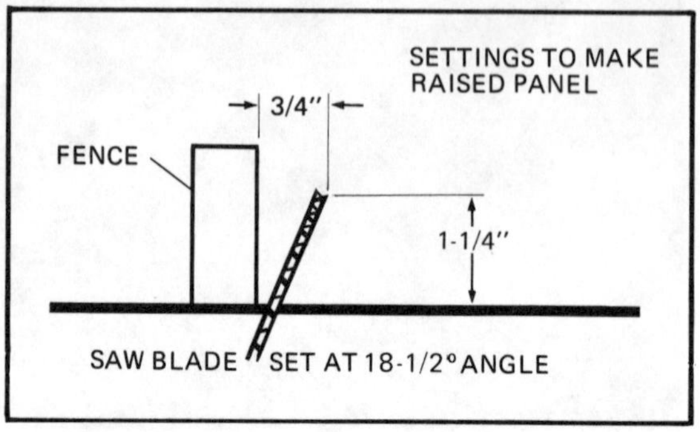

THE SETTINGS shown here were used to make the panels at the left. The resulting shoulder gives a shadow line.

BEVEL CUTS are made across the end grain first, then along the lengths. To saw panels, use a planer blade.

THE VERTICAL BLADE is lowered and the fence adjusted so angled strips can be cut off neatly and accurately.

through a predrilled hole in the workpiece into the jig.

The nail must be centered over the saw arbor and rigidly fixed so that there is no chance of workpiece slop. The workpiece, of course, must rotate freely on the pivot nail and be securely held by the operator at all times.

It's best to reach the desired rabbet width with several passes, raising the blade for each pass. When you're satisfied with rabbet *width,* move fence toward the blade so that the next cut will overlap the previous one. Starting again with a 1/16-in. projection, repeat the procedure. Make the necessary fence moves to achieve desired rabbet *depth,* usually no more than half the thickness of the stock being worked. By now, it should be obvious that in all cases of sophisticated sawing with accessories there are two precautions you should always take: Never saw freehand (always use a guide) and always use a

How to bend wood without resorting to steam

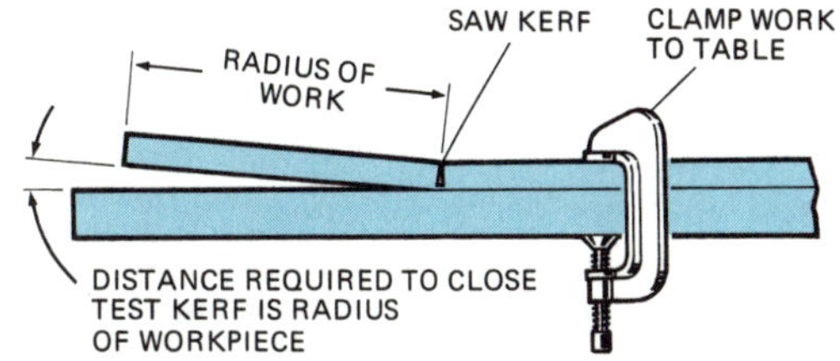

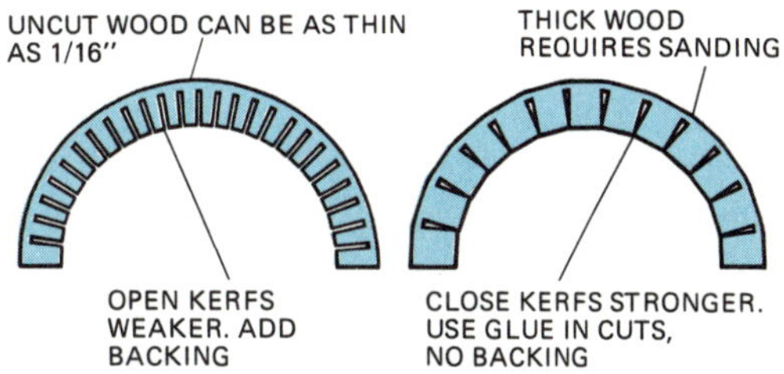

A TEST BEND is made of a scrap piece (top). The amount of the lift at the end is the value in the first column of the chart. For average work, 1/4-in. center-to-center spacing is used (above). The job is set up with a nail (pin) driven into the miter extension to space the cuts. Typical kerfing permits elaborate bending of the wood as shown in the photo below.

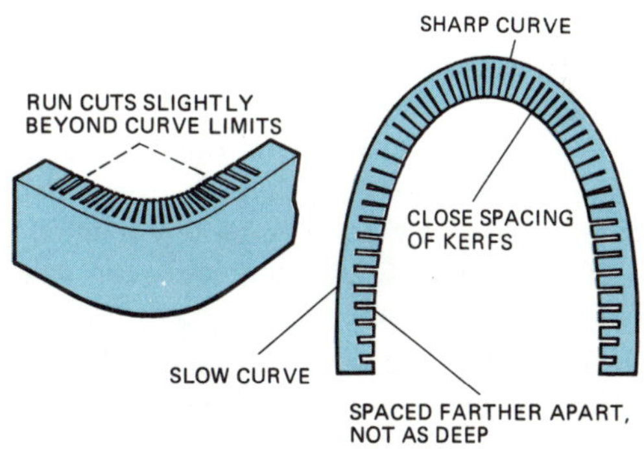

KERFING. The drawings above detail the basic rules. Tack them to your shop wall with the chart below. To use the chart, make a test bend as above. Leave as much uncut wood as possible. Gradually deepen the cut until wood can bend 1/8-in. Now, under "Test Bend," find 1/8 in. Reading across, the number of cuts needed for a full circle is 258 (for a half circle, 129). Under 12-in. radius 9/32 in. is center-to-center spacing. 1/64 in. is the proper kerf width. Since this kerf is impractical, use a wider kerf than that suggested.

SPACING OF CUTS

TEST BEND	CUTS IN CIRCLE	KERF TO CLOSE	RADIUS OF WORK IN INCHES													
			3	4	5	6	7	8	9	10	11	12	13	14	15	16
1/8"	258	.018 (1/64)	1/16	3/32	1/8	5/32	5/32	3/16	7/32	1/4	1/4	9/32	5/16	5/16	3/8	3/8
3/16"	171	.027 (1/32)	3/32	1/8	3/16	7/32	1/4	9/32	5/16	3/8	3/8	7/16	7/16	1/2	9/16	9/16
1/4"	129	.036 (1/32)	1/8	3/16	1/4	1/4	5/16	3/8	7/16	1/2	1/2	9/16	5/8	11/16	3/4	3/4
5/16"	100	.047 (3/64)*	3/16	1/4	5/16	3/8	7/16	1/2	9/16	5/8	11/16	3/4	13/16	7/8	15/16	1
3/8"	83	.056 (1/16)	3/16	1/4	3/8	7/16	1/2	9/16	5/8	3/4	13/16	7/8	15/16	1	1 1/8	1 3/16
7/16"	72	.065 (1/16)	1/4	5/16	7/16	1/2	9/16	11/16	3/4	7/8	15/16	1	1 1/8	1 3/16	1 5/16	1 3/8
1/2"	63	.074 (5/64)	1/4	3/8	1/2	9/16	11/16	3/4	7/8	1	1 1/16	1 3/16	1 1/4	1 3/8	1 1/2	1 9/16
9/16"	56	.084 (5/64)	5/16	7/16	9/16	5/8	3/4	7/8	1	1 1/8	1 3/16	1 5/16	1 7/16	1 9/16	1 11/16	1 3/4
5/8"	50	.094 (3/32)†	3/8	1/2	5/8	3/4	7/8	1	1 1/8	1 1/4	1 3/8	1 1/2	1 5/8	1 3/4	1 7/8	2
11/16"	46	.102 (7/64)	3/8	1/2	11/16	13/16	15/16	1 1/16	1 3/16	1 3/8	1 1/2	1 5/8	1 3/4	1 7/8	2 1/16	2 3/16
3/4"	42	.112 (1/8)	7/16	9/16	3/4	7/8	1	1 3/16	1 5/16	1 1/2	1 5/8	1 3/4	1 15/16	2 1/16	2 5/16	2 3/8

*Average bandsaw †Average circular saw

bench saw know-how, continued

slow feed rate and multiple (repeat) passes.

The remainder of the techniques given here are tricky, yet nonetheless satisfying saw exercises when successfully executed. They require a careful setup of saw and accessories and, mostly, some practice on scrap. Charts shown for kerfing and compound cutting will reduce your time making test cuts. Depending on your saw, the various settings shown may vary somewhat, but by using the charts, you'll start test cuts close to, or right on, the required settings.

Decorative raised panels are frequently called for and add to the charm of Early American furniture. Such panels are now commonly used on cabinet doors, drawer fronts and house doors.

The bench saw lets you raise your own panels—and more. For example, the finished cabinet door shown was completely readied for assembly on this saw. All techniques for making such a door are included here: ripping, crosscutting, edge-rabbeting stiles and rails to let in a panel and shaping the inside edges of stiles and rails with a molding head.

Actually, a raised panel is simply a deep, narrow chamfer cut around all four edges of a block of wood. The cut is made in the same manner as a chamfer cut except that blade and rip-fence settings are altered to get the desired raised panel.

The settings used to produce the raised panels shown are detailed in the drawing. These panels have a slight shoulder to create an architectural shadowline. This can be eliminated if you raise the blade so it completely saws through the wood when you're making the chamfer cut. It's strictly a matter of personal taste.

As with most precision cutting, a hollow-ground planer or fine-tooth plywood blade is the best choice for panel raising. But no matter which blade you use, always cut the chamfers across the end grains first, then make the two passes with the grain. It is also important to use a slow feed rate.

Do-it-yourselfers at some point are sure to find it necessary to make a turn with a piece of wood. Steaming will let you bend wood around a radius, but it is timeconsuming and sloppy. Kerfing, often called the undertaker's cut (by pros)

Other cuts you can make

CUTTING COMPOUND MITERS is tricky and requires good planning. A work hold-down is a must here.

THE PIECE being fashioned above is for a four-sided box with a bottom that's let into edge-rabbets.

Work Angle (slope of side)	For Four-Side Box		For Six-Side Box	
	Blade Setting	Miter-Gauge Setting	Blade Setting	Miter-Gauge Setting
15°	43¼°	75½°	29°	81¾°
30°	37¾°	63½°	26°	74°
45°	30°	54¾°	21°	67¾°
60°	21°	49°	14½°	63½°

NOTE: Settings shown above for most commonly used miter cuts are close approximations of settings required to achieve the desired angle/slope. Test on scrap first; adjust the settings if required.

FACET CUTS are made using a hollow-ground planer or a fine-tooth plywood blade. Use a slow feed rate.

CUTS ARE MADE across the grain first, then with the grain. Countless panel designs can be created.

PATTERN T-JIG

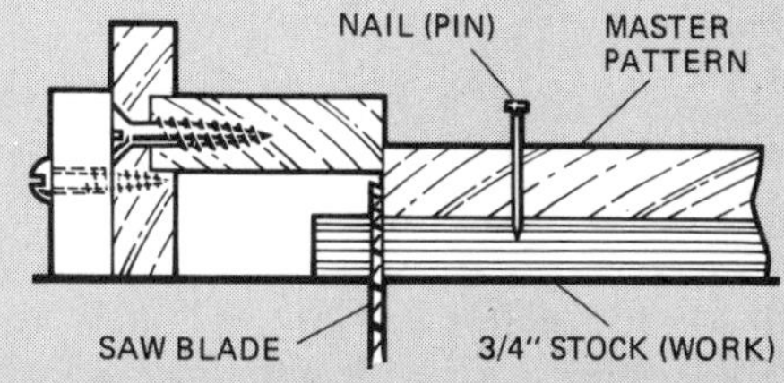

PATTERN SAWING is a fast and accurate way to cut exact duplicates of straight-sided work.

A TENONING ATTACHMENT simplifies cutting tenons. You can feed stock with your hand far from the blade.

because casketmakers originated the idea for turning out the curved top of a casket, is the answer.

With a little practice, kerfing will allow you to make the tightest turn with minimum effort. In fact, the biggest chore about kerfing is the boredom that can easily set in while you make the repeated passes necessary to bend a long piece of wood. Acquire the habit of staying alert; *do not let your attention wander*.

Kerfing, as the name suggests is a series of equally spaced, kerf-wide dadoes sawed across a board so that the board can be bent back on itself. If the board is weakened in the kerfed area, the kerfed segment can be beefed up with glue blocks after it has been bent to shape. Many craftsmen strengthen weak kerfs by pouring in white glue and sawdust, or by filling open kerfs with a wood filler. Either method is satisfactory, but for maximum strength use the glue blocks.

To set up for kerfing, run a saw kerf through your miter-gauge extension and drive in a nail to act as a guide for spacing. The first cut is made with the end of the board butted against the pin, and the balance of the cuts are made by placing the newest kerf over the pin to make the next kerf.

As seen in the chart, the tighter the turn, the closer the kerfs are spaced. As the turn becomes gentler, distance between kerfs can be increased. Use the chart to determine number of cuts, kerf depth and spacing.

I've found that bending a kerfed piece of wood is easier to accomplish, with less chance of breakage, if it is dipped into warm water prior to making the bend. If white glue is to be used as a strengthener, it can be applied immediately. With nonsoluble glues, leave the wood clamped in a web clamp until dry and then apply reinforcing.

You can use faceting to create decorative blocks of original design on doors, cabinets, drawer fronts and so forth. Like panel raising, faceting is similar to chamfer cutting; the rip fence and blade settings are simply varied.

Your best bet is to sketch a plan of your design; then, using scrap, make a test piece. Use a hollow-ground blade and feed the work slowly. And because faceting is, in effect, blind cutting, use a work hold-down and push stick. *Never* make a facet cut any deeper than three quarters of the thickness of the stock being cut.

creating your own designs

Faceted plaques can be cut using the dado and molding heads as well. Just make certain that you follow the safety rule mentioned above and feed the work even more slowly. The number of designs is virtually unlimited. By moving the rip fence in either direction, changing blade elevation, altering the arbor's bevel setting—or with any combination of the three—you will create a new design. That's the fun of facet cutting. If you hit upon a design that you feel you will want to repeat in the future, make a sketch with all saw settings listed.

For a fast way to duplicate straight-sided work, try pattern sawing. Whether you want to make 2, 20 or 100 pieces, each will be exactly alike. The setup requires an overhanging (T-shape) wood fence clamped to the rip fence and a master pattern of the part to be duplicated. Drive two nails through the pattern so that the points can be embedded in the part to be duplicated.

As shown, the plywood fence is aligned flush with the saw blade, and the blade is elevated just high enough to handle the thickness of the workpiece. Clearance under the fence must suit the thickness of the workpiece and the pattern must be of stock thick enough so that it will ride against the fence.

To minimize waste and make the job go faster, the workpieces should be cut close to finish size beforehand. For safety on large duplicating runs, stop the saw from time to time and clear away the cut-offs. Pick the blade to suit the chore, and use a normal feed rate.

The techniques presented here cover most cuts that an average home craftsman will ever want to make. Basically, good bench-saw technique consists of careful thinking, good safety habits and common sense.

Good saw accessories for an active workshop include the tenoning attachment shown. It is available at minimal cost and is well worth the investment if you do a lot of joinery. Another is the dial-type dado head that lets you quickly select dado widths because you don't have to break down the setup to make a change. Finally, as you add blades to your collection, seriously consider buying the carbide-tip type. A good quality carbide blade will last about 20 times longer between sharpenings. That can make quite a difference over the long haul.

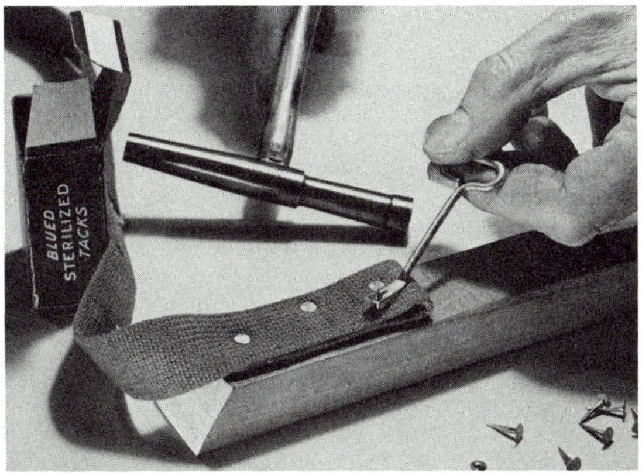

YOUR FINGERS won't feel pinched when you drive tacks if you hold them with a tool made from a can turnkey. Simply snip off the end to open up the slot and slip a tack between the prongs.

A FENCE STOP for use either to the right or left of the blade on a radial-arm saw can be made by welding a C-clamp to a piece of channel iron. It clamps anywhere along the fence.

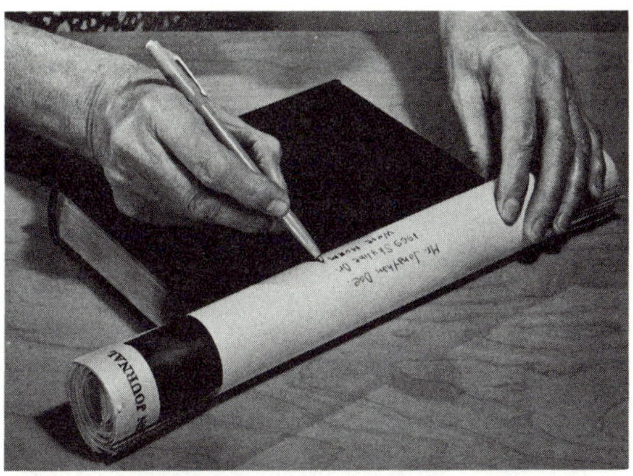

YOU'LL DO a neater job of writing a mailing address on a rolled magazine or newspaper if you will rest your hand on a book. The bigger the roll, the bigger the book, of course.

THINK TWICE about throwing away that old garden hose. Cut into 5-in. lengths, it will provide dozens of neat, handy holders for many of your shop tools. Form a tab at the top for hanging.

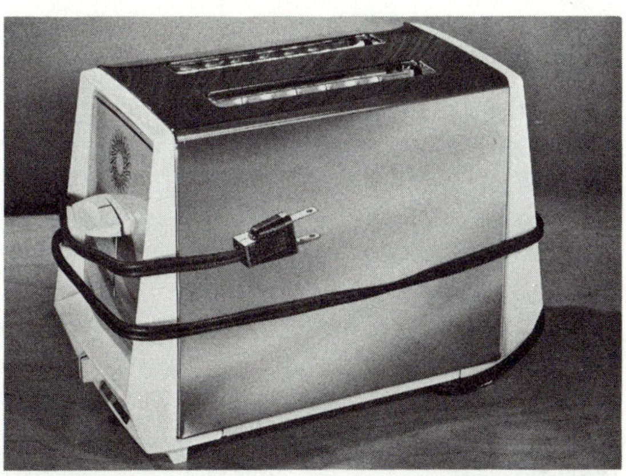

CEMENT A MAGNET from a cupboard catch to the side of the plug of a toaster, and you'll find it handy as can be when you coil the cord around it for storing. The plug will stick to the metal side.

CARRYING A PAIL of water or a paint bucket by its wire handle for any distance is hard on the hand. A more comfortable grip can be provided if you use an open-end wrench as shown in the photo.

Cutting narrow strips on a table saw always calls for a pusher stick. Here's a version that gives maximum leverage and safety. You'll use it often

Make this supersafe pusher jig

By ROBERT K. WALLACE

SEE ALSO

Circular saw blades . . . Power-tool stands . . . Table saws . . . Workbenches . . . Workshops

IF YOU HAVE ever ripped narrow strips on a table saw—utilizing a conventional push stick—there are moments when you feel that you don't have complete control of the workpiece—especially if the wood is thin. Not so with this version. Since the adjustable portion can be set to snuggle the work, control is positive at all times and leverage is greatly increased over that of its less versatile predecessor. And, since good shop practice calls for the use of a pusher when the rip fence is within 3 in. of the blade, it will see plenty of use in the average home shop.

Designed for use on a table saw with a rectangular fence (such as the one shown), the pusher can be cut on the table saw with the exception of its handle. The model shown is of ¾-in. lum-

HANDLE FOR PUSHER is factory-made Spindleflex section which is sold at lumberyards. Its hefty size fits hand comfortably, gives good control.

WINGNUT AND WASHER hold adjustable half of jig securely at desired height. Fixed half is assembled with screws so it can be replaced as needed.

ber-core plywood, but you can use any other type of plywood or a solid stock, such as maple or walnut. The handle that was used here is a section of Spindleflex purchased from the local lumberyard. You could, however, hand-fashion a handle of 2x2 stock by rounding the corners for hand comfort.

In use, the pressure foot of the jig is adjusted to the thickness of the workpiece and clamped in place by tightening the wingnut. The jig then provides a hold-down for the stock as well as a push stick. The operator's hands (photo, right), are completely away from the blade, even when ripping narrow material.

For photographic reasons we show the jig slicing narrow strips, off a piece of stock. In practice, when ripping a lot of like strips the fence is normally set to the desired width and the same piece of wood is repeatedly fed into the blade. To do that with this jig, set the blade to just clear the top of the wood being ripped and push the jig clear through the blade to complete the pass. Eventually, the pressure foot and pusher bottoms will be chewed up, but replacing these parts is simple. *Caution:* Don't try this procedure using a wide plank. In our tests, wide boards had a tendency to "walk" from the fence at the lead edge. This can cause binding; that, of course, is unsafe.

CUTTING NARROW STRIPS this way means moving the fence after each pass. If fence is set desired distance from blade, bottom of jig will be kerfed.

LUMBER-CORE PLYWOOD was used to build prototype, but solid pine or hardwood could also be used. Build the jig so that it will clear the boltheads on the rip fence (see photo at top of facing page).

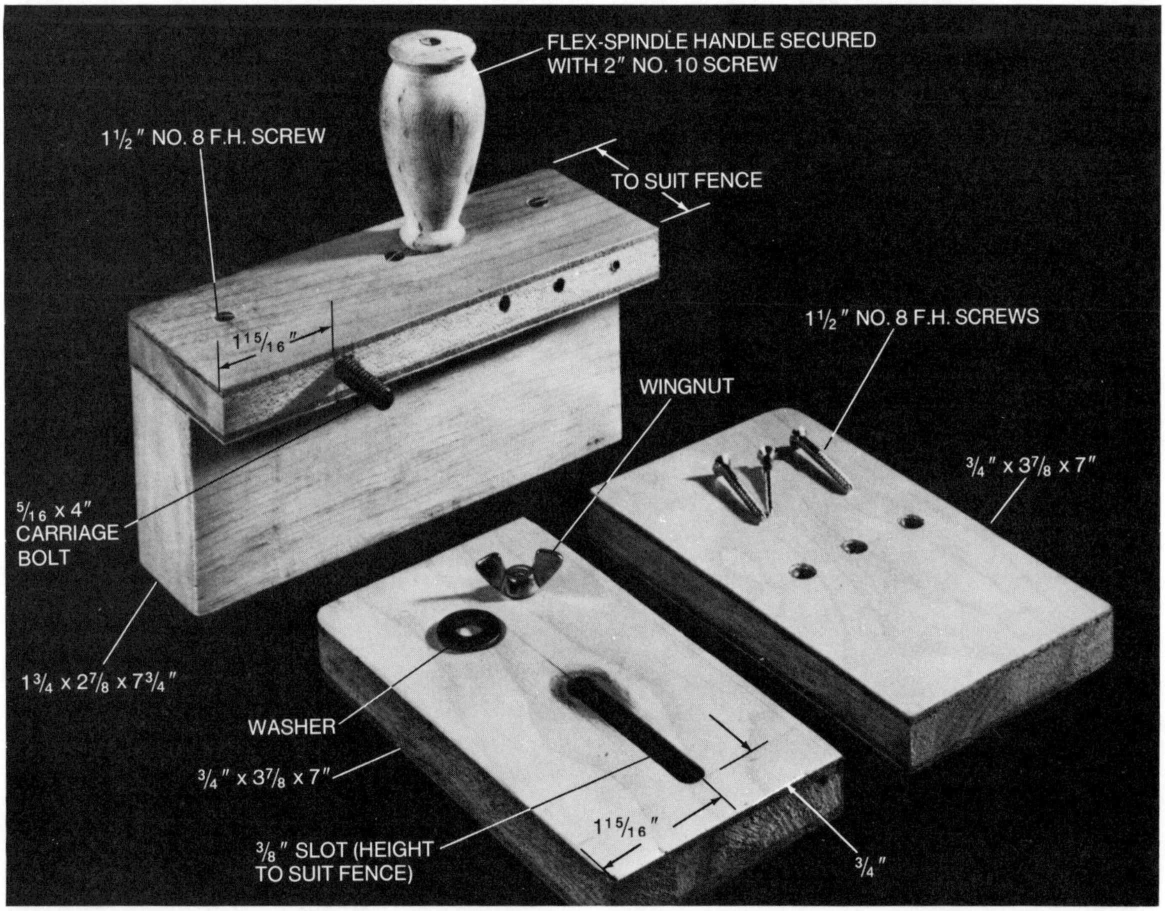

Roller support for a bench saw

This sturdy work support serves as a "third hand" when you are ripping or crosscutting long boards

By C.E. BANISTER

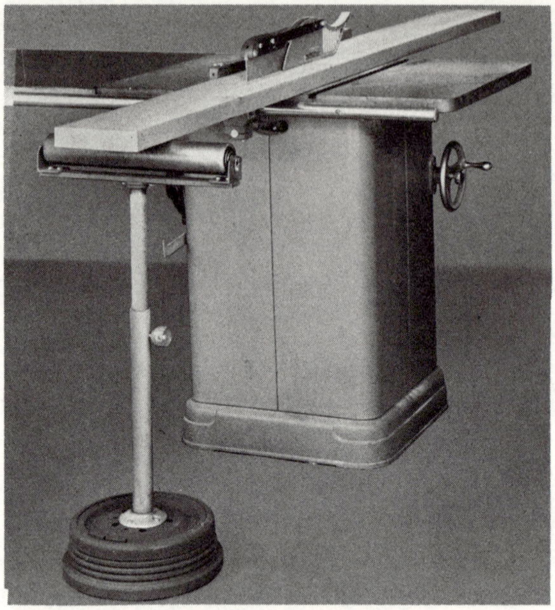

THIS RUGGED work support, which is tip-proof because of the design of the base, is a safety "must" when you rip or crosscut long pieces. (To do the latter, support is repositioned at the saw's side.)

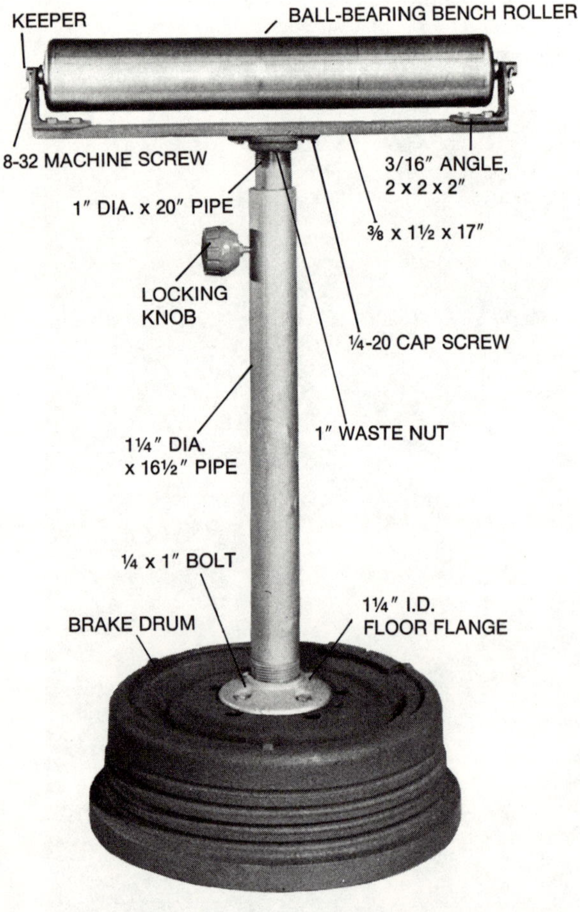

■ HERE'S A ONE-EVENING, easy-on-the-wallet project that will be a valuable "third hand" in your workshop. The work support boasts an adjustable roller top, which greatly simplifies ripping and crosscutting of long boards and large sheets of plywood on a bench saw.

The steel ball-bearing bench roller can be purchased from Belsaw Machinery Co., 315 Westport Rd., Kansas City, Mo. 64111 for about $6.50. All other parts are inexpensive and readily available locally. The two lengths of pipe can be bought cut to length and each threaded at one end. A standard replacement knob for existing equipment would make a good locking device for the pipe uprights. (A piece of 5/16-in. rod threaded at one end and bent to a 30° angle would also work well.) Automotive brake drums can be obtained from brake service shops or junk yards.

The roller cradle consists of a ⅜-in.-thick iron bar, drilled and tapped to receive ½-in. ¼-20 capscrews that attach the waste nut and the two angle irons. Each angle iron is notched and filed with a three-cornered file to allow the seating of the ½-in. hex roller shaft. After each angle iron is drilled and tapped to receive ⅜-in. 8-32 machine screws, two short lengths of coathanger wire for "keepers" are threaded through the ⅛-in. factory-drilled holes in the shaft ends and wrapped under the machine-screw heads to form continuous loops and hold the roller in the cradle firmly.

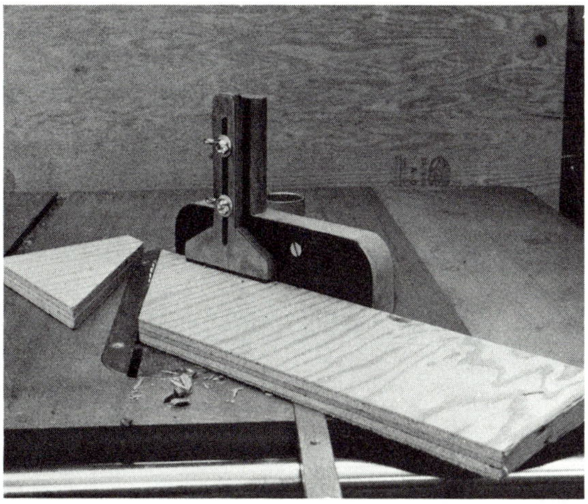

THIS SAW AID grasps firmly to keep workpieces from creeping—especially on angle cuts. At left, business side of hold-down; at right, how it's attached.

Miter-gauge hold-down with a supergrip

By JOHN BAINBRIDGE

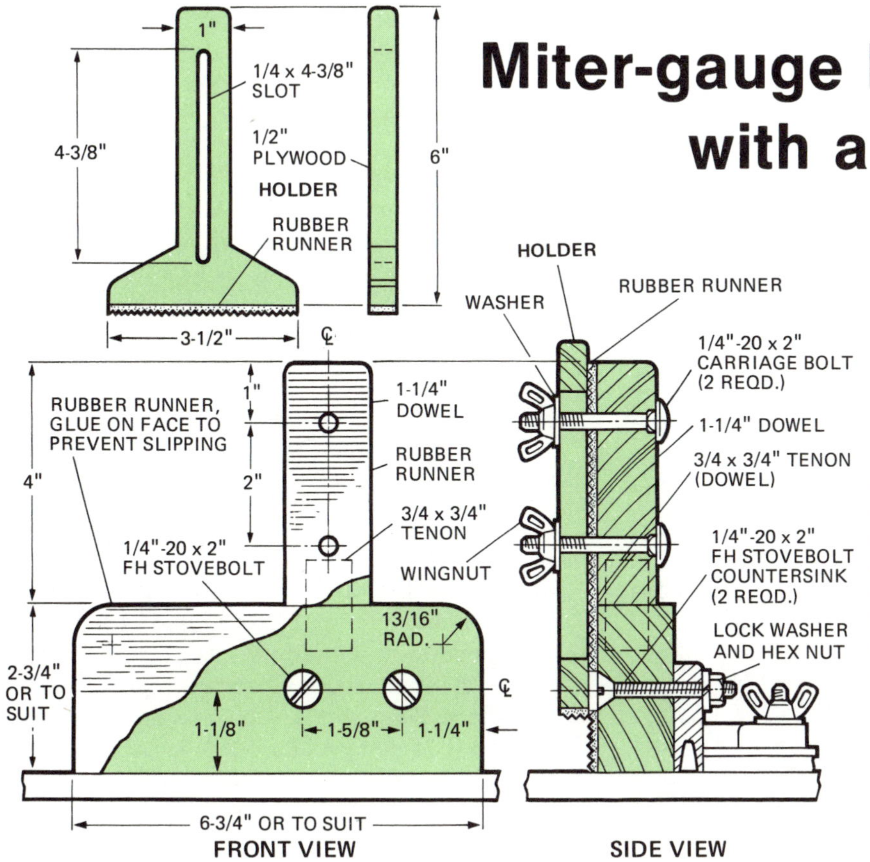

WORKPIECE CAN'T move when the slotted holder is forced down against the work and tightened to the dowel handle with two wingnuts. Hold-down will accept work up to 2 in. thick and can be quickly removed from the miter gauge when it is not needed.

WHEN I SPOTTED the supersafe pusher jig (on page 292) I quickly made one for my saw. The safety this clever ripping device has since afforded me inspired an equally safe jig for crosscutting with the miter gauge.

I made it from clear pine to suit my AMT miter gauge, although it can be made to suit other makes such as Rockwell's (above). I faced the front and the end of the slotted holder with pieces of rubber stair tread. Two stovebolts hold the hold-down securely to the gauge, yet allow it to be quickly removed when desired. What I like about it, besides the way it securely holds the work, is the handle which keeps my hand clear of the saw blade.

SEE ALSO

Power-tool stands . . . Shapers . . . Table saws . . . Workbenches . . . Workshops

How to build a bicycle built for two

By EUGENE A. SLOANE

UNTIL YOU RIDE a tandem you will never know the joy a bicycle can bring to the two of you. You can comment on the passing scene without having to shout or ride dangerously close together to be heard. Two-up riding is easier because two wheels instead of four offer less rolling resistance, and the tandem weighs less than two single bikes. When the wind is gusty a tandem is far steadier and easier to pedal than a single bike.

The trouble with tandems is their great expense. You can buy one that sells for as little as $150 but it weighs almost twice as much as the one you can build yourself, and looks, rides and feels like a truck. (All prices are estimates and were current at the time this was written). A really good ready-built tandem sells for upwards of $750.

You should be able to build this lightweight, comfortable and responsive tandem for a maximum of $390 out-of-pocket and a minimum of $190 if you use less costly components. You can cut costs still further if you already have some of the parts such as saddles, wheels, tires, tubes, frames, derailleurs, brakes and handlebars from old bikes. The old frames you will need you can often scrounge from local bike shops which have no need for wrecked frames.

TOOLS YOU WILL NEED

- Brazing outfit, with a dozen or so 1/16-inch bronze rods and brazing flux. I prefer the Tote-Weld Mapp gas outfit made by Airco which costs about $125 including tanks of Mapp gas and oxygen, rods, lighter, safety goggles and carrying case. The Mapp gas replacement cylinders are available from Sears, Roebuck and you can get oxygen from any welding supply house. A very adequate brazing and welding manual comes with the Tote-Weld setup, and you can learn to braze from it.
- Metal-cleaning equipment, including flat and rat-trail files, sandpaper and a ½-inch carbide burr bit.
- Hacksaw and blades.
- Frame alignment equipment. This includes a carpenter's level, 4-foot straightedge, ruler, roll of twine, I.D. and O.D. caliper rule.

SEE ALSO
Minibikes . . . Tune-up, bicycle

how to ride a tandem

If you follow all the build-it steps, you should have a high quality tandem with excellent shock-absorbing and steering qualities for long distance touring comfort.

Now, some advice about riding your new tandem. Learn to coordinate push-off from a standing start. Pedals on one side should be at two o'clock. Push down on that pedal and push up into the saddle and pedal a few strong strokes to get going. Stop for a second and get the other foot into the toe clips. Never stop pedaling without warning the other rider; never turn without letting the "stoker" at the rear know about it; never stop without informing the stoker. The stoker should never shift bodily weight because this can throw the front man off balance, especially during a turn. Some shifting about is okay, but don't overdo it. If you get along well in other departments, you should be a joy to each other, and to watch, as you harmoniously pedal away!

Now here are the steps for building the tandem:

step one

Remove all parts from both frames except fork from the front frame.

step two

Prepare the rear frame section. Cut headtube in two places (dotted lines on drawing) at Point 1. With torch, unbraze and remove headtube and top tube. Apply heat to Points 2, 3 and 4 as neces-

PARTS YOU WILL NEED

■ Two frames, preferably of high quality tubing such as Reynolds '531', Columbus, Super-Vitus or Vitus. Try to get a man's frame for the front and a woman's frame for the rear that fits your "stoker." If all you can get are two men's frames, steps here show you how to convert one to a woman's step-through frame. Rear frame can have a bent fork, since you need but one. Front frame fork must be straight, as should all main tubes. Prices vary according to how badly they are wrecked and the steel they are made of. Certainly $50 for a pair of old, beat-up frames should be reasonable.

■ A pair of caliper brakes with levers and one short and one extra-long tandem length cable for the rear brake. Mafac brakes are very adequate, cost about $18 with levers. Extra long cable, about $2.

■ Three seat-post lugs, about $2 each from Proteus Designs, Inc., 9225 Baltimore Blvd., College Park, MD 20740. Give O.D. of old front frame seat tube and rear frame down tube to get fit—73° lugs are fine.

■ Headset (if you need one for front frame). These are all cups, bearings and locknut. Measure I.D. of head tube to get set that fits. Strong-light headset is fine, for about $8.

■ Pedals. Two pair of reasonably high-quality-alloy body pedals, such as KKT, with toe clips and straps. These must be threaded to fit your cranks. About $60 for two pairs.

■ Wide gear-ratio rear derailleur and two front derailleurs (one for chain tensioner). Any Shimano GS rear derailleur will do. With dual down-tube levers, cables and stops, about $35. One extra rear derailleur wheel (for tensioner), $1.

■ One front and one rear wheel with steel rims, bolt-on hubs, $1\frac{1}{4}$ x 27-inch tires and tubes. $50.

■ Five-speed rear freewheel, 14-34 teeth preferred, such as made by Shimano. $11.

■ Special Schwinn stem for rear handlebar; fastens on rear seat post. Schwinn Part No. 55-755. $8.50.

■ Fork. This should come with one of the frames. If not, measure length of head tube, buy a fork about 1 inch longer and threaded same as headset threads. New forks come to fit largest frame, cost about $30. It is the practice to cut them to fit smaller frames.

■ Chainwheels and bottom-bracket sets. You can use old chainwheels, *only* if the chainwheels to be used with the chain connecting front bottom bracket to rear bottom bracket have the *same number of teeth.* If not, rotation of each crank will be at different speeds and front and rear pedals will collide after one or two revolutions.

If you use old chainwheels, you can have only a five-speed tandem—okay with a wide gear-ratio freewheel. If you buy new bottom-bracket and chainwheel sets, use the T.A. special tandem set designed for tandems. It includes bottom-bracket sets (spindles, cups and cranks) front and rear, and gives you a 10-speed tandem. The T.A. set costs about $125. You provide bearings, 11 to a side (total 44 $\frac{1}{4}$-inch bearings). If you use old chainwheels designed for a one seater, you'll have to shim out the rear set to allow for chain clearance. Conventional chain ring sets were not designed to carry two chains at once, one chain on each ring. Longer washers or spacers and fixing bolts are available from good bike stores to fit most chainwheel makes.

■ Two chains. This is the derailleur $\frac{1}{2}$ x $\frac{3}{32}$-in. chain with 122 links. Make sure the bike store has extra links to fit the same make of chain; you may need them. About $11 for both chains.

■ Two saddles and seat posts. I prefer leather saddles with steel seat posts. About $30 with posts for both saddles.

You can spend much more than indicated here if you upgrade to the finest components. I have tried to compromise between price and quality.

In listing tools you'll need to build a tandem, I want to make two assumptions. One is that you know how to disassemble, reassemble and adjust every part of a bicycle. The second assumption is that you know how to braze metal. If not, I suggest you stick to the Mapp gas outfit listed.

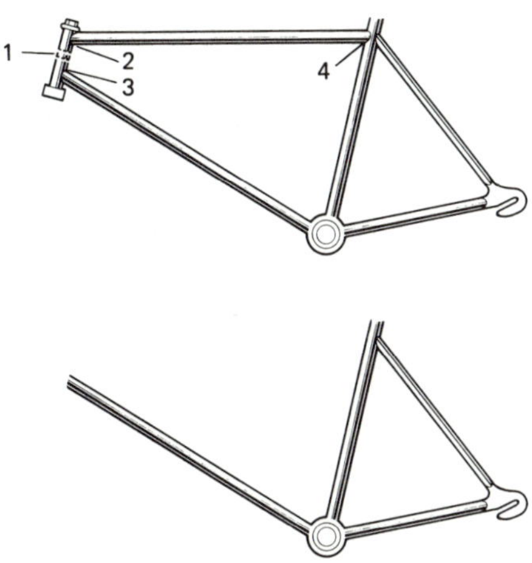

sary. Do not overheat tube, use only enough heat to melt the bronze, *not* the steel. When through, the frame should look like the bottom drawing in this step.

step three

Prepare the front frame section. Apply heat at Points 1 and 2, removing both seat stays from the seat tube first, then removing the seat stays and rear dropouts. When you're through, the frame will look like the drawing below.

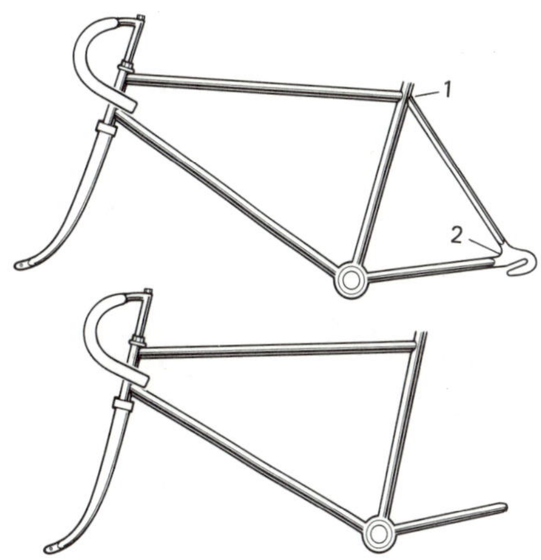

step four

On the front frame section, clean off all paint, grease and dirt from the chain stays down to the bare metal, and for about one-third the length of each stay. Clean another pair of stays from another old frame or new from Proteus (see the parts section). Clean inside of the stays to shiny metal, as well as the outside at least to 3 inches inside of the stays. Braze on these extra stays right over the old stays on the frame, at F on

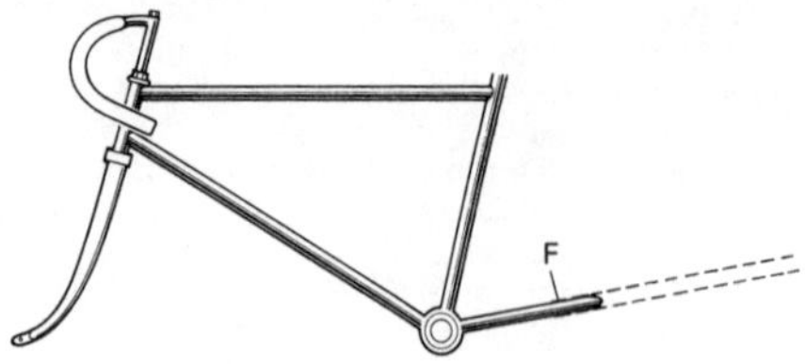

drawing, so that you will get extended-length stays.

Don't worry about the length or the spacing of the stays at this stage. The front frame will now look like it appears in the drawing below.

step five

This is an optional step to take if you wish to convert the rear frame to a shorter one. If the rear frame is a 24-inch size (measured from the top of the seat tube to the centerline of the bottom-bracket spindle) and your "stoker" gal is only 5 feet 2 inches, you should have a rear-frame size of around 18 inches for her.

To shorten the rear-frame section: Unbraze the rear-seat stays at the seat-tube lug, then cut off enough of the seat tube to shorten the frame to the size you need and braze on a new seat-post lug cluster. File off the top tube part of the lug; you won't need it. (Always clean lugs and tubes inside and out to the bare metal before brazing them.)

Fill the rear-seat stays with a fine white dry sand and cap them at the top with corks. Unbraze the rear-brake bridge. Carefully, with the torch always in motion and starting about 4 inches below the bridge, bend the stays—one at a time—until the ends come to just below the top of the seat tube. Remove the corks, dump out the sand, wrap ends of the stays around the seat tube and braze them in place. Rebraze the bridge between stays. The bridge will be at a new angle, so

you will have to use a side-pull brake and install it on the front of the bridge instead of the rear, as shown.

You could use an old section of a seat stay—miter it to fit the rear stays, drill it for the brake bolt and install it with the bolt hole parallel to the ground—but that's a lot of work. Bent and brazed stays are shown in the photo.

step six

Cut in half the three seat-post lugs noted in the parts section. Clean to bare metal inside and out. Slide one of the lugs upside down onto the rear-frame down tube. Clean ends of the down tube. Slide the other two lugs over the down tube you removed from the rear frame in Step 2. Clean all metal. Lugs should be upside down.

Place the rear frame's top tube alongside the front-frame seat tube with its other end on the rear-seat tube; check to make sure that this tube is mitered so both ends will fit snugly on both seat tubes. If not, re-miter. Now fill front frame chain stays for bending later as shown in Step 9.

step seven

Align both frames as follows:

Place each frame on a flat surface. Fork can be in the front frame to help hold it. With level on the front frame top tube, level the front frame. Align both frame bottom-bracket hangars with straightedge on both sides, so hangars are exactly in line with each other. Lightly clamp frames through (or above) the bottom-bracket hangars. (Be careful not to mangle the bb threads).

Make sure that both sets of chainstays are at the same angle with respect to work surface by scribing a mark on all four stays exactly 7 inches from the bottom-bracket hangars; measure the distance that front frame stays are from the work surface and adjust the rear frame so its chainstays are the same distance from the work surface as the front stays (see drawing). Now when wheels are on the tandem their axles will be the same distance from the ground.

Final frame alignment is done with string. Wrap string at the top of the front frame-head tube so that it parallels and passes both frame seat tubes. Wrap another string about halfway down the front-frame down tube and back to the rear-frame seat tube. Adjust frames on the work surface so that the strings either touch all tubes or are at same distance from all tubes they pass (see drawings). Recheck all other alignments (bottom brackets, headtube level and stay distance from

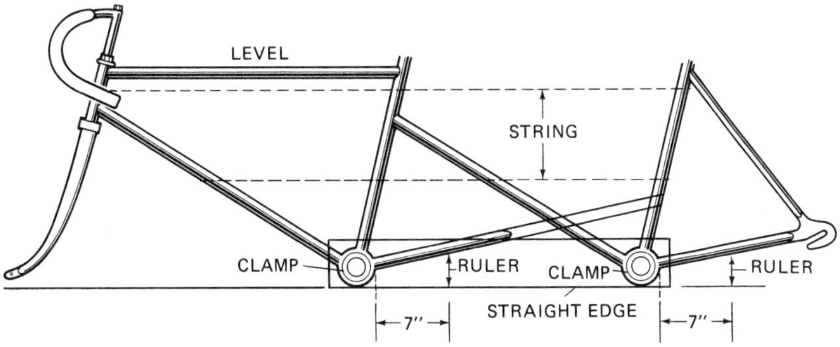

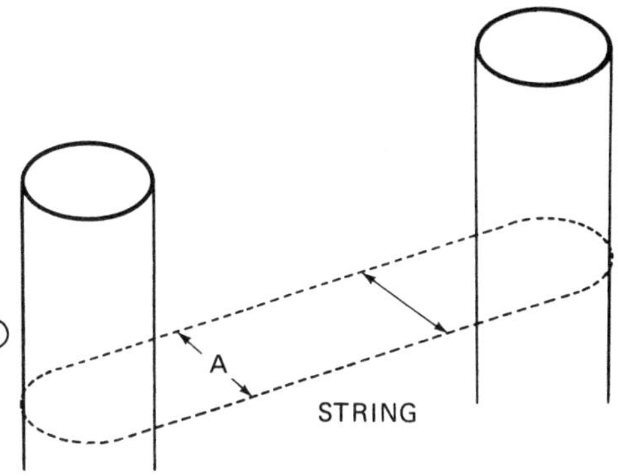

work surface), make any necessary adjustments and firmly clamp both frames to the work surface. Again, recheck all alignments.

step eight

Braze the rear-frame down tube to the front-frame seat tube (A on photo), first brazing the tube with a thin fillet, then a lug. After this and each brazing operation below, recheck alignment at all points. Place the second down tube (formerly the rear-frame top tube) in place with lugs and braze at B and C as above. Be sure that the tube miters fit opposite the tubes snugly before you braze them.

step nine

In Step six we said that the front chain stays, with brazed-on extensions, are filled with sand. Using a torch, you should carefully and slowly bend

each stay, one at a time, until it meets the rear frame bottom-down tube and the seat tube as shown at A and B in the photo. Clamp the parts at both places and braze in position, building up generous fillets at each joint as shown.

step ten

Remove all old paint and repaint.

step eleven

Assemble the parts. Step 9 photo shows a chain tensioner, made from a front derailleur and one rear derailleur wheel, installed in place of a chain guide stop on the front derailleur. When the chain is mounted, both sets of pedals must face in opposite directions. The front chain should have about ½ inch of free play. The chain tensioner can be adjusted by sliding the converted front derailleur up and down the down-tube. Lateral-chain tension is adjusted with the converted chain-tensioner adjusting screws. The drawing shows the correct chainline for both T.A. and conventional chainwheel sets. The chain line for T.A. is accurate when third rear gear is lined up between the double, rear chainwheel. Conventional chainwheel alignment is correct when rear third gear is in line with inner small chainwheel. Some chainline adjustment can be made by adding or removing thin spacing washers under the rear-wheel freewheel-side axle locknut, thus moving this gear cluster laterally. If you add or remove spacers, the rear wheel should be redished for accurate alignment. Assemble all other parts.

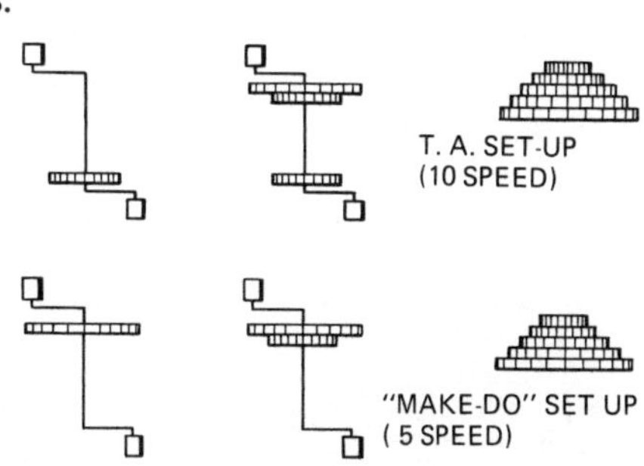

Carrier transports family bikes

By HOMER G. WOLFE

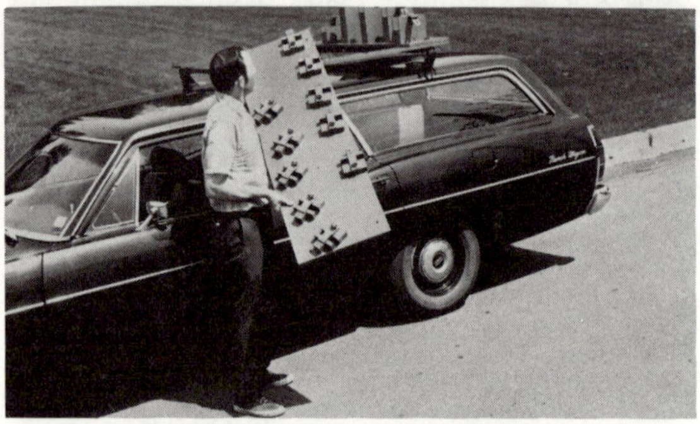

BICYCLES for two adults and three children are mounted without disassembly on the carrier. A wire passing through the eyebolts attached to the bike frames gives extra security. The unit is fastened to the luggage rack with wingnuts. It can be installed by one person and comes apart for convenient storage.

■ TRANSPORTING THE family's bicycles to a distant starting point can be a chore. It usually means either partially dismantling the bikes or fussing with a tangle of tie-down straps. With a carrier like this, you and the family will have more time for bike riding since loading and unloading can be done in no time at all.

The clamps, consisting of garage-door hasps and turnable spring-loaded eyes, hold each bike firmly by its handlebars and rear wheel. I made the plywood carrier in one weekend for about $29; it is mounted on an inexpensive removable luggage rack.

Three clamps are used to hold each bike. To locate them, place the bikes upside down on the carrier in the desired positions. The handgrip clamps are located and screwed down first. Then the height and location of each rear-wheel clamp is determined by blocking up the back fender until the bike seat is about even with the carrier platform. The distance from platform to fender minus ¾ in. gives dimension A in the drawing on the opposite page. Dimension B is calculated by measuring the distance from the outside of the bicycle fender to the inside of the wheel rim, then adding ⅜ in. allowance for compressed sponge rubber. Since all clamps are custom fitted to individual bikes, they should be fastened to the carrier with screws only—you may later replace a bike. The spacers shown in the drawing are not structural; they're designed to prevent wind noise.

SEE ALSO
Minibikes . . . Motorcycles . . . Tune-up, bicycle

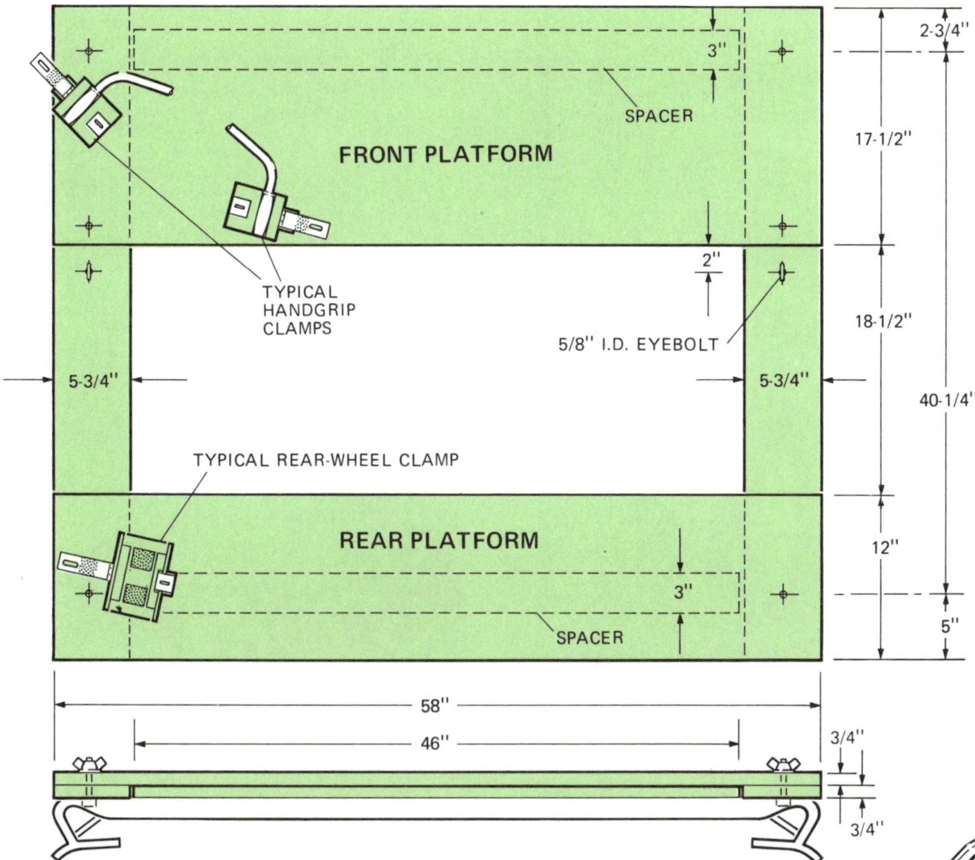

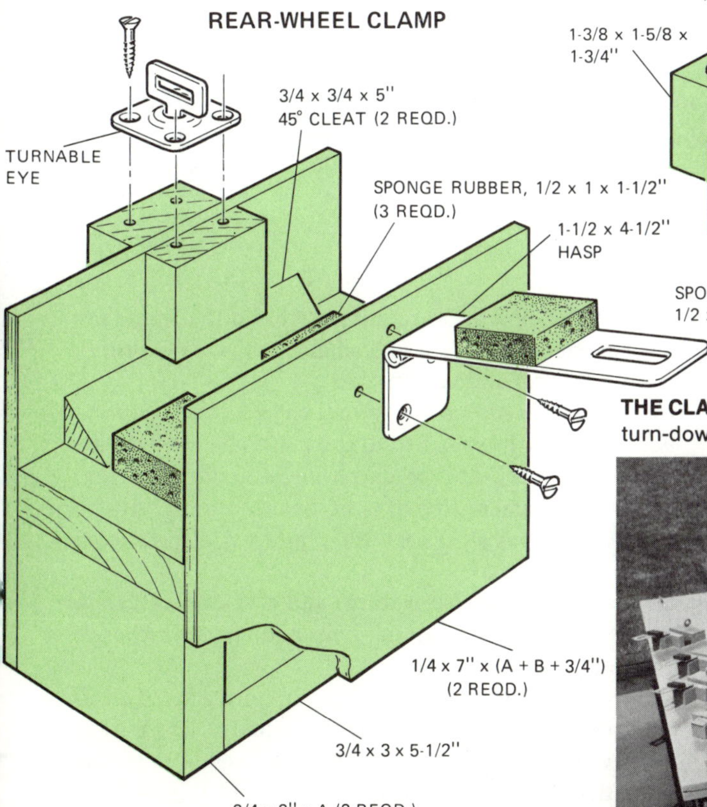

REAR-WHEEL CLAMP

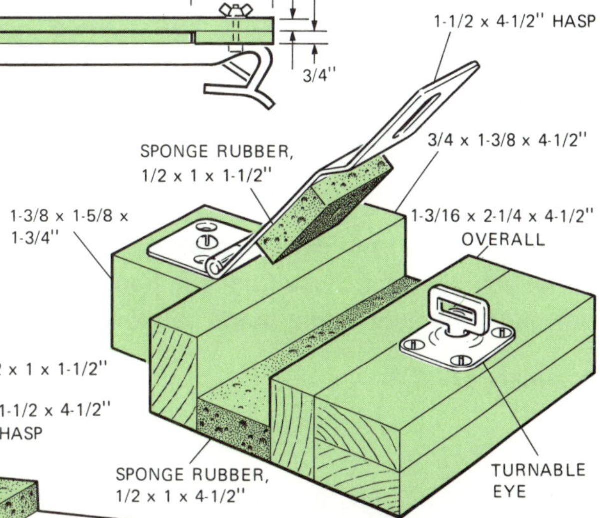

HANDGRIP CLAMP

THE CLAMP SETUP below is for flat handlebars, but the turn-down type of handlebars can also be fitted.

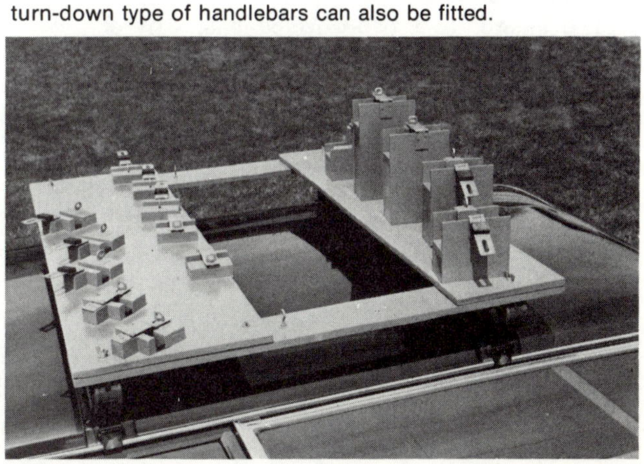

Build a cart for your bike

A bike cart made from easy to work polyvinyl chloride (PVC) plastic pipe may be just what you need for those family outings or a trip to the grocery store. This cart is tough and lightweight but is still low in cost compared to commercial units

By J.H. BRENNECKE

FAMILY CYCLING trips can be a lot of fun, but what do you do when your child outgrows tot-sized carriers and is still too young to keep up on his own bicycle?

The answer is a two-wheeled bike cart designed for toting kids 3 to 7 years of age. Commercial units are available, but cost between $140 and $200. The one shown here can be built for around $75.

To keep the construction cost low, polyvinyl chloride (PVC) plastic pipe was used to construct the cart frame. PVC is tough, lightweight, flexible, requires no finishing and is very easy to work with.

SEE ALSO
Minibikes . . . Tune-up, bicycle

The only tools required to build the frame are a hacksaw, a drill and small cans of PVC primer (cleaner) and cement.

To construct the frame, cut all of the pipe to the lengths specified in the materials list. Dry-assemble the unit to check all parts for fit before using cement to make the final assembly. Attach the canvas sling seat, hitch and wheels as shown in the plans.

You may also want to add a safety feature to your cart—a retaining belt made from leather or canvas.

This cart is designed to support almost all of the payload on its own two wheels. The tongue weight is light because the load weight is evenly distributed over the wheels. The result is free and easy pulling. But go slowly, and don't make sudden stops.

FLEXIBLE JOINT is made with tire-wall rubber. Safety cable from seat post to part C can be added.

MATERIALS LIST—BICYCLE CART

Key	No.	Size and description
A	1	1¼″-dia. × 8″ PVC
B	1	1″-dia. × 6¼″ PVC
C	1	1¼″-dia. × 13″ PVC
D	1	1¼″ × 45° PVC elbow
E	1	1¼″-dia. × 15″ PVC
F	1	1¼ × 1¼″ PVC tee
G	3	1 × 1¼″ PVC reducing bushing
H	1	1¼″-dia. × 10¾″ PVC pipe
I	1	1¼″-dia. × 3⅜″ PVC pipe
J	1	1″-dia. × 3¼″ PVC pipe
K	1	1″-dia. × 7¾″ PVC pipe
L	3	1″ × 45° PVC elbow
M	1	1″-dia. × 5″ PVC pipe
N	7	1 × 1″ PVC tee
O	6	1″-dia. × 11½″ PVC pipe
P	4	1″ × 90° PVC elbow
Q	2	1″-dia. × 10¼″ PVC pipe
Q1	2	1″-dia. × 9⅜″ PVC pipe
R	2	1″-dia. × 3⅝″ PVC pipe
S	1	1″-dia. × 2⅜″ PVC pipe
T	2	1″-dia. × 5⅞″ PVC pipe
U	2	1″ × ¾″ PVC reducing bushing
V	2	¾″ i.d. nylon bushing to fit U*
W	1	¾″-dia. × 36⅜″ aluminum rod*
X	2	cotter pin*
Y	2	eyebolt to suit seat belt
Z	2	eyebolt to hang warning sign
AA	1	½″-dia. × 2½″ bolt with wing nut
BB	1	½ × 2 × 6¼″ tire-wall rubber or belting
CC	4	5/16″-dia. × 2″ bolt, washer and nut
DD	†	⅛ × ⅝″ masonite (stiffener strips)
EE	†	½″ sheet-metal screws
FF	1	26 × 70″ canvas (sling seat)
GG	2	1⅜ × 26″-dia. wheels with ¾″ i.d. axle hubs*

Misc.: PVC primer, PVC cement.
*Available in kit for $45 postpaid (tires not included). J.H.B. Kits, 10405 Wallace St., Kansas City, Mo. 64134. † As required.

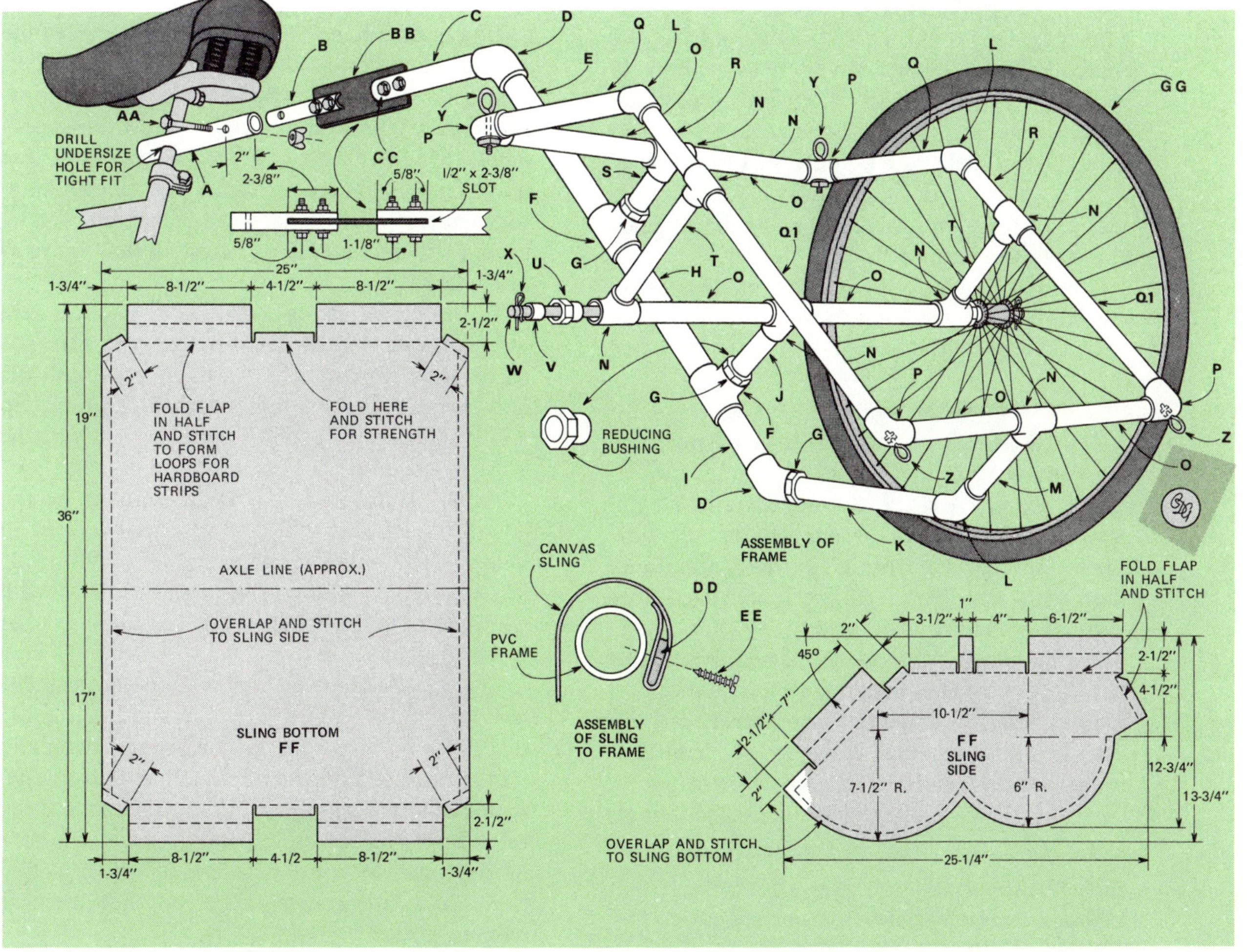

How to choose the right bike for you

Before joining the ranks of ten-speed riders, take a look at the three-speed and the coaster-brake bikes. Then if you still want a ten-speed, here are some things to look for

By DICK TERESI
Author of the *Popular Mechanics Book of Bikes and Bicycling*

YOU'VE ALREADY decided what kind of bicycle you're going to buy. You want a ten-speed, right? Most folks do.

Before you plunk down your money, consider a few things. Ten-speeds need a lot more maintenance than either three-speeds or coaster-brake bikes. The extra care a ten-speed demands is well worth the trouble if you're planning to take long trips over varied terrain. But if you're not, consider first the coaster-brake bike and the three-speed.

you're joking! A coaster-brake?

A coaster-brake bike is one that you stop by slamming the pedal backward to engage the brake. This kind of bike is very heavy (about 40 pounds), with thick tires. A coaster-brake bike has only one gear, is unresponsive, and is a pain to pedal. But don't rule it out. It's slow but indestructible transportation. Its heavy wheels rarely get out of true. And there are no brake or gear-shift cables to snap or foul up.

However, if you need a bike for day-to-day commuting and you want to ride in a little more style, I'd recommend you . . .

give the three-speed a look

Your most serious choice will be between the three-speed and ten-speed. Generally, three-speeds are heavier than ten-speeds and do not have the advancements in engineering available on ten-speeds: high-pressure tires, aluminum alloy parts, etc. However, the three-speed does have some distinct advantages:

1. Its shift mechanism is protected. It's tucked inside the rear hub where there's less chance of it getting mortally wounded or excessively dirty.

2. The three-speed is easier to use. You shift the bike by moving the selector lever to one of three gears, and the shifter is marked so you always know when you are in gear. There are no marks on a ten-speed—you shift by feel, and it's easy to miss a gear (or two).

3. Three-speeds generally have heavier wheels which, while slower, are sturdier and less likely to develop wobbles.

4. A three-speed is cheaper. Because there's such emphasis on ten-speeds today, prices of three-speeds remain at least reasonable.

SEE ALSO
Minibikes . . . Motorcycles . . . Tune-up, bicycle

finding a good ten-speed

Well, here we are at last—but where are we? You can pay anywhere from $60 to $2500 for a ten-speed.

To begin with, let's lop off both extremes of the market. Forget about those expensive models over $500—they're intended for racing. And forget about the cheapos entirely—most ten-speeds under $150 are toys for around-the-block use only. That's right. I don't think you can get a decent ten-speed for under $150. Your aim will be to find an adequate bike as close to that figure as possible.

To size up a ten-speed quickly, look at five things: frame, wheels, total weight, pressure rating of the tires, and gear ratios. These aren't the only things that count, but together they make up a key that separates the serious bikes from the toys.

Frame. A frame's size is determined by the length of the seat tube and is usually stated in inches (most bikes measure between 19 and 25 inches). Don't confuse this measurement with wheel size, which on adult bikes is always either 26 or 27 inches.

In any case don't worry about the numbers; the best way to measure a bike is to straddle the top tube with both feet flat on the ground. Don't sit on the saddle. You should have one-half to one-inch clearance between your crotch and the top tube. If you're buying a woman's-style bike with no top tube, fit yourself to a man's bike to find the right numerical size, then buy the same size woman's bike.

Try to get a frame that's made with seamless steel tubing. The heaviest, weakest, cheapest tubes are just flat steel rolled into a tube and welded. Better quality tubes are drawn through a form, so they have no seams. They're stronger, and usually lighter. A superior frame will have double-butted tubes—thicker (on the inside) at both ends than in the middle. Double-butted tubes compensate for increased stress on the ends of the tubes where the joints are formed, and for any loss of strength when the tubes are heated during manufacture. The two best-known brands of double-butted tubes are Reynolds 531 and Columbus. If a bike is built with either of these, you'll know it, because the dealer will advertise it like crazy.

Wheels. Make sure they are true (no wobbles). Spin the wheels, watching each rim as it passes a brake pad. This will show up any wobble; some are correctible, some aren't. If the dealer can't true the wheel for you, try a different bike. Wheels should also be full size—27 inches or metric equivalent.

Total weight. Weight should not be your biggest concern, as it is with many new cyclists. However, any bike much over 30 pounds should be given a hard, critical look. Most ten-speeds suitable for touring are in the 26- to 30-pound range. To get much below 26 pounds means shelling out more than $300. A few superbikes are under 20 pounds (and over $2000)!

Tire pressure. This area is often overlooked, yet it probably has the greatest effect on the pedaling ease of the bicycle. The higher the pressure a tire will hold, the rounder it is, and the faster and easier your bike will roll.

There are two kinds of tires: clincher, or regular tires, and sew-up, or tubular tires. Clincher tires have a bead that fits into the rim, like a car tire, and they hold an inner tube that is removable. Normal clinchers are rated from 55 to 75 pounds of air pressure.

Sew-ups have no bead, and their tubes are actually sewn up inside the tire. Sew-ups must be glued to special rims that have a smooth, curved surface. Sew-ups make for faster, easier pedaling because they are lighter, narrower, and they take higher pressures—100 pounds per square inch and higher. But sew-up tires and rims add a lot to the price of a bike, and they're much more fragile than clinchers—they get a lot of flats. A good compromise is the new high-pressure clincher. This tire can take up to 100 pounds of pressure, and it costs about the same as a regular tire. Try to get tires rated at 90 pounds or more, but accept 75-lb. tires if you like everything else about the bike.

Gear ratios. A ratio is properly stated in numbers, like 3:2. For bikes, most people use the term gear *values,* and these are stated in inches. The way these inch-values are reached is complex; just remember the fewer the inches, the lower the gear, and the easier it is to pedal. One popular ten-speed, for instance, offers a range from 39 to 100 inches. The 39 is for uphill, when you need easier pedaling; 100 is for downhill; the mid-range gears (70s) are for flat country. Make sure the bike has a low gear of 39, preferably lower. If necessary, the dealer can change the gears by changing the freewheel cluster on the back wheel, though it's reasonable to pay a few bucks extra for this.

other stuff to look for

After you've made sure the bike meets the criteria above, you can look at some fine points:

Derailleurs. Try to get a metal one rather than a plastic one, for durability. Lots of bikes are equipped these days with high-quality, moderately priced Japanese derailleurs.

Brakes. Consider equipping your bike with a set of high-quality side-pull brakes. Good side-pulls are more sensitive and give you better control than the center-pulls that come on most ten-speeds. Campagnolo, Shimano, Sun Tour, Universal, and Weinmann all make good side-pulls.

Saddle. Your best bet is a traditional leather saddle. It'll feel hard at first, but with neat's-foot oil and a couple hundred miles of riding, it'll break in to fit your bottom. Ideale and Brooks are the best traditional models. Nylon or plastic models, or even padded steel ones, may feel softer at first, but they never really break in, and if the padding spreads, look out!

Cranks. Average bikes have steel cranks held onto their axle by cotter pins. Better bikes have cotterless cranks—no cotter pins to get bent or fall out.

Alloy components. Average bikes have steel handlebars, stem, derailleurs, chainwheels, brakes, wheel hubs, rims and seatpost. Superior bikes have components made of lightweight aluminum alloy.

get the most for your money

So there you have it: a simple checklist to help you get the most for your money. If you shop carefully you can get just as much bike as you want at a reasonable price. The bike you end up riding should reflect your own interests and desires.

How to hit the road on a bike

Bike touring isn't just for youthful athletes and cycling fanatics—it's for everyone. There are several groups waiting to help you get started in this fun sport

By DICK TERESI

UPHILL with a full load: handlebar bag, panniers and sleeping bag. The triangular fanny bumper reflects light for safety.

THREE touring moods are shown: left, the serenity of a country road; top, the camaraderie of group cycling; and above, the misery of rain.

■ BICYCLE TOURING is beautiful, romantic and healthy. Cycling gives you a sense of freedom and adventure that car travel cannot. It lets you see the countryside up close, lets you explore back roads and places you would not visit otherwise. On a bike colorfully packed with gear you draw friendly attention, so you tend to meet people as you travel. And you develop a closeness to those with whom you're cycling.

Bike touring is perfect for a vacation or even just a weekend. In fact, you've probably already considered its possibilities. So why haven't you tried it? Here's why:

■ You don't think your body can handle it.

■ Bike touring is for kids, and you're not a kid.

■ Bike touring means camping. And you're very fond of hotels. In fact, you developed a psychotic fear of tents in the Army.

■ You also fear the unknowns of

BACKGROUND: a cyclist climbs a long hill in Montana's Glacier National Park. Clockwise from above: helmeted rider takes a swim; woman enjoys a scenic rest stop; cyclists ride ferry for reduced rates; and the time-honored task of map reading.

TANDEM RIDING makes efficient use of pedaling power, but requires great coordination of both riders. Not for beginners.

cycling: how to find your way over country roads, where to eat, where to find shelter.

■ Finally, you're not a nut. And cyclists are nuts. They wear funny striped shirts, silly little hats; they sit on hard, skinny seats and like it!

Frankly, these are all pretty good reasons. Or rather, they used to be. Because bicycle touring is changing fast. A recreational activity that was once the domain of athletic teenagers and a few fearless, fanatic adults, bike touring is now opening up to the rest of us.

Organizations have sprung up over the past few years that have taken many of the fears out of cycling. There are organized tours—many tailored to adults—that cover as little as 10 to 20 miles per day. Some arrange for overnight stays in hotels, inns or other shelters so camping isn't necessary. "Sag wagons" are becoming more popular. These are vans or station wagons that carry all personal gear so bikers need not weigh down their bicycles with heavy packs. Sag wagons can also give a lift to sagging cyclists who need a break, and carry spare parts and tools for on-the-road repairs. And new cycling maps—with details you absolutely need but cannot find on regular highway maps—are now available.

"A novice's main worry," says John Freidin, director of Vermont Bicycle Touring (VBT), "is whether he can physically make it, whether he can keep up." This fear, in most cases, is unjustified. Freidin, whose organization led 2200 cyclists through rural Vermont in a single year, es-

UPGRADE YOUR BIKE . . . AND GO TOURING

HERE'S THE LATEST in bicycle equipment. Most items may be purchased separately at sporting goods or specialty bike shops as replacement parts to upgrade your present bike.

Teflon-coated brake cables. Regular brake cables get very sticky with age and are hard to lubricate. But permanently lubed Teflon-coated cables slide back and forth inside a plastic-lined housing cutting friction by a claimed 40 percent—meaning smoother, faster, safer braking. There are two brands: Elephant and Ultra-Glide.

Comfortable saddle. Saddle sores have driven many tender souls away

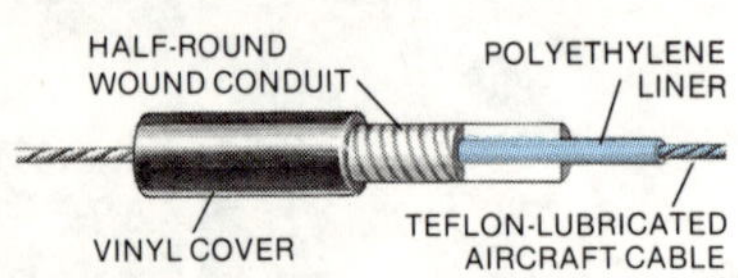

TEFLON-COATED brake cables are permanently lubricated; reduced friction means much less effort.

from cycling. If this is your problem, bicycle experts recommend the new Avocet touring saddle. Its special contour gives pelvic bones extra support while minimizing contact between soft parts of the crotch and the saddle. There's also a wide-profile woman's saddle.

Easy shifting, Part 1. Many novices can't get used to the way you shift a 10-speed: you must always be pedaling as you change gears. Shimano has introduced a system called the FF (front freewheeling) that let's you shift while coasting . . . or even backpedaling! The system is somewhat complicated because it has an extra freewheel up front in the chainwheel, making it very difficult to add to your present bike. But many brands now offer the FF as standard.

Easy shifting, Part 2. Shimano also makes the Positron, a derailleur that has definite click-stop positions on its lever for each gear, like a car. A conventional derailleur has no definite positions (you must move the lever until you feel the

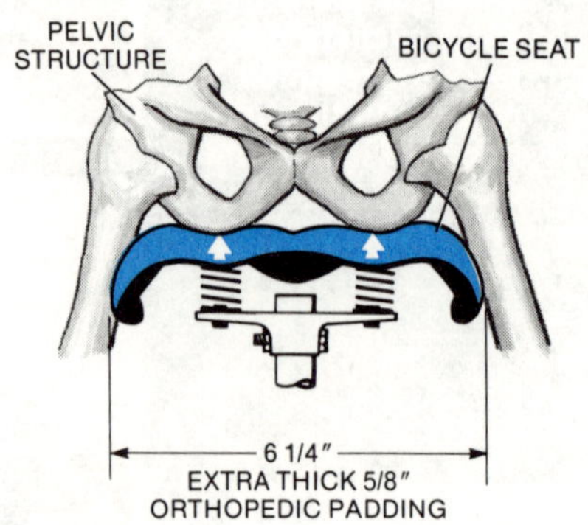

AVOCET touring saddle is designed to provide critical support points for human pelvic structure.

chain fall on the right gear—often difficult for the beginner). The Positron may also be shifted more than one gear at a time or even while the bike is stopped. It's often combined with the FF system (above) as standard equipment or may be purchased separately.

High-pressure tires. The higher a tire's air pressure, the harder it will be and the faster it will roll. Standard tires may be inflated to 70 pounds per square inch. But now there are tires that will hold 90, 95, even 100 pounds. They are also lower in profile so less rubber meets the road. Many brands available.

Antipuncture treatments. The biggest repair problem is still the flat tire. While nothing will make a tire puncture-*proof*, there are many sealants that will improve a tire tube's puncture *resistance*. Most work on a similar principle: a fluid—often containing fibers, minerals and sometimes a vulcanizer—is injected through the valve into the tube. When a sharp object punctures the tire, the fluid seals the wound and prevents a flat. Does it always work? No, experts say, but sometimes it's better than nothing. However, a tube so treated is sometimes hard to patch.

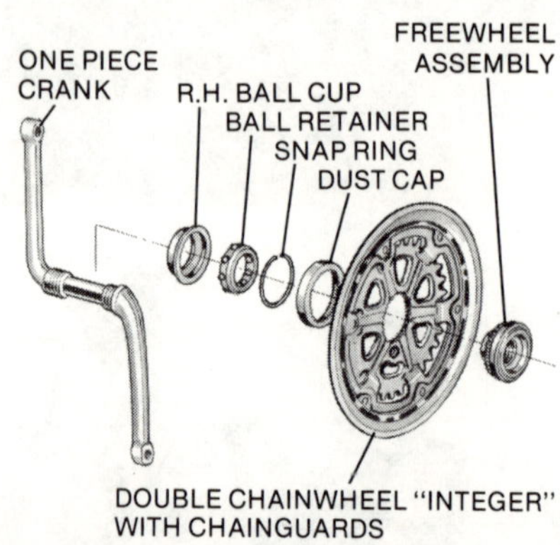

SHIMANO front chainwheel "freewheeling" allows shifting free of pedal movement—even on hill climb.

Small panniers. In 1970, Hartley Alley, a veteran cycle tourist, designed TC panniers, the first really modern bike bags—waterproof, easy to attach, lots of outer pockets, with mating zippers that could be joined together into a sin-

timates that 98 percent of his riders completed the route they had chosen. Freidin's customers are not kids, either. The bulk of them are between 25 and 45 years old, many making their first bike trip.

The secret, if you're a beginner, is to plan an undemanding route. VBT offers 115 supervised trips of varying difficulty. There are weekend, three-day, five-day and week-long tours. No camping is necessary. Cyclists stay overnight at country inns. Sag wagons are provided on all tours of three days or longer.

Bikecentennial, perhaps the most publicized touring organization in the country, is also reaching out to beginners. In 1976, Bikecentennial pioneered the TransAmerica Bicycle Trail—a 4250-mile route of mostly scenic, low-traffic roads stretching from Oregon to Virginia. Though Bikecentennial made its reputation leading some 3000 cyclists over this 90-day cross-country trail, it's now offering seven shorter routes in various parts of the United States. Three of these supervised trips take eight days or less. Some require camping, but others book cyclists into hotels.

For many bicyclists touring means independence—*not* having to stick with an organized group. There's also good news for these individuals.

Bikecentennial sells special, ultra-detailed maps so you can plan your own trip anywhere along its 4250-mile trail. There are also maps

gle piece of airline carry-on luggage. But they're basically for the long-distance cyclist and cost $55. Now Alley's come up with smaller panniers, using the same design, for the front of the bike. However, they can just as easily be used on the rear for short hauls. For a catalog, write The Touring Cyclist Shop, Box 4009, Boulder, CO 80306.

Fanny Pads. Alley also makes Fanny Pads: four-inch square adhesive, felt pads. Saddle sores? Just pop one on where it hurts.

HANDLEBAR BAGS provide a place for things you need quickly. However, too much weight affects steering. Mount bag behind seat with accessory called Seat Post Thing as shown below.

SPT. That stands for Seat Post Thing. It's made by Eclipse and it's a clamp that attaches to your seatpost and lets you suspend a handlebar or other type of bag behind your saddle. Normally, bags that hang behind the seat tend to dangle annoyingly. But SPT is rigid. Available at bike stores.

SMALL panniers can be used on front or rear of bike. They are ideal for shorter trips.

AMONG new gear that makes bike touring a breeze are items like FasTent. It weighs 4 lbs., has spring supports.

Instant tent. Take the four-pound FasTent out of its stuff sack, throw it on the ground and it immediately springs open. An internal steel coil unfolds as the tent is pulled taut and staked at the corners. Available at camping outlets.

Slick touring derailleur. The touring cyclist has always had to settle for second best when it comes to derailleurs because good racing derailleurs handle only higher gears. Touring derailleurs that will shift into lower gears (they need to be longer to do this) are generally not as well made. But recently Sun Tour introduced the Cyclone GT, a touring derailleur patterned after the same design and made of the same alloy as its Cyclone racing derailleur. We tested the Cyclone GT over mountains, through prairies, in rain and in snow. It shifted smoothly at all times with little need of adjustment.

ECLIPSE rain cape has elastic loops to keep it snugged down front and back.

available for other areas: in Oregon, Montana, Kentucky and Virginia. The maps give directions from a cyclist's point of view and feature very detailed drawings of difficult intersections or other problem areas. Camping sites and grocery stores are well marked. Accompanying guide books point out historical landmarks, prevailing weather and wind conditions and warn of special problems, such as a scarcity of campgrounds, grocery stores or water.

Bikecentennial also serves as a clearing house of information for its members. Members can find out about touring services (bike trip organizers, bike trails, public cycling programs) in their part of the country by writing Bikecentennial (address on page 312).

Vermont Bicycle Touring will also plan individualized trips for people, supplying customized maps and booking cyclists into hotels.

No discussion on cycle touring is complete without mentioning the International Bicycle Touring Society. The IBTS, founded in 1964 by California surgeon Clifford Graves, is for adults only (21 and older). The society runs 21 different tours in the United States and Europe, and is unusual in that all organizational duties are done on a volunteer basis—there are no paid leaders.

Though the society warns its members they must be prepared to ride 50 miles a day, it believes cycling should be done with style. Club members are often professional people—doctors, lawyers, businessmen—and generally do not favor staying in cut-rate hotels or eating in fast-food joints. As an example, one of their famous trips of the past was labeled the "Truffle Tour of France" and included much wine tasting and extravagant dining.

Okay, we've covered just a few of the organizations that are making the world a better place for bicyclists. Now here are some tips to help get you started on your own bike tour. It's really quite simple.

The standard touring bicycle today is the 10-speed. But if all you have is an old three-speed, why not give it a try for a two-day trip and see how it holds up? You'll have at least one built-in advantage. Three-speeds invariably come with fenders; few 10-speeds do. Fenders are great in the rain. You can always spot fenderless cyclists by the muddy stripe up their backs caused by a rear wheel throwing up road water.

If you're going to buy a 10-speed, be prepared to spend at least $135 to $150 to get one that's tour-worthy. And be sure to ask your bike dealer what the "gear value" of the lowest gear is. He'll cite you a figure in *inches.* The lower the figure, the lower the gear and the easier it will be to pedal your bike up hills. A rule of thumb is to get

AN OLYMPIAN'S RULES FOR SAFE CYCLING

OLIVER MARTIN JR., road-racing coach of the U.S. Olympic cycling team.

OLIVER MARTIN JR. is the national road coach of our U.S. bicycle racing team. In the summer of 1976 he took his team to the Olympic Games where it placed higher than any other modern American team.

When it comes to bike racing, Oliver Martin knows about winning. But there's one other thing he also knows well—*falling.* In 13 years of racing, Martin estimates he has had major crashes at least seven or eight times—and more spills while training than he can remember.

Accidents are inevitable for the racer because of the high speeds and wild competition. But the bike tourist need rarely fall, especially if he follows Martin's advice. Here's what he had to say about eight important bike safety topics:

■ **Paying attention.** "The biggest problem is lack of attention," says Martin. "Anything can happen on a bike. You can hit a rock, a dog can run out, another rider can bump into you . . . and you have to maintain control at all times."

■ **Speed.** The faster you go, the more care you must take, says Martin, who also points out that many new riders don't see their bikes as vehicles capable of real speed and therefore real danger. A cyclist going down a steep hill can approach 50 mph. But Martin also tells cyclists to be careful at any speed. Recently Coach Martin saw a racer fall while slowly circling a track. He was going only about three mph, yet he broke his jaw in five places.

■ **Brakes.** Marin tests his brakes at the start of every ride. He hits both brakes at low speed to make sure they're adjusted well enough to skid the tires. (Brakes can be adjusted by pulling the cable more taut to bring the brake pads closer to the rims, or by replacing the pads them-

a bike with a low gear under 40 inches. Thirty-five or lower is even better for the beginner.

Ask the dealer if he can slap on a pair of cheap fenders—unless you plan to tour only in arid regions. And get a carrying rack for the rear of the bike. You'll need this for your . . .

■ **Rear pannier bags.** These are the two bags which will hold most of your gear. They attach to each side of your rear carrying rack. Panniers come in a variety of sizes and styles and cost from $25 to $60. Check for three things: The bags should be made of waterproof nylon, have outside pockets for small items and attach and detach from the bike easily.

■ **Handlebar bags** must pass the same tests as pannier bags. Handlebar bags are for carrying items you want to get at fast while riding: food, wallet, camera and film, a sweater. For this reason, be sure the bag opens *away* from you. A handy feature is a transparent plastic map holder on the top of the bag so you can read as you ride. Handlebar bags cost from $10 to $25.

There are also bike bags that hang behind the saddle and *front* panniers that attach to a rack installed over the front wheel, but these are clumsy for most people.

If you buy the cheapest acceptable tour-worthy 10-speed (about $135), rack ($7), panniers ($25) and handlebar bag ($10), you'll have an initial investment of $177. You can squeak by for that, but a total of $200 to $250 would be more realistic, at the time this was written. If you plan to start out with a sag-wagon tour, you could skip the panniers and just buy a handlebar bag, throwing the rest of your gear into a bag to be carried by the wagon.

For those who have never camped, it's sometimes wise to make that first bike trip a *non*camping one with nights spent at hotels or inns. But if you do camp, of course, you'll need a tent and sleeping bag. The ones made for backpackers are ideal. Backpackers and cyclists have at least one common need—lightweight equipment. As a rule, the lighter the tent or sleeping bag, the higher the cost (same as for the bicycle itself). Two-man tents weigh in these days at three to eight pounds; sleeping bags weigh about half as much. When two people travel together it usually works out fairly if one carries the tent and the other both sleeping bags.

You'll probably want two accessories for your sleeping bag: a foam sleeping pad (or air mattress) and a waterproof stuff sack. This latter item is controversial because many experts say a waterproof sack doesn't let the bag breathe and it then gets clammy inside. On the other hand, a sleeping bag becomes awfully soggy when it gets rained on. An alternative is to keep the bag in a

selves if they are worn.) He also wipes the brake pads and rims clean with a cloth so no slippage occurs.

■ **Going down a hill.** Steep hills or mountains can be especially scary to the beginner—especially if you've got 30 pounds of gear in your bike bags. The first thing you should do is give your brakes a quick squeeze before making your descent to be sure they're working. After that, Martin says the most important thing is to *stay away from the side of the road!* True, most bike safety manuals tell you to hug the right side of the road in most instances. But throw this rule out the window when it comes to hills. By staying toward the middle you can swerve either way and are less likely to hit rocks, gravel or other road garbage.

What about traffic coming up behind you? "Don't worry about it," says Coach Martin. Your main concern should be controlling the bike. Besides, you may be outrunning any other vehicles.

■ **Blow-out or flat tire on a hill.** If your *front* tire goes flat you've essentially lost your steering. Martin advises riders to pump the rear brake (never the front) and to bring the bike to a stop while keeping it in as straight a line as possible. Remember, he says, that the tire is flat so you have no gripping rubber on the sides. If you try to turn you'll fall. If the flat is in the *rear* you're in better shape because you can still steer. Martin warns, however, that the rear wheel will lose traction and can start sliding, so he advises moving forward slightly on the bike. And use the front brake only.

■ **When you really have to stop.** In an emergency, hit both brakes hard simultaneously. And if things are really desperate, you'll stop faster if you purposely flop yourself and your bike on the road. Martin recalls racing with the Army team in California back in 1968. They were coming down a steep descent toward Malibu Beach when one rider's rear tire blew out as he approached a sweeping left turn. The racer flopped to keep himself from going off the road. "He left some epidermis on the pavement," says Martin, "but he survived." When Martin and the others looked over the shoulder of the road they discovered an 800-ft. drop—with a wrecked car at the bottom in which several teen-agers had been killed the previous weekend.

■ **And if you do fall.** The biggest mistake a cyclist can make, according to Coach Martin, is to keep his hands on the handlebars. "When you realize you're going to fall, let go of the bars and try to come down on your forearm and then roll." If you freeze on the handlebars, you're likely to come right down on your shoulder, and possibly break your collarbone.

■ **Helmets.** You don't see many racers in hard helmets, but Martin recommends them for the tourist. While too cumbersome to race in, they can save your skull.

conventional breathable stuff sack and slip it inside a plastic garbage bag at the first sign of rain.

And if it rains . . .

. . . you get wet. One way or the other. There is no perfect rain outfit. Those that seal off every part of your body do keep out the rain, but also retain perspiration, so you end up wet anyway. The best advice: Get out of the rain; find shelter. But often you can't, so you can try one of two get-ups, both of them compromises:

■ **A hooded poncho,** or rain cape, protects your torso and part of your head. If you don't like wet legs you can combine a poncho with rain chaps. A poncho solves the sweat problem. It's roomy and lets air circulate, but the wind can swirl it up around you (the funhouse effect) and the rain can splash up underneath.

■ **A rain suit** comes with separate pants, jacket and hat. It keeps you dryer than a poncho, but allows your legs less freedom and, because it encloses you totally, is much hotter (the steam bath effect).

Do you need a striped shirt?

No. You don't need any of those special and expensive clothes that bike racers must wear and fanatic tourists like to affect: wool shorts padded with chamois, tight jerseys with bright stripes, hats with pushed up brims, or those racing shoes with metal cleats that are impossible to walk in. Any comfortable clothes are fine. Sneakers with semihard soles seem to work for most people—as do regular leather shoes.

The first thing to prepare for a trip is your body. Of course, if you've been physically inactive for a few years, it's wise to check with your doctor before setting off. But taken easily, cycling is a great exercise for the heart, lungs and circulatory system. In fact, it's one of the exercises recommended by the American Heart Assn. for maintaining a healthy heart. The AHA even recommends it for patients recuperating from a heart attack, provided they are under the supervision of a physician who prescribes the level of activity.

The more cycling you do before a trip, the more you will enjoy it when you go. And people planning to pedal 50 miles a day had better work up to it gradually. But frankly, it doesn't take a superior physical specimen to do it. A month or two of weekend cycling should be enough. And if you're an avid jogger or swimmer, perhaps even less. As for 10- to 15-mile-per-day trips, you can probably jump right in with practically no preparation.

Age is rarely a problem. Bikecentennial has had riders up to 86 years old. A 67-year-old man finished its entire 4250-mile Trans-America Trail (as did two 9-year-olds).

loading bags and bike

We haven't mentioned *all* the things you should pack for a bike trip, but such lists are readily supplied by touring organizations.

As for packing stuff in your panniers, just let common sense prevail. Put items you need often at the top of your panniers or in their outer pockets. Since it's easy to forget what's where, you might take the time to make two lists: items in the left pannier and those in the right. Put each list in the top of the main compartment of each pannier. Another precaution is to line the main compartments with plastic garbage bags. "Waterproof" nylon sometimes surrenders to the rain. And, of course, get equal weight in the two panniers—this is easier than riding a bike that lists to one side.

Don't put too much weight in your handlebar bag. It seriously affects the steering.

take a shakedown cruise

Take a short, trial ride with the bike *fully loaded* before setting off on any trip. This is really essential. You'll be amazed at how many problems—albeit minor—you'll find and correct. For instance, you may discover that the heels of your shoes bump your panniers when you pedal. You can fix this by adjusting the panniers, changing shoes, or maybe even getting a longer rack. Problems like this are easily solved at home—but can ruin an entire vacation if you wait until you're on the road.

But don't let these things keep you from cycling. Lots of people will help you. Here are some of them:

Bikecentennial, Box 8308, Missoula, MT 59807.

International Bicycle Touring Society, 846 Prospect St., La Jolla, CA 92037. Trip information supplied to members only. Minimum age, 21.

Vermont Bicycle Touring, R.D. 2-H, Bristol, VT 05443.

American Youth Hostels, Inc., National Campus, Delaplane, VA 22025. Sponsors many trips in the United States and abroad. Geared mostly towards younger riders, it's a good information source. Check your phone book for a local chapter before writing the national headquarters.

Keeping your bike running is a simple matter—if you have the tools and follow a few easy procedures

By DICK TERESI

Author of the *Popular Mechanics Book of Bikes and Bicycling*

Basic bike repairs you can make yourself

THE WISEST APPROACH to bicycle repairs is not to do any. Or as few as possible. You avoid repairs by keeping your bike from breaking. Four common maintenance problems are

- Flat tires
- Rough running rotating parts
- Gear shifters that don't shift
- Brakes that break

Don't let these things happen and you won't have to worry about repairs. The first two problems are common to all bikes; the last two refer to multi-gear bikes rather than coaster-brake one-speeds and other less expensive bikes. Here's how to avoid the worst of these problems.

Flat tires. Inflate your tires to the proper pressure. If you have standard clincher tires, the maximum pressure is almost always stamped on the sidewalls (usually between 55 and 90 pounds). If you have expensive tubular (sew-up) tires, see your manufacturer's specifications for recommended pressure (usually between 90 and 115 pounds). You can safely pump your tires up to the maximum unless it's over 80 degrees out, in which case you might want to back off about five pounds (to allow for heat expansion).

If you're caught without a gauge and have to guess, I would lean toward overinflating rather than underinflating. Underinflated tires cannot take bumps, rocks, and other road shocks. Not only can these damage the tube and cause a blowout or leak, they can bruise the tire and even inflict a flat spot on the rim.

Another tip: Your biggest danger is a puncture—caused by glass or other sharp objects. However, most of these threats don't puncture your tires immediately, but work their way into your tire as you ride. Therefore, brush those treads off from time to time.

Rough running. This is a problem that sneaks up on you gradually and erodes the pleasure of cycling. What happens is that moving parts get gummed up, either because they get clogged with dirt, or because their lubrication dries out, or both. This results in a slower and rougher running bike. The parts you should be most concerned with are those that bear a load—the chain and the parts with bearings: wheel hubs, bottom bracket (the assembly of spindle and bearings that your cranks revolve on), headset (the bearing assembly that holds your fork in the head tube), and the pedals.

SEE ALSO

Minibikes . . . Tune-up, bicycle

AFTER EVERY day's ride, wipe the dirt off the chain. Don't worry about wiping off the lubricant, too. Lubricant on the outside isn't doing any good anyway.

OIL THE CHAIN every month or two or whenever the chain is dry enough to make a rasping sound. One drop of any light oil on each roller should be plenty.

When any of these bearing assemblies gets really dried out or gunked up, you have to overhaul it, a procedure that involves taking everything apart and repacking the bearings in grease or oil. And if your chain gets ridiculously dirty, you'll have to disconnect it from the bike, soak it in kerosene, lubricate and then re-install.

To avoid these hassles, keep everything clean and then lubricate. I make it a practice to wipe off my chain with a rag after every day's ride. You can wipe as hard as you want to get rid of dirt. A lot of people worry that they're also wiping off lubricant. While this is true, don't worry about it. Lubricant on the outside of the chain is just collecting dirt. The only lubricant doing any good is inside on the rivets, plates and rollers. The same goes for other parts of the bike. Clean out that dirt from hubs, bottom bracket, etc.

Then lubricate sparingly. A couple drops of light bicycle oil will do for each part. Then wipe dry again. If your chain seems really dry, you might want to try one of the new chain spray lubricants available in most bike shops, but regular old oil will work fine here, too. How often you should oil depends on how much you ride, whether you ride in the rain a lot, etc. But for most folks, once every couple of months should do it. Do not overlubricate. If everything seems smooth, leave it alone. Extra oil simply attracts more dirt and defeats your purpose. (See drawing for lubrication points.)

Gear shifter problems. You three-speeders can laugh at this one—three-speed internal-hub shifters are relatively problem-free. But you derailleur ten-speeders are going to have trouble. To avoid it, first remember to treat your derailleur right. Only shift while pedaling and never back-pedal while shifting. Try to shift down *before* you reach that killer hill to avoid jamming the chain into low gear and straining the derailleur cage. Use common sense. Don't drop your bike on its right side, the derailleur side.

Brakes. This is one area of the bike that you cannot forever avoid making repairs on, not because brakes have a habit of out and out dysfunctioning, but because they inevitably lose efficiency due to wear—brake pads get worn and cables stretch. However, cables sometimes get sticky, impeding smooth braking action, and *this* problem can be avoided. Periodically squirt a couple drops of oil into the ends of the cable housing and then pump your brakes to work the lubrication through the housing.

what if all this fails?

Fix the poor beast. For the repairs described here you'll need a few simple tools:

- Crescent wrench (adjustable). Get a good one—this is your workhorse.
- Screwdrivers. Get one with a ¼-inch blade and a Phillips.
- Tire irons.
- Pliers. Both regular and needle-nose.

Depending on how much more of the work you want to do yourself, you can also get some of these optional tools:

- Spoke wrench. But talk to a mechanic *before* you use it—you might save your wheels.
- Chain tool. For removing links so the chain can be taken off the bike.
- Allen key wrenches.
- Cone wrench. Flat wrench to fit where normal wrenches won't.
- Any other wrenches to fit particular parts of your bike (like crank bolts or seat bolts).
- Patch kit. They're not the same for clinchers and sew-ups, so be sure to get the right kind.
- Vise-lock pliers.

ARROWS SHOW POINTS requiring lubrication. Use a light oil and don't over-oil!

Okay, let's get to work on those common bicycle repairs.

patching those flat tire blues

Every cyclist experiences that depressing sound "psssssst" or, worse yet, "BLAM!" that means a tire is going flat or blowing. There are two types of tires: clinchers, which have tubes, and sew-ups, which do not. We leave you richer sew-up owners to your own devices. Sew-ups are awful to patch; get yourself the special patch kit needed and follow the hard-to-understand instructions in it. We're devoting ourselves here to the more common clincher tire.

But, before you get to the tire itself, you must take the wheel off the bike. So let's discuss that first. (There is one kind of flat that doesn't require you to remove the wheel. See number 1 under "finding the culprit" for more information.)

Rear wheel removal (derailleur bikes). This really scares most people. They look at the chain, the shifter and all those sprockets back there and they figure there's no way to get that wheel out of there . . . and back in. Well, it's not that big a deal.

The biggest favor you can do yourself is to get the bike off the ground. This is more important than in front wheel removal. Suspend it from the roof, a rack, anything. Don't turn it upside down, as this can hurt your brake cables.

Off the ground? Okay, release your brakes if you have the quick-release kind. Now you have to get the chain on the smallest rear sprocket (the outermost gear). Spin the cranks and push the right shift lever all the way up. The chain should now be on the small rear sprocket.

Now pull out your quick-release lever or loosen your nuts or wingnuts just like you would with the front wheel. The wheel is now technically loose. But it ain't goin' nowhere, is it? To free it, stand behind the bike and pull the cage of the derailleur (the part with the little wheels in it) backwards. Don't worry, you won't hurt it—the derailleur is spring-loaded. With the derailleur pulled back, push the wheel down and forward with your other hand. This will get the wheel past the shifter and you can disentangle the chain from the small sprocket by hand.

Rear wheel removal (three-speeds). Shift the bike into high gear and get if off the ground. Now take a look at the assembly leading away from the right axle nut of your three-speed hub shifter. Sticking directly out from the axle nut you'll find the barrel-shaped part. Running from the barrel toward the front of the bike you'll find a chain which leads into a sleeve. Connecting the chain and sleeve is a locknut. Loosen this locknut. Now remove the sleeve from the chain by turning the sleeve counterclockwise.

Now you can loosen the barrel and then your two axle nuts. Pull the wheel from the drop-outs, free the chain from the sprocket and your wheel is loose.

Rear-wheel removal (coaster-brake bikes). First, disconnect the coaster-brake bracket from the frame. The bracket is held to the chain stay by a clamp held by a bolt and nut. Remove the clamp. Turn the bike upside down (no brake cables to worry about). Remove axle nuts and washers. Free the wheel from the frame and chain.

finding the culprit

Now, you're ready to look for what it was that made your tire go flat:

1. Check the valve stem first. Pump up the tire and put some saliva on the valve end. See bubbles? You have a loose stem. You'll have to buy a metal valve cap, which has two prongs on top. Stick the prongs into the valve and rotate the cap until you catch hold of the stem. Now tighten the stem.

2. No bubbles in your saliva? Then the valve is okay, and, congratulations, you have a *bona fide* flat. Remove the wheel as described above. Quickly check the outside of the tire for tacks, nails and other obvious intruders. If you find one, pry it out and mark the spot with chalk or something. If you can't find the problem right away, don't labor over it; go on to the next step.

3. Make sure the tire is totally deflated. Pry one side of the tire off the rim with your tire irons. Get just one bead with the iron. If you get both, you'll squeeze the tube in between. Pry the iron down and hook the handle on a spoke. With a second iron, pry out more of the bead two inches away from the first. The bead will now probably stay out of the rim, but if it wants to snap back, make a third pry with your final iron. Now run your finger around the inside to loosen the bead all the way around. Don't take the tire all the way off. Leave the other bead seated in the rim.

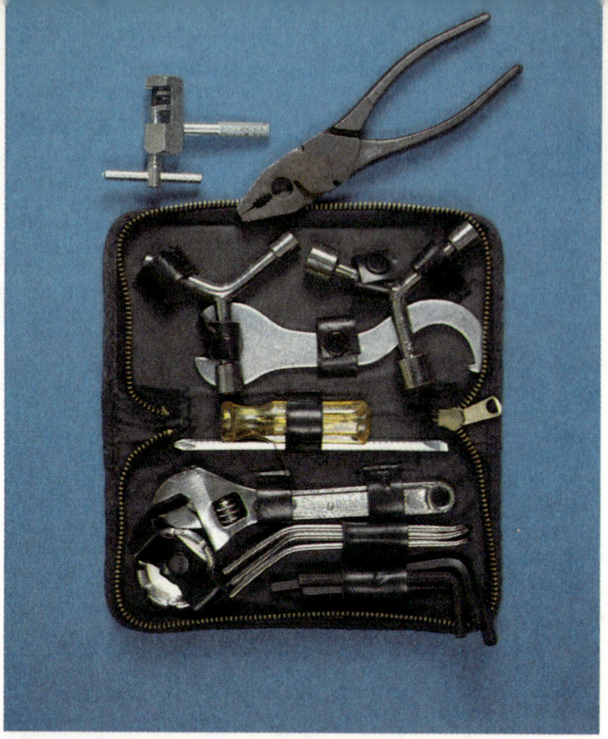

HERE ARE the tools you need to make simple repairs yourself, including all the necessary wrenches. This kit is available commercially, but you can make up your own with tools you already have.

4. Pull the tube out of the tire, starting at a point on the other side of the wheel from the valve. But don't pull the valve out yet. Pump the tire up, overinflating it by about 50 percent. This will help you find the leak if you haven't spotted it yet. Can't pump it up? Either your pump's broken or your puncture is so gigantic you must replace the tube. If you can pump it up, feel around the tube to find the point where air is escaping. If I can't find the leak by hand, I remove the tube completely and dump it in some water to look for telltale bubbles.

Now if you didn't have to remove the tube completely to find the leak, mark it. Then place the tube next to the tire. You haven't pulled the valve out yet, right? Then the tube will line up with the tire just the way it was when you got your flat. This will help you find the culprit. Look for glass, tacks or thorns on the tread, a sharp burr on the rim or a spoke sticking through the rim strip. Remove the glass, file down the spoke or whatever.

5. Now you can take the tube out of the tire completely (deflate it first). You have to do that so you can apply the patch. Run down to your local bike store and buy yourself a patch kit. Make sure you get the kind for clincher tire tubes. Apply the patch following directions on the kit: usually these will say to clean the puncture area and rough up the surface; spread

on some of the kit glue and let it dry; take the backing off a patch, making sure you don't touch the sticky side; and then press the patch on as hard as you can.

6. Okay, put the tube back in the tire. It helps to inflate it slightly sometimes. Poke the valve in its hole and stuff the tube around inside the tire with your hands. Got it neatly in the tire? Okay, put the tire bead back into the rim. Work in both directions at once with your hands. The last couple of inches might be tough, but try to do it with just your hands instead of a tire iron if you can (an iron could pinch the tube). One trick is to push the bead on the opposite side of the wheel more deeply into the rim by pushing the wheel into the ground. While doing this, pull that troublesome couple of inches of bead on top up and into the rim with your hands.

7. Make sure the valve is straight and that the bead is securely in the rim. Inflate the tire. All done? Not quite.

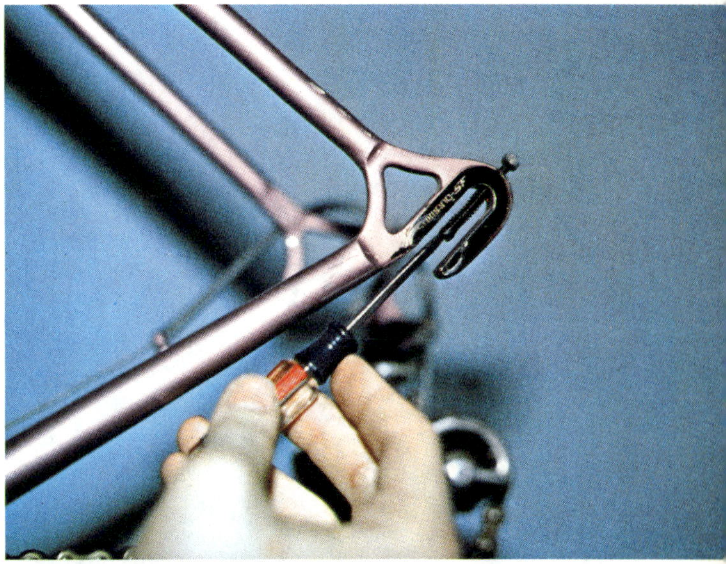

SOME FRAMES have adjustable stops in the rear drop-outs to help you position the rear wheel quickly. You can also adjust chain tautness and wheel position by screwing the stops rearward.

put the wheel back in the bike

Rear-wheel replacement (derailleur bikes). Get the bike off the ground. The derailleur is still in high gear, right? Stick the axle into the drop-outs. Get the chain over the smallest sprocket. If you have a standard wheel, hand-tighten the nuts or wingnuts against the drop-outs. If you have quick-release, and you liked the way it was set before, leave it alone.

Now pull the wheel back until the axle seats against the stops in the drop-outs. Keeping the right end of the axle seated, move the left end until the wheel is centered between the chain stays. This is more difficult than lining up the front wheel as you have more play in the rear drop-outs. Wheel centered? Okay quick-release owners: push up your levers. You others tighten

TIRE REPAIR

YOU MAY NOT have to remove a wheel to fix a flat if the problem is a bad valve. Check it out with saliva. If you do have to take the tube out, remove only one bead from the rim with a special tire iron. If you have none, a spoon handle will suffice, but be careful. When you find the leak, mark the spot and then line up the tube and the tire to find the intruding object in the treads. When you find the culprit, pluck it out! Then, gently stuff the patched tube back inside the tire, making sure the tube isn't twisted or pinched against the rim by the tire bead.

THE GEAR SHIFT levers are held on by a wing nut, knurled knob, D-ring, or other screw-on device. If the levers are too tight, take them apart and clean them.

THIS DERAILLEUR has three adjustments: The top screw limits inward travel; the bottom one, outward travel; the hex bolt holds the cable from the shift lever.

your nuts or wingnuts. Reset brakes if necessary.

Rear-wheel replacement (three-speeds). Get the bike off the ground. Throw the shift lever into high gear. Spin the axle nuts to the ends of the axle. Slip the chain on the sprocket and pull the axle into the drop-outs. Three-speeds don't usually have stops in their drop-outs to guide placement of the axle. Look for nut marks on the drop-outs to show you where the axle was last set. Okay, center the wheel between the chain stays and tighten the nuts. Now tighten the shifter barrel. Connect the indicator sleeve to the chain, and tighten the locknut. Reset brakes if necessary.

Rear-wheel replacement (coaster-brake). Same as above, only instead of reconnecting gear shifter, re-attach the brake clamp with its nut and bolt.

when a drippy derailleur derails your fun

A malfunctioning derailleur is one of the most common (and annoying) problems on ten-speeds. However, sometimes you'll think something is terribly wrong with your shifter when actually your problem is simple. I'm thinking of the following two cases:

Uncontrolled shifting. Your derailleur keeps shifting the chain onto the smaller sprockets when you haven't even touched the lever. Don't worry. Your levers are just too loose, letting out slack cable, which allows the spring in your shifter to pull the chain onto those small cogs. So look at the side of your levers. You should find a wingnut, a knurled knob, a screw or something to that effect. Tighten it. You're all set.

Hard shifting. Just the opposite of the above. Your levers are too tight. Maybe you can fix it by loosening the wingnut or whatever, but I doubt it since these parts don't usually tighten by themselves. Probably the lever is tight because it's crudded up with dirt inside. Take the unit apart by unscrewing the wingnut, but record the order of parts as you remove (and clean) them, so you can put everything back together properly.

the fine art of derailleur adjustment

Adjustment is necessary when you have one of two problems: You cannot get the chain on either the highest or lowest gear, or your shifter throws the chain right off the sprockets. The first thing to do is get that bike, or at least the rear wheel, off the ground.

Rear derailleur adjustment. You'll need a screwdriver, maybe a Phillips, depending on your shifter. What you have to fool with are two throw-adjusting screws which limit how far the derailleur can push the chain. One screw determines outward throw toward the small sprocket, and the other, inward throw toward the big sprocket. On most derailleurs, the low-gear screw is the top screw, but there are many exceptions. The only way to tell which is which is to experiment while turning the pedals (except for those shifters whose thoughtful manufacturers have labeled their screws "L" and "H").

SEE THE TWO screws at the top of this front derailleur? The inside one is almost always for inside travel, the outside one for outside travel.

THE FIRST THING to look for when your brakes don't stop you is worn brake pads. If the pads are okay, as these are, your problem is most likely a stretched cable.

The rear derailleur should always be adjusted with the chain on the small chainwheel up front.

Let's say your derailleur throws the chain too far outward—off the smallest sprocket and against the chain stay. Put the chain back on the smallest sprocket and turn the high-gear screw in ¼-revolutions (usually clockwise) until the derailleur no longer throws as you turn the pedals. When you think you have it, shift the chain all the way in to the largest gear, then all the way out again to make sure the chain won't throw. Obviously, if your problem is that you can't get the bike into high gear, you'll have to loosen that high-gear screw.

If your derailleur is throwing past the large sprocket, you'd better fix it before you ruin your wheel, derailleur, chain or all three. Put the chain back on the sprocket and follow the same procedure as above (but using instead, of course, the low-gear adjustment screw). More common is a derailleur that can't put the chain far enough inward so you lose that crucial low gear that you need for killer hills. It could be a matter of simple adjustment (so loosen the low-gear screw), but it could also be a loose or stretched cable. But we'll cover that in a moment. First, let's look at . . .

Front derailleur adjustment. On most European shifters, the inside adjusting screw is for inward throw, the outer for outward throw. (If there is only one screw, it's for outward throw, and you have my sympathy. To control inward throw, you must move the front cage on its shaft and tighten the cage locking screw.)

To adjust inward throw, put the chain on the largest sprocket in back. Adjustment in the front is a bit more difficult, because you want to set the throw to allow a slight clearance between the chain and the inside of the front derailleur cage (to avoid rubbing). Again, turn the adjustment screw in ¼-revolution increments. Now shift the chain in the rear to high gear and adjust for outward throw in the front. Again, avoid rubbing by getting some clearance between the chain and the outside plate of the cage.

Now, test it out by shifting back and forth a few times. You should be able to jam the lever all the way in either direction without throwing the chain. After shifting onto a chainring, you should also be able to move the front shifter to a position where the chain is centered between the inner and outer plates so that there is no rubbing. The only way to test this aspect of your adjustment is to shift your bike into each of its 10 gear combinations and see if you can center your front derailleur over the chain for each one.

There may be, however, two gears that you can't get perfect: the gear in which the chain is on the large chainring and smallest rear sprocket and vice versa. Using these two gears is called "cross chaining" and subjects the chain to a severe angle. Most experts recommend you use neither of these gears, so if you cannot adjust your front derailleur for either of them, forget about it.

PULLING OUT SLACK is no problem on a high-quality side-pull brake. See the screw and disc at the left? Simply turn the disc and it screws the cable tighter. Nice, huh?

Cables and other problems. If all this fails, perhaps maladjustment isn't your problem. Is the derailleur cage bent? Perhaps the spring in the rear shifter is weakening? Are the little wheels in the rear derailleur gunked up with dirt? And perhaps, as mentioned earlier, your cables have stretched with age. If this is the case, you won't be able to shift onto the big sprocket in back or the big chainring in front. To tighten most cables, you shift the derailleur to get the chain on the smallest sprocket, loosen the anchor bolt on the derailleur and pull the cable taut with pliers. Tighten the anchor bolt and try shifting again.

One exception: On some Sun Tour front derailleurs, a stretched or slack cable will mean that you won't be able to shift the chain onto the *small* chainring. So put the chain on the large chainring before pulling the cable tight.

solving simple brake problems

Your brakes lose stopping power for two main reasons: The brake pads are worn or your cable has stretched. In either case, the result is a pair of pads too far from the wheel rims. The solution: Take up slack in the cable or replace the pads.

Replace brake pads. You can either buy whole new shoes or just the rubber pads. Both are fairly cheap. Just make sure that when you install them, the shoes are positioned so they strike the rim, not the tire. They should be about ⅛ inch from the rim when the brakes are open. Make sure the closed ends of the shoes are facing forward when you install them. (If you look closely at a shoe, you'll notice that one end is open to allow you to slide pads in and out. If the open end is positioned forward, when you hit the brakes the force of the wheel will shoot the pads right out of the shoes.)

On some brakes the pads toe-in slightly—the front of the pad is closer to the rim and strikes it before the rear does. If the pads are equidistant all the way, that's fine, too. But if the rear is closer, no good. Try bending the brake arms very carefully with vise-lock pliers to rectify the situation.

Stretched cable. If your pads are not worn and they're still too far from the rim, most likely your cable has grown a few millimeters. No problem. You just have to pull the slack out. Tie the brake arms closed so the pads are flush against the rim. This can be done with twine, a special tool called a "third hand" or with the hands of a patient friend.

Now, loosen the nut (see photos) and pull the cable end down with pliers to remove the slack. Tighten the nut when the cable is taut. This is easy if you have side-pull brakes; the cable connects directly to the brake arms through the nut. But on center-pulls, the cable and nut are connected to a carrier which in turn is connected to the brake arms through a transverse cable. What this means is that you must hold the carrier *up* while you pull *down* on the cable and at the same time tighten that nut. If you have no friends handy, I've found a good substitute to be a small socket wrench that will let you tighten the nut and hold up the carrier in one motion while you pull down the cable with the pliers in your other hand.

rough running

After a while, especially if you ride a lot in the rain and over dirt roads, your bike is going to ride rough. The rotating parts are going to balk at rotating; the chain gets kinky with grime. The lubricant in the hubs dries out and their bearings may even be pitted. And the same thing can happen to the headset, the bottom bracket, even the pedals. You have two choices. The time-consuming job of overhauling all these assemblies will be performed by many shops—the one in my neighborhood charges $20 for the job—or you can do it yourself; but you'll need more detailed instructions than we have space to present here. For such instruction, get the *Popular Mechanics Book of Bikes and Bicycling* and follow the directions given there.

METRIC CONVERSION

Conversion factors can be carried so far they become impractical. In cases below where an entry is exact it is followed by an asterisk (*). Where considerable rounding off has taken place, the entry is followed by a + or a - sign.

CUSTOMARY TO METRIC

Linear Measure

inches	millimeters
1/16	1.5875*
1/8	3.2
3/16	4.8
1/4	6.35*
5/16	7.9
3/8	9.5
7/16	11.1
1/2	12.7*
9/16	14.3
5/8	15.9
11/16	17.5
3/4	19.05*
13/16	20.6
7/8	22.2
15/16	23.8
1	25.4*

inches	centimeters
1	2.54*
2	5.1
3	7.6
4	10.2
5	12.7*
6	15.2
7	17.8
8	20.3
9	22.9
10	25.4*
11	27.9
12	30.5

feet	centimeters	meters
1	30.48*	.3048*
2	61	.61
3	91	.91
4	122	1.22
5	152	1.52
6	183	1.83
7	213	2.13
8	244	2.44
9	274	2.74
10	305	3.05
50	1524*	15.24*
100	3048*	30.48*

1 yard =
.9144* meters
1 rod =
5.0292* meters
1 mile =
1.6 kilometers
1 nautical mile =
1.852* kilometers

Fluid Measure

(Milliliters [ml] and cubic centimeters [cc or cu cm] are equivalent, but it is customary to use milliliters for liquids.)

1 cu in = 16.39 ml
1 fl oz = 29.6 ml
1 cup = 237 ml
1 pint = 473 ml
1 quart = 946 ml
= .946 liters
1 gallon = 3785 ml
= 3.785 liters
Formula (exact):
fluid ounces × 29.573 529 562 5*
= milliliters

Weights

ounces	grams
1	28.3
2	56.7
3	85
4	113
5	142
6	170
7	198
8	227
9	255
10	283
11	312
12	340
13	369
14	397
15	425
16	454

Formula (exact):
ounces × 28.349 523 125* =
grams

pounds	kilograms
1	.45
2	.9
3	1.4
4	1.8
5	2.3
6	2.7
7	3.2
8	3.6
9	4.1
10	4.5

1 short ton (2000 lbs) =
907 kilograms (kg)
Formula (exact):
pounds × .453 592 37* =
kilograms

Volume

1 cu in = 16.39 cubic centimeters (cc)
1 cu ft = 28 316.7 cc
1 bushel = 35 239.1 cc
1 peck = 8 809.8 cc

Area

1 sq in = 6.45 sq cm
1 sq ft = 929 sq cm
= .093 sq meters
1 sq yd = .84 sq meters
1 acre = 4 046.9 sq meters
= .404 7 hectares
1 sq mile = 2 589 988 sq meters
= 259 hectares
= 2.589 9 sq kilometers

Kitchen Measure

1 teaspoon = 4.93 milliliters (ml)
1 Tablespoon = 14.79 milliliters (ml)

Miscellaneous

1 British thermal unit (Btu) (mean)
= 1 055.9 joules
1 calorie (mean) = 4.19 joules
1 horsepower = 745.7 watts
= .75 kilowatts
caliber (diameter of a firearm's bore in hundredths of an inch)
= .254 millimeters (mm)
1 atmosphere pressure = 101 325* pascals (newtons per sq meter)
1 pound per square inch (psi) = 6 895 pascals
1 pound per square foot = 47.9 pascals
1 knot = 1.85 kilometers per hour
25 miles per hour = 40.2 kilometers per hour
50 miles per hour = 80.5 kilometers per hour
75 miles per hour = 120.7 kilometers per hour